Sanctioned
Ignorance

Sanctioned

The Politics of Knowledge Production and
the Teaching of the Literatures of Canada

Ignorance

PAUL MARTIN

THE UNIVERSITY OF ALBERTA PRESS

Published by

The University of Alberta Press
Ring House 2
Edmonton, Alberta, Canada T6G 2E1
www.uap.ualberta.ca

LIBRARY AND ARCHIVES CANADA CATALOGUING IN PUBLICATION

Martin, Paul, 1968 April 9–, author
     Sanctioned ignorance : the politics of knowledge production and the teaching of the literatures of Canada /
Paul Martin.

Includes bibliographical references and index.
Issued in print and electronic formats.
ISBN 978-0-88864-545-6 (pbk.).—ISBN 978-0-88864-732-0 (epub).—ISBN 978-0-88864-734-4 (Amazon kindle).—
ISBN 978-0-88864-735-1 (pdf)

     1. Canadian literature—Study and teaching (Higher). 2. Canadian literature—History and criticism—Theory, etc.
3. Canon (Literature). I. Title.

PS8031.M37 2013   C810.9   C2013-905282-8
                                  C2013-905283-6

Index available in print and PDF editions.

First edition, first printing, 2013.
Printed and bound in Canada by Houghton Boston Printers, Saskatoon, Saskatchewan.
Copyediting and proofreading by Joanne Muzak.
Indexing by Adrian Mather.

The University of Alberta Press is committed to protecting our natural environment. As part of our efforts, this book is
printed on Enviro Paper: it contains 100% post-consumer recycled fibres and is acid- and chlorine-free.

The University of Alberta Press gratefully acknowledges the support received for its publishing program from The Canada
Council for the Arts. The University of Alberta Press also gratefully acknowledges the financial support of the Government
of Canada through the Canada Book Fund (CBF) and the Government of Alberta through the Alberta Multimedia
Development Fund (AMDF) for its publishing activities.

To Mona, Emily, and Aidan

Contents

Acknowledgements

WHETHER AS A STUDENT at the University of Alberta and the University of Western Ontario, a bookseller and entrepreneur at Northwest Passages, or as an assistant professor of English and director of Canadian Studies at the University of Vermont, one of my constant preoccupations over the last twenty years has been with the place of the literatures of Canada in the national and international psyche. My perspectives on these issues have been shaped by so many people I have met and worked with along the way that a mere thank you seems hardly tribute enough.

In particular, the unusual approach I took to the early stages of this research project—travelling from coast to coast and interviewing nearly one hundred professors of Canadian literature—continues to remind me of how much of my success and knowledge has been thanks to the generosity of others. Over the course of those six weeks of interviews, I had memorable conversations with many people, but I would be remiss if I were to fail to mention the helpfulness, hospitality, and insightful responses offered to me by Bernard Andrès, Dennis Cooley, Burke Cullen, Gwen Davies, Dennis Duffy, François Dumont, Carole Gerson, Terry Goldie, Sherrill Grace, Seymour Mayne, Roy Miki, Jean Morency, Pierre Nepveu, John O'Connor, Malcolm Ross, Donna Smyth, James Steele, Marie Vautier, and Lorraine York. Many of the conversations I had with them make their way into this book and continue to shape my work as a teacher and scholar.

The study of the teaching of the literatures of Canada is still a relatively unexplored field—especially in English Canada. It is important, then, for me to note the influence of those who broke considerable ground before I even envisioned working in this area. Clearly, I would not have been able to accomplish what I have without the benefit of the books and articles written by Diana Brydon, Frank Davey, Margery Fee, Nicole Fortin, Barbara Godard, Robert Lecker, Joseph Melançon, Clément Moisan, Heather Murray, Lucie Robert, Max Roy, and Denis Saint-Jacques. I am also grateful to the following professors whose teaching and mentorship was equally influential: Anthony Purdy, Ted Bishop, Frank Davey, Stan Dragland, Paul Dubé, Ray Morrow, Fred Radford, Marilyn Randall, Paul Robberecht, and Janice Williamson. Most of all, I am grateful to Ted (E.D.) Blodgett for his sage advice and guidance in the writing of the dissertation that forms the basis of this book. His encouragement and mentorship was deeply important to the success of this project, as was his openness to my idea of travelling across the country before I knew precisely what I was looking to find. There are few who know the literary landscape of Canada as well as he and it was my great privilege to work with him.

At a number of key moments in my writing and research, I also received much appreciated assistance from Lu Ziola, Janet Friskney, Louise Ladouceur, and from countless administrative staff of literature departments across the country. I must also thank the following organizations for the support, monetary and otherwise, that they have provided me with at various stages in the writing of my book: the Social Sciences and Humanities Research Council of Canada, the Province of Alberta, the University of Alberta, Mount Royal College, the University of Vermont's Canadian Studies Program, and MacEwan University. I am especially grateful to the University of Alberta Press for their unwavering support and patience. In particular, I cannot thank enough Peter Midgely, Linda Cameron, and Cathie Crooks for their belief in this project. A special thanks to Joanne Muzak for her thoughtful and skilled copyediting of the manuscript and to the external reviewers for their insight and helpful suggestions. This book is much improved because of their contributions.

The people who are best acquainted with the commitment of time, thought, and energy required to write this book are my friends and family, who occasionally try to recall if there was ever a time when I was not working around the clock. I have had tremendous support and encouragement from many friends, colleagues, and members of my extended family, especially Stephen Abbott, Sarah Bagshaw, Philip Baruth, Pablo Bose, the Derby Circle gang, Chris Gibbins, Richard Harrison, David Massell, Dale Jacobs, Marc Jacques, David Jenemann, Peter Jones and Terri Donovan, Kiera Ladner, Tony Magistrale, Tom McGrath, Ken Meadows, the Paquin family, Helen Scott, Lisa Schnell, Rob Stocks, Robyn Warhol, Nancy Welch, and Luis Vivanco. I am thankful for the support and endless encouragement I have received from my sister, Heidi LM Jacobs, and my parents, Jerome and Merle Martin, whose enthusiasm and belief in my abilities has never wavered.

Finally, I wish to thank the three people with whom I share my life and my love: Mona, Emily, and Aidan. This project began during the first year of my marriage and witnessed the birth of our two children along with several moves across the continent. It would never have been completed without Mona's love, faith, and strength. This accomplishment is ours.

Introduction

Points of Departure

THIS BOOK IS THE PRODUCT of nearly two decades of reading and research, taking and teaching courses on the literatures of Canada, and a coast-to-coast journey to visit twenty-eight university literature departments and interview nearly one hundred professors.[1] Much of the formal research for this book began with that exploratory trip in 1997–98 and became a core part of my 2001 PHD dissertation. That text, however, was only an intermediary point to this revised and expanded volume. On its own, the dissertation provided an important snapshot of what I found on my trip and my observations of how the shapes and functions of courses on our literatures are inextricably linked with our literary histories and institutions. The data I gathered in 1997–98 is a valuable historical record in itself, for no one else has ever made an effort to assemble such information in so complete a way. As I demonstrate in Chapters Three and Four of this book, the course data and interviews from that year reveal a tremendous amount of information about what we teach, how we teach, and why we teach the courses that we do. Looking at that snapshot of our field in isolation, however, can only tell us so much, which is why I have not published the results of that initial research until now. Incorporating, as I do in Chapter Five, corresponding data from a full decade later enriches our understanding of that first data set significantly. It is only when we have an understanding of at least two points in time that we can attempt to gauge the direction or rate of change between them; the later data, then, reveals much about the earlier and vice versa. For instance, if the data from 1997–98 reveals something about the processes of cultural and institutional reproduction at work at that time, then in which ways have our teaching practices and departmental structures developed in the decade that followed? Would the pressures described by the interviewed professors to accommodate the growing and vibrant literatures in Canada alter the direction of their praxes over the next decade? What kinds of courses would the most promising undergraduates of the mid-1990s teach when they had a chance to enter the classroom as professors?

The middle of the 1990s was a period of significant commercial and critical success for Canadian writers and publishers both nationally and internationally, especially for those working in English. Anglophone writers such as Rohinton Mistry, Ann-Marie MacDonald, Anne Michaels, and Eden Robinson gained international attention as Canada suddenly appeared to be a hotbed of young talent, even prompting bidding wars among publishers trying to discover the next great talent from Canada. At the same time, writers like Michael Ondaatje, Margaret Atwood, and Alice Munro were cementing their international reputation as some of the best writers working in the English language. Within Canada, there was also a clear growth in the number of interesting works being written by minority writers, including Native writers like Thomas King and Tomson Highway, and immigrant writers such as Mistry, Dionne Brand, M.G. Vassanji, Ying Chen, and Sergio Kokis. In the interviews I conducted as part of my "field" work, I asked professors about how they were meeting the challenges of incorporating some of these newer and internationally acclaimed writers while also addressing the growing body of minority and immigrant writing in Canada. As I discuss in Chapter Four, many professors during that era struggled with the challenge of fitting in newer and more diverse works within the course and department structures that had been in place for some time. The challenge of removing "classic" works that had been on the syllabus for years in order to make room for newer and in some cases "unproven" works was a dilemma that professors raised with me again and again.

Only time would tell how departments and professors would respond to this. As I reveal in Chapter Five, when we compare the list of books and courses taught in the 1997–98 academic year to the corresponding data from 2007–08, we can see some clear and provocative answers to these questions.

Over this same decade, the critical landscape in Canada has also changed in many ways that are germane to this project. In the introduction to my 2001 dissertation, I wrote,

> the challenge for anyone studying the literary institution in English Canada is that there has been relatively little work done on the topic. Moreover, much of what has been written, save the work of a few scholars, including Frank Davey, Robert Lecker, and Heather Murray, either takes the form of articles in lesser known journals or, like Margery Fee's influential thesis "English-Canadian Literary Criticism, 1890–1950: Defining and Establishing a National Literature," remains unpublished. (Martin 3)

This statement was true in 2001, but in the years to follow, as Cynthia Sugars argues in her introduction to *Home-Work: Postcolonialism, Pedagogy, and Canadian Literature*, "postcolonial revisionings and pedagogical interrogations of the discipline of English literature have become more readily accepted" (6). This growing current in Canadian literary criticism was particularly nurtured by two key conferences and the essay collections that emerged from them. The 2000 "Is Canada Postcolonial?" conference, organized by Laura Moss at the University of Manitoba, revolved around the ongoing debates over the applicability of postcolonial theory to the study of primarily anglophone Canadian literature. Two years later, the University of Ottawa's "Postcolonialism and Pedagogy: Canadian Literature In the Classroom" conference, organized by Cynthia Sugars, foregrounded the vital question of how pedagogy was being shaped, if at all, by these discussions. The edited essay collections that developed out of these meetings, Moss's *Is Canada Postcolonial?: Unsettling Canadian Literature* (2002) and Sugars's *Home-Work*, each contain a number of important and provocative essays, such as Diana Brydon's "Cross-Talk, Postcolonial Pedagogy, and Transnational Literacy," that have had a continuing impact on our understandings of the discipline (or disciplining) of Canadian literary studies.

As debates about the shape and future direction of our field came further to the fore during the first half of the decade, Smaro Kamboureli and Roy Miki also staged a significant intervention with the creation of the TransCanada project. One of the primary goals of this project, as Kamboureli writes in the preface to *Trans.Can.Lit: Resituating the Study of Canadian Literature* (2007), was to "undertake a major rethinking of the assumptions that had governed the field of CanLit studies and to rejuvenate the field through a renewed sense of collective purpose" (xiii). It is hard to look at the TransCanada project as being anything other than a prolific success. Since its conception in 2004, the TransCanada project has yielded three conferences (in 2005, 2007, and 2009), one collection of essays (*Trans.Can.Lit*), and the establishment at the University of Guelph of the TransCanada Institute, funded "with the support of [Kamboureli's] Canada Research Chair (Tier 1) in Critical Studies in Canadian Literature and a Canada Foundation for Innovation grant" (TransCanada Institute). Like the scholarship that has emerged from the two previously mentioned conferences, the TransCanada Institute (which closed in 2013) and its publishing and conference projects have also grounded themselves in postcolonial approaches to the study of "Canadian Literature." Despite what now seems to be a flourishing preoccupation with questions of pedagogy, the literary institution, and the aim of "unsettling" (Moss) or "resituating" (Kamboureli and Miki) the study of "Canadian Literature," there remain huge gaps in our understanding of the literary institution and how it affects and is affected by the study and teaching of "Canadian Literature" at anglophone universities across the country. These gaps are not caused as much by burning questions that remain unanswered as they are by simple, yet foundational questions that, conveniently, remain unasked.

This book asks, what happens to our understanding of the complexity of Canada as a site of literary production when we confine its study to university departments organized (and deeply compromised) by the premises of Romantic nationalism that were so fundamental in their founding? In other words, to paraphrase John Willinsky, how has the way scholars have "learned to divide the world" shaped the biases and blind spots we bring to our understandings of the literatures of Canada? While postcolonial theory and its preoccupations with indigenous and minority cultures may seem to be a productive lens through which to view some of these issues, the complete absence of any consideration of literary production in French or other minority languages in most of the work published in these three essay collections reflects the notion that, as Kamboureli puts it, "notwithstanding the various attempts to insti-gate and maintain a dialogue between anglophone and francophone literatures in Canada, CanLit has, more or less, always functioned as a referent to Canadian Literature in English" (ix). The extrapolations made throughout all three volumes (and, as I will discuss in the fifth chapter, two prominent anthologies published in 2008 and 2009) from the synechdocal use of "Canadian" in place of "English-Canadian" to pronouncements about how crucial our national *literature* is to under-standing Canada and its postcoloniality (or lack thereof) is deeply problematic for anyone who tries to work and read in both of Canada's official languages or any of the many other languages actively spoken within our country's borders. It is only through an active, "sanctioned ignorance," perpetually reinforced by this country's predominantly unilin-gual literary institutions, that scholars and students (whether anglophone or francophone) are able to justify such perspectives (Spivak 3).

: My longstanding interest in the question of how we frame and practise the teaching of the literatures of Canada dates back to my experiences as an undergraduate pursuing a combined honours degree in English and French language and literature at the University of Alberta. Faithfully following the requirements of my program, it was not until my final year that I took any courses on the literatures of Canada. I anticipated at the time, particularly with regard to my English course in "Canadian Literature," that these courses might be the ones that could bridge the gulf between my studies of English and French literatures. For reasons that I will spend much of this book exploring, this was not to be the case. My English and French professors rarely, if ever, alluded to works written originally in the other official languages, nor did they appear to have much knowledge of them. Taking these two programs at the same time, then, offered me a considerable opportunity for reflection, not only about the literatures themselves, but also about the nature of the literary institution and the way these departmental divisions arbitrarily fracture our knowledge of literary production in Canada primarily based on the language of expression and instruction.

Anyone in a university setting who has the opportunity to work out of two departments or to pursue any serious type of interdisciplinary research quickly comes to understand that there is no such thing as "*the* ivory tower." Rather, there sit side by side numerous windowless towers of knowledge, each seeming to have only a small entrance and no discernable exit. As with any closed society, the motives of anyone more than politely interested in what goes on elsewhere are often deemed questionable by those content and secure in their own confinement. As Frank Davey observes,

> The Arts faculties of anglophone-Canada's universities have adopted disci-
> plinary structures similar to those that developed at Johns Hopkins and
> Indiana late in the nineteenth century. These structures replicated the nation-
> alisms of the time particularly in their language and literature departments,
> which even today in many universities have boundaries and customs posts
> around them, if not Maginot and Siegfried lines. The norm in such a structure
> is that one nation has one language and one national literature. Translation
> is viewed as a questionable or impure practice, one usually to be contained as
> much as possible within departmental boundaries. ("'and Quebec'" 9–10)

It is precisely this lack of interaction between colleagues, departments, universities, and the disciplines themselves that has had the greatest influence on the nature of my work in this book. My experience travelling across the country over the course of six weeks in 1997 and 1998 to visit twenty-eight different departments and to interview an incredible array of scholars in the field gave me a perspective of the discipline I could not have achieved otherwise. Of an equally profound effect—and what has become inseparable from my current understanding of the literature— was the chance to experience, albeit fleetingly, life in every province of

Canada. Visiting much more of the country than I had ever seen before tempered my previous cynicism about the nationalistic notion that, by reading works by Canadian writers, our students should gain a broader sense of Canada and *all* of its peoples. The more departments I visited, the more convinced I became that we lessen our potential understanding of our own literatures by restricting our students and ourselves to the confines of departments of either English or French.

Robin Mathews makes this very argument in his 1972 essay "Research, Curriculum, Scholarship, and Endowment in the Study of Canadian Literature," first presented at that year's meeting of the Association of Canadian University Teachers of English.[2] In this fiery and, as we will see, prophetic essay, which Barbara Godard cites as one of the inspirations for the founding of the Association of Canadian and Québec Literatures (Godard 32), Mathews criticizes the "seriously impoverished" situation of the literatures of Canada in the nation's literature departments (Mathews 39). One of the fundamental causes of this deficiency, he contends, is that

> foreign models [of literary studies] have assumed that the literature of a country is written in one language only, and the study of Canadian literature has suffered as a result....The literature of francophone Canada ought to be studied as a major part of Canadian literature in anglophone universities. It has been avoided partly because...of unilingual foreign models. (41)

"Those models," Mathews adds, "have also shut out or restricted areas of Canadian experience not found in the model literatures" such as "the literature of exploration,...the literature of the immigrant populations...—in and out of translation—[and]...the literatures of the native peoples of the land" (41). The rise of postcolonial studies in English departments seems to have assisted in allowing these latter two literatures a place at the table in the curriculum of English departments, but only when they fit within the dominant paradigm of English studies. As Davey notes, "postcolonial studies is an academic field that closely resembles Canadian literature in its having gained a place in university English departments while being at best problematically suitable to them. Like Canada, postcoloniality is polylingual rather than unilingual" ("'and Quebec'" 22). With "no strong models available for theorizing and studying a bilingual or polylingual national literature," ("'and Quebec'" 10) the use of the term "postcolonial" in English departments functions similarly to how Kamboureli describes the commonplace use of the term "Canadian Literature," as "at once a troubled and troubling sign. Troubled because 'Canadian' minus any qualifiers evokes the entirety of the geopolitical space it refers to, but it also siphons off large segments of this space and its peoples into oblivion at worst, and circumscribed conditions at best" (Kamboureli ix). In the past, francophone critics in Québec routinely used the term "Québécois" as a totalizing descriptor that excluded writing in other languages from its vision of Québécois literature and ignored the presence of writing in French outside of Québec. Since the 1990s, as Québec's politicians and intelligentsia refigure the term to be more inclusive, critics and professors have increasingly included both "littérature anglo-québécoise" and "littérature migrante" in their widening view of the literary landscape and history of Québec. They have also begun to pay closer attention to francophone writing from outside of Québec, seeing it as part of a larger North American contribution to "la francophonie," a terminology that escapes the "sanctioned ignorance" at the core of the synechdocal constructions of the terms "postcolonial" or "Canadian" so common in English departments across the country.

In many ways, then, the place of the literatures of Canada in today's departments of English seems fundamentally similar to what Mathews described over forty years ago. The study of "Canadian Literature" frequently remains yoked to a nationalist, unilingual model of literary history that continues, as it did in the nineteenth century, to reflect "a considerable sense that Canada was a unilingually anglophone country, in which francophone culture was a minor phenomenon, something like Welsh in Britain" (Davey, "'and Quebec'" 10). In other ways, however, the increasing racial and ethnic diversity of the authors whose texts are included in both English and French courses on the literatures of Canada indicate that the parameters of our fields have also expanded since the early 1970s. As many professors who began their careers during that period told me, the fields of "Canadian Literature" and "littérature québécoise" seem more open and heterogeneous than ever before. Furthermore, they reminded me, the literatures of Canada have earned such a degree of respect in both academia and the literary marketplace that very few people, if any, question the value of their inclusion in the curricula of departments of English or French. As Leslie Monkman has warned, though, this apparent state of success has also led to "a failure [on the part of our discipline] to acknowledge the *actual* status of Canadian writing in our curricular structures" (Monkman 121). When one looks at these curricular structures more closely, it soon becomes apparent that, with a few changes here and there, Mathews could publish nearly the same article today. The hard truth of the matter is that, as Monkman boldly stated in 2004, "the study of Canadian literature has not been 'a very powerful force' in our discipline over the past twenty-five years" (121).

Since the 1990s, critical discourse in English Canada has increasingly turned its attention to the literary institution, but much of this conversation has suffered greatly from a profound lack of one thing: data. While we may assume that we have a sense of what is taught in classrooms across the country, truthfully, as members of the same field, we have been terrible at sharing information about what we do at our own institutions. Many of us meet at least annually at conferences to present our current research, yet we rarely share syllabi or discuss in detail how and why we choose to teach some texts over others. This lack of shared knowledge hinders our growth as a field tremendously. My interviews made it clear to me time and again that in English Canada we have not done enough to combat the isolation that develops while we teach in our own institutions, focus on our own research, and devote much of our attention to our own students. As for the two literary solitudes of our country, the walls between francophone and anglophone scholars and scholarship seem thicker than ever. With a few notable, longstanding exceptions such as the Association for Canadian and Québec Literatures, and the journals *Tessera*, *Ellipse*, and sometimes *Canadian Literature*, we have made few meaningful efforts in recent years to bring together scholars and students of the French and English literatures in this country to share ideas and common concerns. To put it bluntly, since the mid-1990s, anglophones have learned more about Québécois literature from the Giller Prize and CBC's Canada Reads than they have from virtually any English course on "Canadian Literature" taught during that time.

My aim in writing this book is not primarily to argue that "my Canada (and its literatures) includes Québec, and yours should too."[3] Rather, I seek to explore how the ways we allow(ed) our field to be shaped have a profound impact on the type of knowledge that it produces and perpetuates. The lack of dialogue and even awareness between anglophone and francophone scholars of the literature produced within our country is but one aspect of this problem. From my interviews across the country alone, it was clear to me that each of these scholarly communities would benefit immensely from a greater awareness and understanding of the literature, criticism, and literature curricula of the other. The same can also be said for the scholars separated by regions rather than language, or, for that matter, between teachers of literature at the primary and secondary level and professors from our post-secondary institutions. Once those of us studying and teaching any or all of the literatures of Canada can enter into such a dialogue with one another, we can begin to make the types of meaningful curricular and institutional change needed to broaden dramatically our knowledge of the literatures of Canada. As someone whose education, research, and teaching has routinely taken me between the majority and minority literatures of anglophone Canada, francophone Canada and Québec, not to mention the First Nations, I am not content to settle for the explanation that these divisions are too firmly established to be dislodged or, at the very least, troubled.

: With the aim of examining both the history and current practices of the teaching of the literatures of Canada, I begin this book with a chapter on the history of English and French studies and the eventual place of the literatures of Canada in university-level literature programs. The foundations of literary studies in Canada are essential to understand, for they continue to shape the field to this day in ways that we rarely notice. The second chapter complements the first by providing the theoretical basis for much of what I will argue in Chapters Three and Four. By rooting much of my work in Pierre Bourdieu's theories of the market of symbolic goods and the process of cultural reproduction and those of Jacques Dubois on the workings of the literary institution, I set the stage for what the quantitative aspects of my research reveal. One of the primary premises of the second chapter, in other words, is that the work of Dubois and particularly Bourdieu offers some fundamental explanations as to why, for instance, the literatures of Canada are represented as they are in literature departments across the country and why there has been such a lack of disciplinary self-evaluation, especially on the part of Canadianists in English departments in Canada. More important, perhaps, is that the specificities of the situation of the literatures of Canada within this country's departments of literature enable us to explore the larger question of the central role within the literary institution played by universities, their literature departments, and the scholars and students they produce and reward.

The third chapter of this book details the research I conducted while visiting the twenty-seven universities and contains my analysis of the collected data. It provides a quantitative analysis of the 1997–98 data, including a breakdown of the place of courses on the literature of Canada in the curriculum of each of the departments I visited. Also part of this chapter is an analysis of the types of courses offered at these institutions and a detailed list and analysis of the books that are taught as part of these courses. This material has never been collected before and offers us, therefore, some insight into how course structures and curricula affect the canon, or at least the canon of texts that we teach in the classroom. Though I have managed to acquire a wealth of information, the exploratory nature of this research also points to a great deal of work that I hope I and others will have the chance to pursue in the future. We have yet, for instance, to produce detailed histories of most of our universities' departments of literature and the process by which courses on the literatures of Canada became part of the curriculum; nor have there been any lengthy studies of the symbiotic relationship between Canada's small literary presses and academia. As with any large research project, then, there are books still waiting to be written from all the gathered material that falls outside the aims of this work.

Although I catalogue in great detail the books taught in English courses on Canadian literature for 1997–98 and, in Chapter Five, for 2007–08, I do not attempt here to do the same for courses taught in French at francophone universities. The most important reason for this lies in the structural differences between these two systems. The Québec system, as I discuss in Chapter Three, is remarkable in two ways that are significant to this study. First, because of the separate college or CÉGEP (Collège d'enseignement général et professionel) system in Québec, which provides students with many of their basic general education requirements, many students entering university to study literature have already completed general literature courses that in the post-secondary system of other provinces remain at the core of the English major and minor. Thus, students interested in studying Québécois literature at the university level have often already taken the broad introductory courses in the field similar to the survey courses that dominate the Canadian literature course offerings at many anglophone universities outside of Québec. Because students at Québec universities move immediately into studying within their area of specialization, that system allows students specializing in literature to take a far greater number of courses in their field than their counterparts can at universities outside of Québec. This also allows literature departments to offer a much wider variety of specialized courses in Québécois and other literatures than departments outside of Québec could ever achieve. For this reason, we also see a much greater diversity of texts taught at those universities. To get a true sense of all the texts students read in courses on Québécois literature in Québec, my study would need to expand dramatically to examine and incorporate all courses taught at the CÉGEP level as well as those taught at francophone universities. For this reason, and because other scholars like Max Roy and Joseph Melançon have written in great detail about the role of the CÉGEPs, I focus here not on the particular texts that are taught in Québec but on what the structural differences between these two systems demonstrate in terms of the connection between course and department structures and the types of knowledge these institutions can be seen to produce.

Some of the most illuminating data I collected over the course of this early research is difficult to quantify, for it comes from the personal interviews I conducted with ninety-four professors and instructors. Rather than focusing on which books were taught and in which courses, as I do in Chapters Three and Five, in Chapter Four I deal primarily with the question of *how* my interview subjects taught these works. Through an analysis of the responses I received to the primary set of questions that I asked every subject, I discuss how the teaching of the literatures of Canada is influenced by factors including the training of the professor, his or her attitude towards the canon, his or her willingness to be influenced by the curriculum and notions of coverage, the location and history of the university, and, finally, the question of cultural nationalism(s). It would be impossible in a single book to address all of the information, stories, and history I recorded in each of these interviews, which together form an incredibly rich, if still a patchwork, oral history of the teaching of the literatures of Canada. For the purpose of this project, what these interviews help to provide is less the details of each professor's teaching practices and more an overall sense of their general attitudes towards the literature and their teaching of it.

Given the nature of this aspect of my research, there is a distinct but necessary shift in tone in Chapter Four both in terms of my own writing and my approach to the qualitative parts of my study. The interviews with professors are clearly the part of my research that surprised me the most, and I try here to let my interview subjects speak for themselves as much as possible. The opportunity to meet ninety-four other specialists in the field was a phenomenal one from which I learned many things, not the least of which was a much greater sense of the field's history than I possessed when I set out on my trip. I had many lengthy conversations on the topic of the teaching of the literatures of Canada with the interviewees, who were nearly all supportive, forthcoming, and enthusiastic. I also gained invaluable mentorship, suggestions for new approaches to my topic that I had not yet considered, and even the occasional free lunch and night's accommodation. It was, in many ways, a strange sensation to visit so many places and meet so many people in such a short time; I frequently visited five different universities per week and interviewed upwards of half a dozen people each day. The more I travelled, the more I felt a kinship with the protagonists of the journey narratives we discuss so frequently in our classes. I was constantly on the move, stopping only momentarily on my own odyssey to encounter new people and experiences, the significance of which I would be left to ruminate on over the course of the journey to my next destination. This fourth chapter, then, aims both to detail the qualitative data I gathered during these interviews and to evoke a sense of my experiences of interviewing everyone from Frank Davey, Clara Thomas, Malcolm Ross, and Denis Saint-Jacques to Roy Miki, Margery Fee, Armand Garnet Ruffo, and Pierre Nepveu. I mention these individuals not as an exercise in name-dropping but to highlight how so many aspects of our field have been shaped by the work of individual professors and critics working year after year in their own institutions to foster a future for the study of the literatures of Canada. The personal histories and perspectives of everyone I interviewed, then, offer crucial context for interpreting the "harder" quantitative data that I examine in Chapters Three and Five. As Barbara Godard has argued, "the relentless presentness of the field" today exists in great part because of "the absence of bibliographies of scholarship which has made much of the pioneering work invisible" (Godard 33–34). This leaves "many younger scholars...unaware of this history of the field" (33). There is, particularly in terms of the history of anglophone universities, much work to be done if we are to document fully the beginnings of our field and the vital period during the 1960s and 1970s when the call for a greater representation of our national literatures was at its loudest. A comprehensive history of the institutionalization of the study of the literatures of Canada has yet to be written and it must be undertaken before we lose many of the key architects who oversaw the development of the field as we know it today.

As I describe in Chapter Four, the experience of conducting all of these university visits and personal interviews continually brought into relief the contrast between the state of perpetual motion in which I found myself and the comparatively static role of the university professors I met. My interview subjects were each at a particular point in careers, begun and likely to end at the same institution, each seemingly confined to their own solitary and unchanging office spaces, while I was never in the same room, let alone town, for more than a day. This same contrast seemed to exist on a psychological level as much as it did on the physical. The more I learned about the state of teaching of the literatures of Canada at each university, the more I was reminded of Edward Said's observation that "confined to the study of one representational complex, literary critics accept and paradoxically ignore the lines drawn around what they do" (20). While this captures perfectly the notion of sanctioned ignorance, it also pinpoints what occurs on a much more local level of the university department of English or French literature. With just a handful of exceptions, nearly every professor with whom I spoke had no knowledge of what types of courses other departments offered in the field. In fact, many had little knowledge of how colleagues in their own department taught their courses on the literatures of Canada, even when their colleague might, for instance, be teaching a different section of the same survey course. It was as if many professors resided in a voluntary state of house arrest. Not only did they seem uninterested in stepping outside to see what their neighbourhood looked like, they were frequently unable to describe to me even the colour of their own house.

While I may seem here to be a making an indictment of our profession, declaiming professors as being mired in self-interest and unwilling to reflect on what they and others do, I am not. My observation, rather, is simply an affirmation of Bourdieu's theories as to the efficacy of the university as a site of institutional and, on a larger scale, cultural reproduction. It deliberately creates and rewards cultural agents whose work is to perpetuate the current system and the dominant culture, both of which could be threatened by accommodating models that work in markedly different ways from their own. As Said contends,

> *a principle of silent exclusion operates within and at the boundaries of discourse; this has now become so internalized that fields, disciplines, and their discourses have taken on the status of immutable durability.... To acquire*

a position of authority within the field is, however, to be involved internally in the formation of a canon, which usually turns out to be a blocking device for methodological and disciplinary self-questioning. (16)

The power relationships involved in these convenient and deliberate blind spots are precisely what Spivak explores through her notion of "sanctioned ignorance" (3). These "blocking device[s]" are incredibly effective in ensuring that the questions any discipline or institution asks of itself will not fundamentally alter the ways in which it currently works (Said 16). One of the goals of this book, then, is to try to answer the question posed by Diana Brydon in her essay "Cross-Talk": "What are the particular forms of sanctioned ignorance encouraged by Canadian literature and postcolonial study in the classroom?" (70). It is only by uncovering and making more visible some of those "lines drawn around what [we] do" that we can begin to challenge and even dismantle the parameters that help us to avoid questioning in meaningful ways how we study the literatures of our own country (Said 20).

One of the most obvious ways in which we structure our knowledge of the literatures of this country, and one which is shaped primarily by this division of knowledge into separate and isolationist fields, is the referents we employ when speaking of them. Throughout this book, I have chosen to speak as much as possible of "the literatures of Canada" rather than choosing other, less satisfactory options, especially the ubiquitous use of the terms "Canadian literature" to refer to everything in this country written in English and "Québécois literature" to represent everything written in French. The latter terms, to my mind, are especially problematic because of the ways they are used to oversimplify these bodies of literature and to exclude those writers and works that do not fall within these narrow definitions. The most notable example of this is the frequent practice of scholars and critics to exclude from their vision of "Canadian literature" all literature written in languages other than English, most notably Québécois literature in French. However, the term "Canadian literature" when envisioned in the most inclusive manner— or reworked as "Canadian Literature(s)" to denote the existence of more than one Canadian literature—is also problematic because the singular nation/notion of Canada remains at the centre.

The terms "Canadian Literature in English" and "Canadian literature in French" have similar connotations with the emphasis that they place on the nation and the suggestion that both bodies of work are a part of a single Canadian literature. Furthermore, one could also understand these terms to encompass works in translation. "Canadian literature in English," for example, could include Gabrielle Roy's *The Tin Flute* or Ringuet's *Thirty Acres* while the French equivalent could include Hugh MacLennan's *Deux Solitudes* or Timothy Findley's *Guerres*, as is clearly illustrated by the fact that the former titles are both part of the "New Canadian Library" series published by McClelland & Stewart (who, not coincidentally, refer to themselves as "The Canadian Publisher") and the latter are part of the "Bibliothèque Québécoise" series of inexpensive paperbacks.[4] This same problem applies to the use of the terms "English-Canadian literature" or "Anglophone Canadian literature" and "French-Canadian literature" or "Francophone Canadian literature," which posits the writer's cultural and linguistic background as a key point of separation between "the two" literatures. Such terminology ultimately lumps together, for instance, Acadian literature, Québécois literature, and other francophone writing from across the country when these are all quite separate literatures with varying degrees of interaction. The greatest difficulty with seeing Canadian literature as characterized by a binary structure of any sort, such as the double helix model articulated by Philip Stratford, is that such a vision works to erase difference between regions and cultures and, more crucially, marginalizes literatures of Canada in other languages, and especially those of Canada's First Peoples.[5]

One of the possible ways to avoid many of these assumptions is to speak simply of the literatures of Canada. As I envisage it, one benefit of this terminology is that it places the literature at the centre and moves the issue of nation(s) and even language more towards the periphery. The distinction between referring to "the literatures of Canada" and "Canadian literature(s)"—a term that in the past has served an important purpose in reminding its audience that one cannot justifiably imagine there to be only a single Canadian literature—may seem to be minimal. Nevertheless, by removing Canada from the centre of the equation and limiting the connotation of some sort of precedence on the part of the nation, my preferred terminology will likely be more acceptable to those constituencies who would reject any vision of themselves as being an example of a *Canadian* literature. Speaking of "the literatures of Canada" also opens the door a bit wider for literary scholars to conceive of Canada more as a highly complex literary space than as a difficult-to-define grouping together of mostly distinct cultures and language groups. More importantly, the use of terminology that, unlike those rooted around a text or author's language of origin, does not immediately identify a text as belonging to either one category or another, makes it easier to imagine that text to be part of more than one category at the same time. The works of Antonine Maillet, for instance, can be considered to be part of Acadian literature, Atlantic Canadian literature, a larger grouping of French-Canadian literatures, while also having affiliations with Québécois literature as she lived and worked in Québec for many years. In other words, by starting to look at literary works from Canada as interacting in complex and non-exclusive ways with everything from questions of nation, region, language, and cultural or ethnic groups, to literary genres, literary movements or styles, and influences from within and without Canada, we can begin to understand the literatures of this country in a way that takes into account its rich intricacies rather than conveniently overlooking them.[6] This type of approach, it is crucial to note here, is rooted firmly within the paradigm of comparative literature, and is one that has been articulated in the Canadian context through the work of scholars such as E.D. Blodgett and M.V. Dimic. Unfortunately, very few anglophone or francophone scholars of the literatures of Canada have adopted this approach in their research or teaching.

The issues surrounding the ways in which we refer to and envision the literatures of Canada are why I continue to be engaged by this research topic. My hope is that my readings of the material I have brought together in this volume will shine new light on some of the dominant forms of sanctioned ignorance at work in how we currently teach, study, and think of the literatures of Canada. The most obvious process through which this occurs in academia, of course, is in the division of the literatures of Canada into two separate subjects, English-Canadian literature or, more commonly, "Canadian Literature" and littérature québécoise, the study of which is handled by two separate departments with little if any inter-action between them. As my book will demonstrate, the primary reason that there have only been scattered attempts to overcome this division, such as through courses in comparative Canadian literature, is that to look at the literatures of Canada through anything other than this sepa-ratist framework undermines the erroneous belief that there is some logical and understandable continuum or pattern of growth in which each literature has developed. The specious unity that such a model imposes on the respective literatures of English Canada and French Québec, and the direct lineage it implies between the "mother" literatures of England and France and their offspring cultures, is crucial for the self-reproduc-tion of the literary institution and the universities' role in it. As I will elaborate in the Afterword, there is a tremendous opportunity for scholars and teachers today to begin to question the myriad assumptions that current course structures and literature curricula make on a daily basis; as Québec's three largest French universities have proven so well with respect to the literatures of Québec, a diversity of courses and a greater place in the curriculum for the literatures of Canada would yield a far greater understanding of the literatures themselves. In this book, I do not presume to have the answers as to how to get there, but I do try to pinpoint some of the questions we need to ask before we can make any significant steps to acknowledging through our literature curricula the tremendous complexity of Canada as a literary space.

The "People's Literature"
Histories of Teaching the Literatures of Canada

1

OVER THE COURSE OF MY VISITS to Canadian universities in 1997–98, it became clear that the vast majority of professors with whom I spoke believed that the study of English and French literatures was more open than ever before—that the presence in their departments of a significant number of courses on the literatures of Canada is in itself proof of the academy's willingness to break the bounds of its formerly restrictive notions of English and French literature. In fact, many professors suggested that the position of the literatures of Canada in the university curriculum of the mid-1990s was accepted and relatively unchallenged, a situation very different from the 1960s and 1970s when many of them or their predecessors were treated by their colleagues as if the literatures of Canada did not merit serious attention. It is my contention, however, that this apparent acceptance is due as much to a gradual shift in approach on the part of Canadianists that aligns them much more with the traditional objectives of a department of English or études françaises as it is to a growing appreciation of the literatures of Canada by non-Canadianists. This is particularly true in English Canada where just a few decades ago scholars fought tirelessly to demonstrate that English-Canadian literature was a national literature worthy of study. A look at English departments in the late twentieth and early twenty-first centuries shows that we have reached a point where English-Canadian literature—or more accurately *contemporary* English-Canadian literature—is considered as relevant and important a subject of study as the contemporary literatures of Britain and the United States. In Québec, this sense of equality arrived quite a bit earlier, in part because of particular methodologies and institutional structures that permitted a more scientific study of Québécois literature. To determine if the place of the literatures of Canada has truly changed since the 1960s, however, one needs to look beyond the plethora of possible courses and critical approaches available to students in the early twenty-first century to the very origins of English and French literary studies at Canadian universities and then to the history of how the two principal literatures of Canada eventually became the subject of dedicated courses within the university curriculum.

Given the history of Canada, it should not be surprising that when, in the second half of the nineteenth century, the study of literature in the vernacular languages began to take the place of the classics, the English-language and French-language universities of Canada focused their respective attention on the national literatures of Britain and France. These literatures became so dominant, in fact, that it was only after decades of debate, that works by Canadian writers ever found their way into the curriculum and much longer before entire courses on Canadian literature were ever offered. Furthermore, once English departments finally put into place such courses, they designated that English majors or honours students could not take them for credit; Canadian literature, in other words, was effectively deemed irrelevant for students specializing in the study of literature and a nice diversion for students without a serious interest in studying English literature. When the surge of nationalism in the late 1960s and early 1970s finally brought a great call for courses in the literatures of Canada, many English-language universities in Canada found themselves ill-equipped to meet the demand. The relative lack of attention previously given by English departments to the literatures of Canada meant that many of the "Canadianists" who began teaching during that era had no formal training in the field.

French-language universities, on the other hand, were undoubtedly better prepared, in part because of their awareness of the need to preserve and further their own culture but also due to the efforts of figures such as Camille Roy, who, early on, saw the need to work towards a "nationalisation de la littérature" (C. Roy 187). This is not to say, however, that scholars of French-Canadian and Québécois literature never felt marginalized in their own institutions. As most francophone professors I interviewed related to me, even in the 1960s, French-Canadian literature was not considered to be material worthy of doctoral research; moreover, a doctorate from a French university earned one much greater academic credibility and respect than one from an institution in Québec. In fact, it has only been since the 1970s that the literatures of Canada have come to be considered by the academic mainstream as being of interest for their literary value rather than simply as representations of the literary production of the Canadian peoples. As I will begin to argue in this chapter, though, in spite of this apparent escape from the shadows of British and French literatures, the eventual incorporation and acceptance of the literatures of Canada in university curricula, and the slow move away from an overtly nationalistic motive for studying them, much of this historical baggage still plays a prominent—and perhaps even dominant—role in early twenty-first-century courses on the literatures of Canada.

: It is not a coincidence that the nineteenth century saw the introduction, in Britain and France, of university-level instruction in the national literatures of those countries. While the classics had long been considered the ideal material for a true humanistic education, certain conditions, both social and political, eventually turned the focus of literary education away from the classics and belles lettres to the literature written in the vernacular of each nation. The French Revolution and the subsequent decades of political turmoil in France made it apparent to the elite, in both France and England, that the only way to have some sort of control over the masses—or at least to be somewhat certain there would be no widespread revolt—was through education and, especially, inculcation of the notion that there were certain common ideals that superseded the class and economic structures that were no longer simply accepted by many. In England, the Industrial Revolution, an increased recognition by the people of their own power, an increasing rate of literacy, and a growing question of the value of empire were increasingly threatening to destroy the metanarratives that placed political, economic, and social privilege as a birthright. For the "educationalists, politicians, and political theorists [searching] for new and more efficient ways of building and disseminating a national sense of ancestry, tradition, and universal 'free' citizenship"—which, not coincidentally, would help to maintain the hegemony and ensure the continuation of England's role and status as a world power—mass education for the working class and for women in the "English subjects," that is to say, English language, history, and literature, seemed the ideal means to this end (Doyle, *English and Englishness* 25).

English literature, then, became an essential component in the adult education movements of the nineteenth century. For instance, the Mechanics' Institutes, of which there were five hundred by 1850, aimed to provide men with a more scientific and theoretical form of vocational training; they nearly always, however, also "included lectures on English literature in their programmes, and through their libraries they enabled many members to develop the reading habit and to make acquaintance with the national literature" (Palmer 31). In fact, as James Hole revealed in his 1853 essay lamenting the decline in the "instructive" subjects at these institutions, "[lectures] on literature had increased to more than half the total" (Palmer 33). As this emphasis on bringing national culture to the masses continued through the extension movement and the founding of institutions such as the Working Men's College in 1854 (Palmer 35), the education of women became another locus of early education in English literature. A significant moment in this movement was, undoubtedly, the founding in 1848 of the Queen's College for Women in London. Charles Kingsley, the first professor of English at Queen's, argued in his opening lecture that the "reading of English literature (to include modern works) would help towards an understanding of the 'English spirit,' thus counteracting the notion that 'the minds of young women are becoming un-English'" (Doyle, "Hidden History" 24).

In both cases, the teaching of English was seen as a sort of "missionary work addressed to the cultural colonization of the great mass of the excluded population" (Doyle, *English and Englishness* 19). "'By means of [English] literature,'" wrote Reverend H.G. Robinson in an 1860 essay entitled "On the Uses of English Classical Literature in the Work of Education," "'it seems to me that we might act very beneficially on the national mind, and do much to refine and invigorate the national character'" (Palmer 45). Importantly, as Brian Doyle reminds us in his article "The Hidden History of English Studies," for "English" to be effective on both social and political levels, it needed to construct itself in such a way that it "carr[ied] the sense of an unproblematic national cultural heritage" (18)—a tendency comically pointed to in Kingsley Amis's *Lucky Jim* when a drunken Jim Dixon concludes his disastrous public lecture on "Merrie England" with the remark that "Merrie England...was about the most un-Merrie period in our history" (Amis 227). "Thus," writes Doyle, "'the English language' and 'the national literature' in dominant definitions, represent ratifications of a selective sense of culture and history, or comfortable affirmations of certain structures and forms of cultural authority" ("Hidden History" 18).

Like the English, the French too used the teaching of an oversimplified concept of cultural history to propagate what Étienne Balibar refers to as a "fictive ethnicity":

> No nation possesses an ethnic base naturally, but as social formations are nationalized, the populations included within them, divided up among them or dominated by them are ethnicized—that is, represented in the past or in the future as if they formed a natural community, possessing of itself an identity of origins, culture and interests which transcends individuals and social conditions. (Balibar 96)

Thus, while the educational reforms of the Third Republic, for example, "reflected the passionate republican belief...that education was the instrument of democracy, social progress, and popular emancipation," they "were also inspired by nationalism, using the school to break down regional loyalties and form French citizens; this entailed the imposition of standard French, and a war against *patois* and non-French languages" (R. Anderson 273). To make French the national language and the cornerstone of the national identity was no small task: a 1790 survey of fifteen million French citizens found that only three million of those people were francophones by birth and six million spoke no French whatsoever (Calvet 166). The Third Republic's emphasis on French as the nation's official language positioned French literature as being superior to that written in other languages: "les autres langues de l'hexagone peuvent produire de la poésie populaire, le français, lui, produit de la littérature: la nuance est importante et caractéristique du siècle" (174).[1] As this quote from Louis-Jean Calvet's *Linguistique et colonialisme* implies, while the dissemination of these constructed notions of a "national" language and tradition—"sans se demander d'ailleurs s'il y a vraiment *une* nation" (174) (without demanding, for that matter, if there really is *a* nation)— allowed France and England to begin to see themselves reflected in the influential Romantic nationalist ideas of Rousseau and Herder, it also permitted them to present a more unified vision of themselves to the world and, particularly, to their colonial subjects. Just as the United States in the twentieth century prospered by creating—out of a complex conglomeration of diverse peoples, regions, and histories—an image for itself as the world's great democratic, freedom-loving, melting pot, France and England found the concept of a single and definable national identity to be a mobilizing force for its own citizens and justification of its superiority as a colonial power.

Given the usefulness of such a national image in the colonial enterprise, it is not surprising that, as noted by critics such as Gauri Viswanathan, Margery Fee, and Heather Murray, the development of English studies in the colonies predates by decades their integration into the curriculum at British universities. Viswanathan, in her important book *Masks of Conquest: Literary Study and British Rule in India* (1989), details how "English" education of the native population "was seen by England to be a colonial intervention" (11) that would "civilize" and thus "free" the people of India. Of course, as Viswanathan points out, "the question of how England [could] serve the people of India blends indistinguishably with the question of how power [could] best be consolidated" (15). The teaching of English literature in India began shortly after the 1813 Charter Act under which Britain assumed "new responsibility toward native education" (23) and was further institutionalized with Governor General W. Bentinck's English Education Act of 1835, which "officially required the natives of India to submit to the study of English literature" (45). Bentinck and other British officials initially viewed English literature as an ideal vehicle for the "dissemination of moral and religious values" while still maintaining the pretense of religious non-interference (44). Eventually, though, it was recognized that religious conversion was not an achievable goal and that English literature was a more effective tool when the focus was shifted "from the centrality of universal Christian truths to the legitimacy and value of British institutions, laws, and government" (95). Of course, this secularization of the goals of public education occurred at home in England and France too, marking "a relocation of cultural value from belief and dogma to language, experience, and history" (117). Still, there was an additional aspect to teaching and promotion of the "national literature" to the colonized; in the case of both England and France, it was hoped that a "grafting of [their] literary achievements onto the cultural system of the colonies [would] further assur[e] the survival of the [national] culture, leaving a 'monument more imperishable than the pyramids of Egypt'" (115).

The early history of English studies in Canada is marked by a similar agenda to ensure that the citizens of Canada would recognize and help to further the greatness of the British tradition. Yet, unlike the situation in India, this was not a case of the colonizer trying to "civilize" the indigenous population, which, in Canada during the nineteenth century, was small compared to the size of the land and, in many cases, had already suffered through centuries of subjugation. It was, rather, more like the situation in Britain where there was seen to be a need to introduce women and the lower classes to the characteristics of the national mind. What is especially striking about the early history of university-level English studies in Canada—and what helps explain why they predate similar courses at most British universities—is that this push for the furthering of Canada's Englishness came from within rather than without. The elite in English Canada saw the study of English as a way to ensure the Englishness of a country that had a significant franco-phone population, an aggressive southern neighbour, and, during the last half of the nineteenth century, a huge growth in immigration. It was not uncommon during this period for newspaper editorials and political speeches to call for English to be *the* national language and culture of Canada and, thus, for the assimilation of all other linguistic and cultural groups (Morgan 290). Those "loyalists" saw a great need for a kind of English education, then, that would focus on "inculcating the ideals of British culture....The primary interests of newly formed English departments, therefore, coalesced with those of the cultural elite outside of English studies programs " (Hubert and Garrett-Petts 14). As George Ross, Ontario's first minister of education and a future premier, stated to the *London Advertiser* in 1900, "There is no antagonism in my opinion between Canadianism and Imperialism. The one is but the expansion of the other. To be a true Canadian, under existing conditions, is to place yourself in harmony with the spirit of the empire" (Morgan 297).

Initially, explains Robin S. Harris in his *History of Higher Education in Canada*, "the arts curricula" at Canadian universities "were purely derivative—the model whether English, Scottish, Irish or American is readily seen" (37). During the 1850s, though, universities began to diverge from these models as they sought ways to "respon[d] to the conditions of Canadian life" (37). While classics remained a primary focus of an arts education, by 1860 the study of English had become mandatory for undergraduates, although at that time "the main concern of teachers of English was with English language" (49). The 1850s and 1860s saw some growth in the place of English in the university. In 1853, for instance, the University of Toronto appointed the first Canadian professor of English, Daniel Wilson (a joint appointment with History), and in 1858—only one year after the first American chair of English was founded at Lafayette College (Shumway 96)—McGill University established a chair of English language and literature (R.S. Harris, *English Studies at Toronto* 7).

It was really only in the 1880s that English studies began to take a prominent position in the Canadian curricula, becoming "the rising subject in the humanities" while interest in Greek and Latin declined noticeably (R.S. Harris, *History of Higher Education in Canada* 138). Appointments of professors of English at Dalhousie, Queen's, and Toronto during this decade reflected the growing demand for English studies (*History of Higher Education in Canada* 138). The first full professorship of English was established at Dalhousie in 1884 with the appointment of W.J. Alexander, who left in 1889 to become professor of English language and literature at University College at the University of Toronto. The fact that by 1890 five major Canadian universities had dedicated English professors is extremely significant when one considers that the subject was only just beginning to be taught at the most important institutions in Britain. As Heather Murray notes,

> By the 1900s, then, while the Oxbridge study of English was in its infancy (although studies at London and the Scottish universities had been in place much earlier), and while cases for vernacular study were still being mustered in the US academy, the study of literature as literature—a so-called "rhetorical" or even "aesthetic" criticism—was as much as sixty years old in English Canada. (198)

English studies continued to grow in popularity and influence in Canada partly because of the impression that it best fulfilled the ideals of Arnoldian humanism; a system in which students were exposed to "the best that is known and thought in the world" (Arnold 38), Arnold and his followers believed, would awaken those students to the political, moral, and aesthetic ideals of their society. By the end of the First World War, English "was a core subject in virtually every arts and science program in English-speaking Canada" (McKillop 227) and during the interwar period had achieved such a status that "no subject enjoyed more prestige" (465).

The rapid and distinct development of English studies in Canada serves as a prime example of what Viswanathan labels the "danger of reading the history of modern English studies as an uninterrupted narrative" (168). From its earliest stages in Canada, in other words, English grew in different directions and for other reasons than it did in other parts of the world. This is not to say, however, that similar concerns over the production and reproduction of "Englishness" were not present throughout the development of English studies in Canada. As mentioned above, when English studies began in Canada it was recognized by its supporters and practitioners as a means of humanistic enlightenment but also as a means of propagating a vision of Canada as a logical extension, both politically and culturally, of the British Empire. This latter understanding of English not only persisted well into the twentieth century, but it also became even stronger after the publication of the Newbolt Report, *The Teaching of English in England*, in 1921. "English," the report argued, "is not merely the medium of our thought, it is the very stuff and process of it. It is itself the English mind, the element in which we live and work" (Great Britain Board of Education 20). Equally important, then, was the notion that the study of English was the key to building and perpetuating a "common" (English) culture:

> *The common right to [such an education], the common discipline and enjoyment of it, the common possession of the tastes and associations connected with it, would form a new element of national unity, linking together the mental life of all classes by experiences which have hitherto been the privilege of a limited section. (15)*

Much like E.D. Hirsch's theories of "cultural literacy," of course, the Newbolt Report does not advocate looking for and finding value in what all segments of society have in common but, rather, promotes imposing on the rest of society those values and traditions deemed important by the cultural elite. As Robert Morgan points out, these ideas were embraced by English Canada's own cultural elite and promoted by departments of English that were continuing to grow in size and influence (316). Even while developments such as the New Criticism saw scholars working to position English as a more professional and scientific discipline, many felt that the aim should still be towards the glorification of the British tradition and the inculcation of a sense of Britishness in students, a notion that was, in Canada at least, as much anti-American as it was pro-British. Exemplars of this attitude during the 1940s and 1950s included University of Toronto professors H.V. Routh and Malcolm Wallace. Routh, as Morgan points out, argued in *The Diffusion of English Culture* (1941) that teachers of English should see themselves as "'British emissaries' disseminating 'British culture' in colonial settings," while

Wallace, in *English Character and the English Literary Tradition* (1952), "revived Kipling's notorious phrase, 'the white man's burden,' remarking that 'it's ceasing to be a phrase for cynicism'" (317). Thus, while English was sometimes touted as developing in students a sort of universal humanism, scholars, teachers, and bureaucrats also clearly saw its potential to counteract and minimize the effect of Canada's non-English and non-white population on "Canadian" identity.

Partly because of a very different educational system, that of the *collèges classiques*, the study of literature developed much differently at French-language institutions of higher learning. The college system in Québec—and, it is important to note, the history of higher education in Canada—began in New France with the establishment in 1635 of a Jesuit college at Québec. While that college initially served as little more than a primary school for the children of settlers, by the 1660s it was offering the full *cours classique*, a seven- or eight-year program leading ultimately to the *baccalauréat ès arts*. A mainstay of education in France, the cours classique remained the basis of higher education in Québec until the formation of the CÉGEP (Collège d'enseignement général et professionel) system in the mid-1960s (R.S. Harris, *History of Higher Education in Canada* 14–15). While the education provided by the collèges classiques— there were seven in existence by 1840 and close to two hundred by 1960 (Melançon, Moisan, and Roy 28)—there was, from fairly early on, some coverage of French literature in the Belles Lettres course. Nevertheless, as late as the 1850s, though, Belles Lettres and Rhetoric were only two classes in the whole eight-year program and these classes used examples from Greek, Latin, and, to a lesser degree, French and English literatures (R.S. Harris, *History of Higher Education in Canada* 38–39). The influence of French language and literature grew in 1880, however, when the French government made changes to the baccalauréat curriculum—such curricular changes were nearly always also enacted in Canada—that replaced Latin composition with French and increased the presence of French poetry, prose, and literary history (Melançon, Moisan, and Roy 239). Ten years later, the "dissertation française" became another required element of the baccalauréat, and French literature increasingly became the subject of this written work (239–40). Still, classics remained the focus of the cours classique, and it was not until the opening of the CÉGEP system in 1967 that the emphasis of literary curricula underwent a fundamental and nearly complete shift from the classics to literature in the vernacular.

Unlike the development of English studies in English Canada, which developed with some independence from the British models of higher education, the collèges classiques nearly always followed the lead of the college system in France. In fact, the system of colleges in Québec "a adopté les mêmes programmes, utilisé les mêmes manuels, et suivi la même évolution" (Melançon, Moisan, and Roy 237).[2] Nevertheless, the cultural, religious, and political elite in Québec who supported the furthering of the cours classique had similar motives to their counter-parts in English Canada in that they too saw a great political and social benefit in the ability of education to create and propagate a "common culture:" "La valeur de l'enseignement classique," stated a 1950s docu-ment on classical education in Québec, "provient en grande partie de ce qu'il représente un foyer culturel homogène pour toute la période de formation de l'adolescent" (cited in Melançon, Moisan, and Roy 63).[3] The founding of the Université Laval (1852) was one means of ensuring this homogeneity,[4] for it came to control the administering of the final examinations for the baccalauréat and the conferring of the degree. This responsibility was also given to the Université de Montréal once it ceased being a satellite campus of Laval in 1920. While the system of collèges classiques was considered to be one of secondary education, it effectively filled the same roles as both secondary and undergraduate education in English Canada. Students completing the cours classique would then be eligible to go to university for a more specialized type of education. When Laval first opened, for instance, there were four facul-ties: Theology, Law, Medicine, and Arts, the latter of which, aside from its role in administering and awarding the baccalauréat ès arts, oversaw the activities of several collèges classiques that chose to affiliate them-selves with the university (Moisan 46). A significant development in the state of literary education in Québec occurred in 1920 when Laval insti-tuted the *licence ès lettres*, a two-year program of specialized study for those intending to teach the literature classes in the cours classique. The newly established Université de Montréal further divided the licence ès lettres into two streams: the first was oriented towards teaching, while the second, the *licence de culture*, followed the same standards but allowed the student much greater choice in courses and was ultimately a "titre d'honneur" (R.S. Harris, *History of Higher Education in Canada* 313–15). Increasingly, then, Québec's universities served as a regulator of higher education, a role that, more and more, saw them set the standards by which the cours classique could help to achieve the uniformity or "cultural literacy" the elite saw as necessary for the greater definition and dissemination of a "national" culture.

While a humanistic education was often lauded by Québec's elite for its ability to open the minds of students to aesthetic and moral ideals, thus, in the words of Arnold himself, "turning a stream of fresh and free thought upon our stock notions and habits" (Arnold 38), it was clear to them that the knowledge produced by a classical education also served as a "'patrimoine national' ['national heritage']. Rationellement et historiquement, le génie latin et français, au Québec, ne peut être que national et religieux, rempart efficace contre le génie saxon et l'hérésie protestante, à la fois" (Melançon, Moisan, and Roy 66).[5] In this respect, then, the value of the cours classique was not so much that it originated in France but that the type of knowledge it (re)produced was distinct from the more contemporary, secular, and scientific education being promoted in English Canada and the United States. One of the strongest proponents of this idea was the Abbé Henri-Raymond Casgrain:

> *Représentants de la race latine, en face de l'élément anglo-saxon, dont l'expansion excessive, l'influence anormale doivent être balancées, de même qu'en Europe, pour le progrès de la civilisation, notre mission et celles des sociétés de même origine que nous, éparses sur ce continent, est d'y mettre un contrepoids en réunissant nos forces, d'opposer au positivisme anglo-américain, à ses instincts matérialistes, à son égoïsme grossier, les tendances plus élevées, qui sont l'apanage des races latines, une supériorité incontestée dans l'ordre morale et dans la domaine de la pensée.[6] (Casgrain 370)*

Unlike the public and higher education systems in English Canada that aimed to assimilate the "other" by not allowing it a voice, the corresponding systems in French Canada worked from the completely opposite perspective. The primary paradigm of English-Canadian education and its promotion of Englishness was one of domination; that of the French-Canadian system was one of resistance and survival. Continuously vigilant against the linguistic, political, and cultural threat of the English other, the collèges classiques worked hard to establish and propagate an understanding of the exact nature of French Canada's own otherness. It was this aim to define further the *difference* of the French-Canadian society that provided the impetus for the inclusion of "littérature canadienne" into the curriculum of the cours classique.

It was not long after the rise of Romantic nationalism in nineteenth-century Europe that Canadian critics began to question if Canada could truly consider itself a great nation without its own national literature. One of the earliest and most influential critics to do so in Québec was the Abbé Henri-Raymond Casgrain who, in his influential article "Le Mouvement littéraire canadien" (1860), argued that French Canada's "avenir national" (national future) was directly dependent on its "avenir intellectuel" (intellectual future) (367–68). French Canada, he argued, should be excused for not yet having produced a body of undeniably "great" literature as its people had until now been preoccupied with war, rebellions, economic development, and the great physical and intellectual hardships entailed in the establishing of a new society in such a large and relatively inhospitable land. This struggle, argued Casgrain, was now nearly over and it was time for the people to focus on the intellectual progress of the nation, to which the furthering of a "native" literature would make a significant contribution. Throughout the second half of the nineteenth century and well into the twentieth, critics and journalists, both anglophone and francophone, continued to debate the relation between literary production and the maturity of a nation and whether the literature of Canada would ever be able to stand alongside those of Britain, France, and, to a lesser extent, the United States. While many, including Casgrain, advocated for more critical and public attention to the literatures of Canada if only to help nurture its growth, few—if any—envisioned higher education as playing any formal part in this process, except as a means of turning out well-educated Canadians who would themselves go on to create literary works. This attitude began to change in 1904 with the appearance of an article by Camille Roy, the first critic and scholar to devote serious effort to creating a place for the literatures of Canada in the higher education system.

In "La Nationalisation de la littérature," Roy argued that if a mature and significant francophone literature was to develop in Canada, it could only do so in conjunction with the literary education provided by the cours classique: "mettrons-nous fin à ce spectacle anormal d'une littérature canadienne qui se développe, c'est-à-dire qui recrute ses ouvriers actifs, surtout à côté et en dehors de nos maisons d'éducation" (200).[7] Contending that the college system "est dans quelques-unes de ses parties trop calqué sur l'enseignement français" (is in some of its aspects too closely copied from French education), Roy proposed that space be created in the curriculum for the study of Canadian literature as well as Canadian history, geography, and politics (198). It was Roy's conviction that a more "national" education system would fight "l'indifférence parfois dédaigneuse qu'ici l'on professe, pour la littérature canadienne" (the sometimes disdainful indifference professed here for Canadian literature) and, on a broader level, work to reverse "cette tendance que nous avons à soumettre trop nos idées, nos jugements et nos goûts littéraires à des influences extérieures, européennes et surtout françaises" (198) (this tendency we have to submit overly our ideas, our judgements, and our literary tastes to outside, European, and especially French influences). Roy's suggestions did not go unnoticed; in 1906 a congress on secondary education endorsed a proposal that, beginning in 1907, "littérature canadienne" be added to the program leading to the baccalauréat (Robert, L'institution du littéraire au Québec 41). To facilitate this curricular change, Roy published the Tableau de la littérature canadienne (1907) as a guide for secondary instructors who might have little knowledge of the literary history of Canada. As the still marginal role of littérature canadienne in the cours classique began to gain some ground—by 1914 one of the subjects of the baccalauréat exam on rhetoric was devoted to littérature canadienne (Moisan 47)—Roy filled the need for a more extensive textbook with his *Manuel d'histoire de la littérature canadienne* (1918). Again oriented towards providing instructors with an overview of the history of Canadian literature—both French and English—Roy's manual quickly became the standard text around which the majority of such instruction was based. In fact, the book was so frequently used that it underwent ten revisions between 1918 and 1945 and remained in print until 1962.

As the education of instructors in Québec became a more formalized process with the founding of the École normale supérieure at Laval in 1920 and the opening of the Faculté des arts at the Université de Montréal in 1921, university-level instruction in "littérature canadienne" began to be offered on a regular basis. The teaching stream of the licence ès lettres at the Université de Montréal, for instance, "required study of the languages basic to the classical course (French, Latin, Greek, and at least one modern language) and French-Canadian literature and history" (R.S. Harris, *History of Higher Education in Canada* 315). The non-teaching stream had fewer restrictions, offering students courses in several optional subjects including Canadian literature (*History of Higher Education in Canada* 315). The first regular Canadian literature course offered at the Université de Montréal was taught by Émile Chartier, the university's first dean of the Faculté des lettres. Chartier's "Cours d'histoire de la littérature canadienne," which employed the historical focus typical of literary studies at the time, was offered regularly between 1923 and 1945 (Fortin 188). The University of Ottawa began offering similar courses in 1925, two years before the establishment of their own Faculté des lettres in 1927. Taught for the next thirty years by Séraphin Marion, an employee of the National Archives with doctorates in literature from both the Sorbonne and the Université de Montréal, these courses helped to lay the groundwork for the establishment of Ottawa's Centre de recherche en littérature canadienne in 1958 (Moisan 48). By 1950, a time when most anglophone universities were just starting to teach Canadian literature on a semi-regular basis, "littérature canadienne"—which in these cases, with very few exceptions, referred only to literature in French—had been the subject of regular courses at Laval, the Université de Montréal, and the University of Ottawa for nearly thirty years.

As with French-Canadian literature in Québec, early calls for a greater focus on English-Canadian literature were rooted in a Romantic nationalist philosophy that tied the greatness of a nation to the maturity of its cultural production. During the nineteenth and early twentieth centuries, many seemingly sympathetic critics, such as Pelham Edgar, essentially reiterated Casgrain's argument from "Le Mouvement littéraire canadien" that "the main reasons why we are not more advanced in letters are that we have been busy setting our house in order, and that we have not as a people, and scarcely even as individuals been vitally concerned with ideas that make for literature" (Edgar, "A Fresh View of Canadian Literature" 479). Nevertheless, it was also argued from early on that there was a significant body of Canadian literature already and it would not be until that work was recognized and, more importantly, that Canadian literature was allowed and encouraged to develop further that Canada could ever truly consider itself a nation rather than a colony. E.H. Dewart's introduction to his 1864 anthology *Selections from Canadian Poets* illustrates precisely the Romantic nationalist understanding that links the fate of the nation to the state of its literature:

> A national literature is an essential element in the formation of a national
> character. It is not merely the record of a country's mental progress: it is the
> expression of its intellectual life, the bond of national unity, and the guide
> of national energy. It may be fairly questioned whether the whole range
> of history presents the whole spectacle of a people firmly united politically,
> without the subtle but powerful cement of a patriotic literature. (ix)

Such a statement, of course, is predicated on two key concepts. The first posits a mature and complex literature as an indicator of true nationhood. The second, however, echoes the desire of the British elite to promote an "official nationalism" (B. Anderson 86) that would help to unite the various classes, assimilate the ethnic minorities, and still maintain the country's hegemonic structures. In her 1881 article, "Education and National Sentiment," Kate Seymour MacLean argues that integrating more Canadian content into the primary and secondary education systems would help to promote precisely such an official "national sentiment":

> In a country whose population is so largely made up as ours is, by the influx of yearly immigration from all the countries of the Old World, the strongest necessity exists for some potent influence which shall unite this vast mass of differing, and often conflicting social and civil forces, and render them coherent and orderly elements of the body politic. That there can be no stronger assimilating power than that of a universal and controlling national sentiment. (Maclean 100)

Although some Canadian content was incorporated into the primary and secondary curriculum, "English Studies" became the primary educational component in this process of cultural reproduction. This was especially true at the university level, where departments of English were exactly that—departments of *English*. Thus, even though influential figures such as Pelham Edgar, head of the University of Toronto's Department of English from 1910 to 1938, believed and wrote publicly that to survive, let alone flourish, Canada would need "a coherent body of literature stamped with our national spirit" (Edgar, "Canadian Literature" 100), he and other people in similar positions of power believed that the way for universities to further Canadian literature was not by lowering its standards and teaching Canadian works that they felt to be of a lesser quality than the British classics. Instead, Edgar and others "took it for granted that the role of the university was not necessarily to teach Canadian literature but, rather, by teaching in an inspiring manner the best of English literature, to encourage undergraduates to write" (Fee, "Canadian Literature and English Studies" 25). Edgar, for instance, even wrote articles on Canadian literature and privately did much to encourage its growth. He saw this, however, as an endeavour separate from his teaching. When Thomas Guthrie Marquis writes in 1913 that "the writers of Canada should be studied as English and American writers are studied," it is quite clear that he is arguing for more critical attention to be paid to Canadian writers and not for the presence of Canadian content in university-level English courses (Marquis 495).

As Fee has demonstrated, this early reluctance among chairs of English to incorporate Canadian literature in the curriculum has often led to a mistaken impression among today's scholars that Canadian literature was not taught at English-Canadian universities until the 1960s when, in fact, it appeared in the English curricula of some institutions by 1907. Until well after mid-century, however, courses on Canadian literature were few and far between and were nearly always oriented towards students not majoring in English. There was, in other words, a distinctly utilitarian quality to these early courses in which the pedagogical aim seems to have been more to promote nationalism and the enjoyment of reading than to engage in a serious study of literature for literature's sake. The first Canadian literature course in English seems to have had precisely this intent. Taught first in 1907 as a summer course to women students at the MacDonald Institute, an affiliate of the Ontario Agricultural College, Canadian literature began to appear regularly on the institute's curriculum in 1910 (Fee, "Canadian Literature and English Studies" 22). While this particular course may have initially served a less literary and more utilitarian purpose, Robin S. Harris's survey of Canadian English curricula in the 1950s reveals that Canadian literature grew to be a fundamental part of the English program at the Ontario Agricultural College. As Harris explains, English literature was a required subject throughout the four-year program and the curriculum was essentially a typical survey of British literature "beginning with *Beowulf* and concluding with Stephen Spender" (R.S. Harris, "The Place of English Studies" 198). What makes the Ontario Agricultural College curriculum remarkable—even by today's standards—is that Canadian literature acted as bookends for this traditional survey rather than as simply an add-on to the "English tradition"; the first term of the first year and the second term of the final year were devoted to the study of Canadian literature, and the latter term also included American literature. Rather than the traditional notion that the study of English literature would act as the groundwork for studies in Canadian and American literature, the Ontario Agricultural College curriculum reversed this hierarchy, causing students to learn about the literature of their own nation before they studied that of the empire. Sadly, this course structure still remains the sole exception to the rule; the place given to Canadian literature by the Ontario Agricultural College made them an anomaly in the study of Canadian literature, not a pioneer.

The first Canadian literature course at a major Canadian university came hot on the heels of the course at the MacDonald Institute. Taught by Susan Cameron at McGill University in the academic year of 1907–08, this course was the first of a long series of courses at Canadian universities that covered both American and Canadian literature. Ostensibly examining both literatures within the context of North American literature, such courses in "AmCan," as they were often known, almost always placed a tremendous emphasis on the American literature at the expense of Canadian, which was, thus, portrayed as its poor cousin. Cameron's course, initially titled "American and Canadian Literature, a Historical and Critical Outline of English Literature in the New World," was not taught every year, but survived in various forms with various instructors until 1948–49 when Arthur Phelps began teaching a half-course on solely Canadian literature (Fee, "English-Canadian Literary Criticism" 218). It was not until after the First World War that other major English-Canadian universities joined McGill in offering some instruction in Canadian literature. In fact, the boom in Canadian nationalism during this period prompted many significant developments in the study of Canadian literature, much like the effect of Canadian and Québécois nationalism during the 1960s.

One of the most important figures in this regard was John D. Logan, a critic and, for several years, a lecturer at Acadia University. While not a remarkable critic—Fee describes him as being "to English-Canadian literary criticism what James McIntyre, the 'Cheese Poet' is to English-Canadian poetry" ("English-Canadian Literary Criticism" 298)—Logan was an outspoken commentator on the lack of courses on Canadian literature at English Canada's universities. After giving what he describes as the "first formal series of lectures on Canadian literature ever given at any university in the British Empire" in December of 1915, Logan left Canada to serve in the war ("Teaching Canadian Literature" 61).

To further his efforts to have Canadian literature added to the Acadia curriculum, and recognizing "the importance of having solid research collections in libraries such as Acadia's so that students and faculty could build and develop beyond the mere curriculum of a university English course" (G. Davies 125), Logan, upon his return from France in 1918, donated his vast collection of Canadiana to the Acadia library. In 1919 Acadia instituted a half-course in Canadian literature and, to assist in this effort, Acadia's Board of Governors appointed Logan as a "Special Lecturer on Canadian Literature" (Logan, "Teaching Canadian Literature" 61). Logan did not teach the course itself, but rather gave a series of lectures over the course of the academic year that he describes as being "more for inspiration and method than for a detailed and systematic study of the genres and qualities of Canadian prose" ("Teaching Canadian Literature" 61). While Logan's lectures that year dealt with both the English and French literatures of Canada, the companion half-course, taught by Vernon B. Rhodenizer, focused on English-Canadian literature. Entitled "English 5A: The History of Canadian Literature," this course was offered every other year, with Logan continuing to deliver his complementary lectures until the mid-1920s (G. Davies 117–18). During these early years, these courses were very popular; in 1931, for instance, Rhodenizer indicated that these courses sometimes had upward of sixty students (Fee, "English-Canadian Literary Criticism" 222). While Rhodenizer did tinker with the course over the years, it remained essentially the same until he retired in 1953 ("English-Canadian Literary Criticism" 222).

Logan's influence on the development of early courses on Canadian literature extended past Acadia to Dalhousie University. An alumnus of Dalhousie, Logan initiated a great controversy when he publicly accused Dalhousie and, specifically, Professor Archibald MacMechan of failing to offer courses in Canadian literature and thus "grievously [sinning] against their country and its cultural development" (Logan, "Teaching Canadian Literature" 62). After the Dalhousie Senate acknowledged his complaints and assured him that a Canadian literature course was in the works, Logan was angered when Dalhousie later announced they would be offering a course on American literature in the 1920–21 year while still no similar course on Canadian literature existed. In response, Logan published in 1922, at his own expense, a pamphlet entitled *Dalhousie University and Canadian Literature*, the subtitle of which reads *Being The History of an Attempt to Have Canadian Literature Included in the Curriculum of Dalhousie University*. While this highly public attack undoubtedly embarrassed Dalhousie into offering a Canadian literature course sooner than they had anticipated, Logan's pamphlet is perhaps more interesting for the argument it makes for the inclusion of Canadian literature in the English curricula of Canadian universities. Logan does not go so far to reject the Arnoldian philosophy at the heart of English studies at Dalhousie and, ultimately, all Canadian universities of the day. In fact, unlike the vast majority of his fellow scholars and critics, he argues that "Canada [has] a body of prose and verse which, at its best, [is] worthy to be included in the corpus of English literature and in the survey of English literature as conducted by our universities" (Logan, "Teaching Canadian Literature" 61). Conversely, Logan also takes a more "Canada First" approach and argues that Canadian universities have an obligation to acknowledge adequately the existence of a Canadian literature and literary history—"whether aesthetically fine or not is not to the point" (Logan, *Dalhousie University* 2):

> A written literature and the written appreciations of that literature are a spiritual history of a people, and...it is the function of a Professor of literature to discover a people's ideals as they are preserved in their own literature, to reveal them to contemporary generations and to hold them up for contemplation by the aesthetic, the moral, and the religious imagination. The literature of a country is the people's literature, and the people have the right to say to their Universities and Professors of Literature that the history and appreciation of their native literature shall be taught to them and their children, and future generations. (Dalhousie University 2)

While Logan's criticism may be overly impressionistic and inadequate even by the standards of the 1920s, he was perhaps the first in English Canada to address systematically the need for including Canadian literature in the English curriculum of Canadian universities. His eagerness to engage the public in this debate, to bring, as Gwendolyn Davies puts it, "the battle for Canadian literature to the streets" (121), demonstrates one of the fundamental aspects of his philosophy, one that appears again in the nationalist rhetoric of the 1960s and 1970s: that the good of Canada and its people were served by the teaching and promotion of Canadian literature.

The surge of Canadian nationalism in the 1920s, of which Logan was obviously a part, led several other universities to bring Canadian literature into their English curriculum. In 1919–20, Alexander W. Crawford introduced a course on "Contemporary and Canadian Poets" at the University of Manitoba. Two years later, Queen's followed McGill's lead by introducing a course in Canadian and American literature, a course structure that lasted there until 1929–30 when the Department of English instituted a half-course on Canadian literature. 1923–24, of course, saw the introduction of the Dalhousie course requested so vociferously by J.D. Logan. Entitled "Literary Movements in Canada," MacMechan's course was unusual—particularly in comparison to the courses of the late twentieth century—due to the emphasis it gave to French-Canadian literature. Novels in French were included on the syllabus and all students were therefore expected to have at least a reading knowledge of French (Fee, "Canadian Literature and English Studies" 224). The next Canadian university that moved to ensure a continued presence of Canadian literature in its curriculum was the University of Western Ontario, which in 1925 began offering a "Pass Course" in Canadian literature every second year (S. King 8). The "Pass" designation here is significant because it again represents Canadian literature used as the basis for a less demanding course designed primarily for students not specializing in English. Other Canadian universities to bring in courses at least partly on Canadian literature during the 1920s included Bishop's University, Winnipeg's Wesley College, the University of British Columbia, and Mount Allison University, which, like Dalhousie, offered a half-course on the English and French literatures of Canada.

Given its prominence as Canada's largest university and the number of other universities already initiating courses in this area, it may seem surprising that the University of Toronto did not begin to teach

Canadian literature until 1934–35. Even then, this Canadian content added to the curriculum was relegated to the very end of a course on American and Canadian literature. While the University of Toronto offered a graduate course on Canadian literature in 1947, it took nearly another twenty years after the institution of the AmCan course before Canadian literature became the subject of an entire undergraduate course in the English department. As Robin S. Harris recounts, English 4G, introduced in 1956, was "a solid course, an excellent introduction to Canadian literature"; the syllabus included seven Canadian novels, a short story anthology, and, two collections of Canadian poetry (*English Studies at Toronto* 120). English 4G, however, in no way represented a fundamental change in the University of Toronto's attitude towards the place of Canadian literature in the discipline of English studies. The course was merely "a one-hour-a-week course available as a religious knowledge option to students in honour courses other than those which included English as an honour subject, for example, Physics or Political Science and Economics. It was not available to students whose major interest was in English" (*English Studies at Toronto* 120). In fact, it was only in the mid-1960s that Toronto brought in a number of changes to the honours and general programs, including the addition of an optional fourth-year course on Canadian literature.

The University of Toronto's conservatism and apparent unwillingness to envision "English" as anything other than British and, to a somewhat limited extent, American literature was not all that unusual. In fact, we can see it as a microcosm of the real struggle waged from the 1920s to the 1960s by the literatures of Canada in universities across English Canada and, to a lesser degree perhaps, in Québec. While the smaller size of universities like Acadia, Western, and the Ontario Agricultural College may have made them more flexible and willing to initiate curricular reform, Canadian literature was still met with similar resistance from the faculty of such English departments. As we have seen from its origins in colonial India, English studies aspires to be seen as having no political aims. To make Canadian literature a matter for study in the Canadian English curriculum, still solidly rooted in notions of Arnoldian humanism, was perceived by many members and chairs of English departments as an attempt to politicize the curriculum by incorporating texts that would be taught for reasons other than their "natural" aesthetic superiority. In the case of Toronto and a number of other Canadian universities, though, Canadian literature was seen to be acceptable content for the more service-oriented courses that were not aimed towards students specializing in literature.

The phenomenon of the American-Canadian or AmCan course also serves to illustrate the complexities of this debate between maintaining the purity of the discipline and making it more responsive to the cultural production of the nation. The first attempt to teach these literatures together appears to have occurred at McGill in 1907–08 and was followed by the initiation of a similar course at Queen's in 1921–22. In both cases—and in almost every other subsequent one—these courses served as transitional structures that eventually led to the separation of the two national literatures into courses of their own. The University of Western Ontario offers a unique twist to this pattern in that after offering biennial courses in Canadian literature starting in 1925, they changed the format to American and Canadian literature in 1934. As Sarah King has documented, this structure stayed in place until 1967 when the course was split in two, though not by national literature but by period: the first pass course, English 38, and its honours equivalent English 338, covered "Literature of the United States and Canada to 1885" while English 48 and 448 covered "Literature of the United States and Canada 1885 to Present." These were finally replaced by separate courses on American and Canadian literature in 1970 (S. King 8–9). While the syllabi for these courses at Western almost always contained at least 50 per cent Canadian content, the far more typical structure for courses in "American and Canadian literature"—employed, for instance, at the University of Alberta and the University of Toronto—placed a far heavier emphasis on American literature. The most widely known of the AmCan courses was, naturally, that offered by the University of Toronto. Throughout its history—it was first offered in 1934–35 and continued until the mid-1960s—the course focused so heavily on American content that Canadian works usually made up less than 10 per cent of what was studied. As Robin S. Harris reports, "the course description in the

1963–64 calendar (basically unchanged from that of 1944–45, indeed from that of 1934–35 when the course was introduced in the fourth year)" lists "selections from" works by seven major American poets, five canonical American novels, and a choice from three others (*English Studies at Toronto* 120). The Canadian content is merely described as "Readings in Canadian Poetry (texts to be specified by individual instructors)" (*English Studies at Toronto* 120). The most revealing part of this description is that the course included department-prescribed "canonical" American novels, "major" American poets, and "Readings in Canadian Poetry" chosen at the instructor's discretion; this suggests that not only were there no "major" Canadian writers or works but also that the Canadian works were of such little importance that the department found it unnecessary to determine which works should be covered.

While the stated rationale for courses in "American and Canadian Literature" was frequently that it was both logical and profitable to study these two North American or "New World" literatures side by side, it is quite clear that in many cases these courses served to appease the demand for Canadian content, and did so in such a way that would not fundamentally alter the structure of English studies and English departments. Moreover, as these courses also often marked the first time a course was devoted primarily to American literature, their introduction brought American literature more firmly into the curriculum without the controversy that would inevitably occur—as it did at Dalhousie— if it were brought in before Canadian literature. On the surface, these courses addressed the need for coverage of American literature without appearing to favour it over Canadian literature. The length of time before University of Toronto English students were ever able to take a course entirely on Canadian literature, though, is indicative of the general suspicion there was towards Canadian literature, which, although likely present to varying degrees at other English and French departments across the country, certainly seems to have been more marked at University of Toronto. Robertson Davies's satiric portrayal of such an attitude in *Leaven of Malice* is undoubtedly true to life. Solly Bridgetower, a junior professor of English at Waverly University, is pushed into writing on the work of Charles Heavysege by the department's head who tells him that "Amcan's the coming thing, and particularly the Canadian end of it" (R. Davies 170). A dismayed and unimpressed Bridgetower asks himself,

> Why do countries have to have literatures? Why does a country like Canada, so late upon the international scene, feel that it must rapidly acquire the trappings of older countries—music of its own, pictures of its own, books of its own—and why does it fuss and stew, and storm the heavens with its outcries when it doesn't have them? (171)

While there were many opinions of this sort to be found in English departments around the country in the 1940s and 1950s, there were nevertheless a number of opposing voices. Perhaps the most progressive of these dissenters was Carlyle King at the University of Saskatchewan, whose ardent demands for courses in Canadian literature would have undoubtedly seemed both curious and annoying to someone sharing the views of Davies's Bridgetower. When, in 1944, King resorted to lobbying the president of the university to allow him to leave the Department of English—where, apparently, Canadian literature was not welcome—to form his own department of North American literatures, the president rectified matters by *suggesting* to the department "that certain classes in American and Canadian literature [be] assigned to Dr. King as part of his teaching work" (Findlay 427). This move paved the way for King to teach in 1945–46 "'Canadian Literature, Music, and Art' as a night class to 160 students" (427) and then, the following year, what Len Findlay describes as "the first full-length university course devoted exclusively to the study of Canadian literature" (Findlay 426). While King's disputes with his department may seem to be simply another example of department politics, they are significant because they perfectly represent the deeply engrained institutional resistance to innovation that awaited any Canadianist attempting to convince his or her university of the need for courses on Canadian literature. What was perhaps the most threatening to the University of Saskatchewan's Department of English, however, was not the incorporation of Canadian literature into the curriculum, for it has always been—and, for the most part, continues to be—simple to marginalize and disarm new and potentially progressive areas of the discipline by adding them on as options to an existing curriculum that will then still remain intact. What made King dangerous—and such a word is hardly too dramatic—to the status of English studies at the University of Saskatchewan was his stated desire to form a Department of North American Literatures. Such a department would have disengaged the study of literature from the study of language and culture and allowed the study of North American literatures—which would likely have incorporated French-language literature as well—to extract itself from this notion of the great British "tradition" and its aesthetic and moral superiority over its less interesting colonial offspring. Thus, the Department of English's eventual acceptance of King's courses on Canadian literature were, at the surface, a desire to resolve a political dispute among its members but also, on a much deeper level, a move to preserve the department and the Arnoldian philosophy on which it was based. In other words, so long as North American literature could not be entirely studied on its own terms, it would remain a rather benign force within the English studies curriculum.

King's progressive vision and successful introduction of a "full-fledged, upper-level, and fully accredited course" (McDougall 264) might have been a portent for the rapid development of similar courses at other universities during the 1950s. Robin S. Harris's 1952 dissertation, "The Place of English Studies in a University Program of General Education," however, proves that it was not. Much like my own journey nearly fifty years later, Harris spent the winter of 1951–52 visiting thirty universities across the country primarily to look at the balance between composition and literature in the English classes required for general degrees. Out of these thirty universities, Harris found only eight that offered a potential for "some, though not all, undergraduates to have some formal contact by way of a prescribed English course, with the literature of their own country. In all but two cases, the content was fleeting" (R.S. Harris, "The Place of English Studies" 253) Interestingly, these two seemingly anomalous cases were the two English-language institutions with the longest history of teaching Canadian literature: McGill University and the Ontario Agricultural College. McGill, Harris found, offered a

lecture on Canadian literature every second week, "the avowed purpose...
[of which] was to arouse interest in the literary efforts which Canadians
have made and are currently making" ("The Place of English Studies"
254). These bi-weekly lectures were given to sections of four hundred
students as a supplement to their twice-weekly lectures on English literature. These Canadian lectures were not exclusively focused on Canadian
literature. Rather, as Harris reports, they were seen "by the instructor as
an introduction to the whole problem of the arts in Canada,...an aspect
of Canadian life about which the undergraduate appears to be largely
ignorant" ("The Place of English Studies" 145–46). As previously noted,
the Ontario Agricultural College seems to have been the only institution in English Canada during the 1950s to devote a significant portion
of its curriculum to Canadian literature. While the Ontario Agricultural
College English program still maintained a full and very typical survey
of British literature over the course of the four years of compulsory
English courses, the reading list for the first term of the first year was
drawn solely from an anthology of Canadian prose and poetry, and the
final term of the fourth year brought students back to that anthology at
the same time as they were introduced to American literature; "Canadian
literature thus greeted the O.A.C. student as he entered the College and
waved a figurative goodbye to him as he took his leave" ("The Place of
English Studies" 254).

   In nearly all the other cases found by Harris, Canadian literature
was most likely to appear in service courses oriented towards students
who were not pursuing an arts degree. Whether in courses at Queen's
or Alberta where students of engineering and agriculture respectively
were required to read a Canadian novel, courses at the University of
British Columbia in which second-year professional students "read single
issues of two Canadian periodicals" ("The Place of English Studies" 253),
or at Dalhousie where the professional students studied a few works of
Canadian fiction and non-fiction, it is clear that the designers of these
courses and the curriculum understood Canadian literature to be an
adequate tool for instruction in critical reading and in composition in
such cases where the study of Literature was not a primary goal. Even in
the cases of the McGill lectures and, though perhaps to a lesser degree,

the Ontario Agricultural College program, the place given to Canadian literature makes it clear that the criteria for its inclusion in the curriculum were different than those applied to British literature. Specifically, Canadian literature appears to have been seen to be more useful for the fostering of citizenship and knowledge about Canada than it was for increasing a student's understanding of literary works. The tension between nationalism and the humanistic understanding of the role of English studies characterized the introduction and development of English courses in Canadian literature. As we will learn in later chapters, this very conflict still plays a role in such courses today and does so in a way that it never has in Canadian courses on British literature.

Carlyle King's course—much like that taught by Rhodenizer and Logan at Acadia in the 1920s—was revolutionary for its time. Nevertheless, as Harris's research clearly demonstrates, it did not have an immediate impact on the course offerings at other English universities in Canada. Moreover, while King's supposed goal of teaching in a department of North American literatures positioned the literatures of Canada, at least in that institutional context, as a threat to English studies, the vast majority of the proponents of Canadian literary studies to follow him had more meagre and, sadly, more realistic demands. Desmond Pacey, for instance, is one of the best-known English-Canadian critics and professors to have lobbied extensively for the creation of courses in Canadian literature. In a number of articles over the course of his career, though, he also disavowed any will to have Canadian literature gain a significant enough place in the curriculum to be seen as equally worthy of attention as British literature. In his frequently anthologized article "Literary Criticism in Canada" (1950), Pacey contends that while Canadian literature "should have a place—a small place" in the English curriculum, it should never challenge the centrality of the English canon: "That the study of Canadian literature should not supplant the study of English literature in our universities is eminently reasonable; but it should supplement it" ("Literary Criticism in Canada" 49).[8]

While such a rhetorical strategy was perhaps prudent at a time when many chairs of English had a hard time believing that Canadian literature should be given a place in the English curriculum, it was also a self-fulfilling prophecy. By articulating a vision of Canadian literature that saw it as an offshoot of the British tradition—Pacey's discussions of "Canadian literature" almost always conveniently omit the consideration of French-language literature written in Canada—and thus being worthy of only being a curricular add-on, scholars like Pacey helped to ensure Canadian literature would be incorporated into the curriculum in such a way that it would never threaten the primary focus on British literature. Pacey's vision—undoubtedly a progressive one for 1950—was that Canadian literature should ideally make up "possibly one term out of the usual eight...in the curriculum of those students who are specializing in English" ("Literary Criticism in Canada" 49). Given that today, over sixty years later, the number of Canadian literature courses at English universities barely meets Pacey's optimum ratio of one out of eight, it appears that the reasonable demands of Pacey and his contemporaries may have actually hindered Canadian literature's ability to grow beyond its position as a "supplement" to the study of British literature.

Certainly, during the 1950s, some professors in the literature departments of Québec's French universities also considered French-Canadian literature to be a "soft option," an adolescent and aesthetically inferior offshoot of the great French tradition. Yet, perhaps because of a self-awareness among academics as to the role education would need to play in protecting and invigorating the French language and culture in Québec, courses in littérature canadienne began to expand and to grow beyond the more general survey courses that had been offered regularly since the early 1920s. In 1955, for instance, Laval offered their first course—and perhaps the first ever course—devoted to a single Canadian text: Philippe Aubert de Gaspé's *Les Anciens Canadiens* (Fortin 196). An entire course on *Maria Chapdelaine* followed in 1960 at the Université de Montréal (197). More revolutionary, though, was Léopold LeBlanc's 1959 Université de Montréal course on André Langevin, a writer in his early thirties whose works had never been taught before. These courses opened the door for a series of courses in the 1960s that dealt with either a single work or a single author (198). In 1958, the founding of the University of Ottawa's Centre de recherche en littérature canadienne by four professors from its French department was also a landmark event in that it gave both a credibility and a distinct institutional presence to the study of French-Canadian literature. It is essential to note, however, that while Québec's universities had come to devote more attention to the literature of its own people, the most frequent form of higher education in Québec, the baccalauréat, still provided a very traditional and conservative classical education, in which the "sujets canadiens" could only play a minor role. In fact, all of modern literature was still very much neglected in the collèges classiques in comparison to the attention devoted to French literature of the seventeenth and eighteenth centuries. As Clément Moisan points out, for instance, it was not until the 1950s that Baudelaire was included in the curriculum, and even Voltaire, "comme tout les auteurs à l'Index, est étudié dans des morceaux choisis ou des textes expurgés" (Moisan 52) (like all authors in the Index was studied through selected passages or expurgated texts). While, by the 1960s, littérature canadienne still did not have a dominant role in the literary subjects of the cours classique, that it had any presence at all was in fact a major accomplishment, due in great part to the efforts and influence of Camille Roy.

Because the Université Laval and the Université de Montréal had allowed littérature canadienne a permanent, albeit minor, presence in the university curriculum since the 1920s and, during the 1950s, had introduced more specialized courses on the subject, these universities— unlike their English counterparts in the other provinces—were fairly well prepared to respond to the surge in Canadian and Québécois nationalism during the 1960s and early 1970s and the resulting interest in the literatures of Canada. At these two universities in particular, the overall zeitgeist of the Quiet Revolution and the specific educational reforms brought in by the Lesage government following the Parent Report helped bring about a rapid expansion in the study and teaching of what was increasingly referred to as littérature québécoise. In 1963, for instance, Laval's Faculté des Lettres created separate departments of études françaises and études canadiennes, the latter of which was "consacrée entièrement au domaine littéraire, au folklore, et à l'ethnologie" (Moisan 50) (devoted entirely to the literary domain, to folklore, and to ethnology). Thanks to the growing role of littérature canadienne in the cours classique, the university had already instituted specialized teaching degrees or *licences*, in which students could specialize in "civilisation canadienne." In 1963, students working for the licence gained the further option to obtain one of the four required certificates in the field of "littérature canadienne-française" (51). While changes at Laval in 1971 reunited the two departments (and integrated several others) in a single "Département des littératures"—the title of which, it is important to note, removes the linguistic and cultural determinants inherent in the nomenclature of all departments of English or études françaises—the study of Québécois literature had eight years to develop in its own department and therefore undoubtedly grew in ways it could not have in the same department as French literature. Moreover, becoming one of the literatures around which a new department of several literatures was constructed perhaps allowed it a status of being worthy of study on its own in a way that can never occur when a department is composed of one major national literature and one that inevitably seems to be minor in comparison.

The Commission royale d'enquête sur l'enseignement au Québec, formed in 1961, was perhaps the single most important event of the 1960s to affect the place of Québécois literature in the university and college curriculum. Released in 1964, the commission's findings, more commonly referred to as the Parent Report, called for the government to take over control of the public education system, replace the system of collèges classiques with a more modern college system, and to found several new public universities. Significantly, in its recommendations on curriculum, it also argued for a greater role to be accorded to littérature canadienne, even if it meant applying different standards to it than were applied to the literature of France: "L'enseignement de cette littérature pourrait s'orienter en partie vers une étude des aspects sociologiques que comportent les oeuvres littéraires et se rattacher, de cette façon, à une sorte d'anthropologie culturelle ou de psychologie nationale" (3, 613: 41).[9] As Melançon et al. point out, the members of the commission were obviously "trop imprégnés de la conception esthétique de la littérature pour proposer une simple intégration des oeuvres québécoises à l'enseignement littéraire" (398) (too imbued with the aesthetic conception of literature to propose a simple integration of Québécois works into literary education). Nevertheless, it is clear that the commission considered the study of its own people's literature to play a vital role in the creation of a provincial educational system that would not only increase the quality of education and thus the province's competitiveness, but also foster the further growth of the French language and culture in Québec.

One of the key places the teaching of littérature canadienne would occur would be at a new level of post-secondary education that would provide both professional and vocational training as well as a more general form of pre-university education. Created in 1967 with the passing of Bill 21, the Collèges d'enseignement général et professionel, or CÉGEPs as they are more commonly known, provided students with a two-year course of general studies that then allows them to enter university directly into their area of specialization. The required CÉGEP courses in French, much like the required first-year English courses at universities outside of Québec, mark the last time students bound for university are ever required to take courses in language and literature. Therefore, these courses became one of the primary sites where the inclusion of works by Québécois writers was deemed essential by critics, scholars, teachers, and administrators. In their *La littérature au Cégep, 1968–1978*, a profoundly detailed study of the role played by literature at this level of education and major achievement in the sociology of literary studies in Canada, Joseph Melançon and his co-authors reveal that between 1968 and 1978 Québécois literature became increasingly important in the curriculum, gaining a status and proportion nearly equal to that of French literature (Dumont 382). A survey of course outlines from a number of CÉGEPs during this period reveals that three of the ten authors most frequently studied were from Québec (M. Roy "Les oeuvres littéraires étudiées dans les cours communs de français" 207). Québécois texts were also among the most frequently used; only Anouilh's *Antigone* (twenty-two occurrences) appeared on course lists more often than Hébert's *Kamouraska* (twelve occurrences) and Borduas's *Refus Global* (Camus's *Noces* also tied for second place). Although this shift to Québécois texts, which were mostly from the twentieth century, was partly due to a deliberate shift away from the Grand Siècle so favoured in the cours classique to the contemporary and seemingly more relevant, its relation to the *projet national* of educational reform and the formation of a "national" identity cannot be underestimated. Interviews and surveys of teachers of literature at the CÉGEP level reveal that this growth in the study of Québécois literature was tied to "l'adoption d'un point de vue socio-historique, d'une part, et à la volonté de susciter un sentiment d'identification, d'autre part. Cette identification a semblé s'être faite par le biais du nationalisme" (Dumont 383).[10] Interestingly, by the late 1970s, most of these same instructors reported finding less of a need to address the relation between Québec's literature and its society and that they had thus shifted their pedagogical focus to the literary aspects of these same texts (383–84).

The growing cultural and political desire of Québec society during the 1960s to define and further its own distinct identity that was neither French nor simply "Canadian"—a term that, more and more, had been appropriated by English-Canadians as being wholly representative of themselves—the study of littérature canadienne and eventually littérature québécoise at the university level passed "d'un enseignement destiné à la formation d'enseignants du secondaire, à une recherche méthodologique et théorique dont le but avoué était d'accréditer le caractère scientifique de la littérature québécoise" (Moisan 56) (from an education aimed at teaching future secondary teachers to methodological and theoretical research of which the avowed goal was to substantiate the scientific character of Québécois literature). As Nicole Fortin has shown, this period saw more courses introduced that went beyond the traditional structure of the historical survey. While courses dealing with particular authors, movements, or texts certainly emerged during the 1950s, these new courses began to address directly the methodologies to be applied in such studies. In Fortin's words, courses with titles such as "Problèmes de littérature canadienne (Université de Montréal—1960)," "Éditions critiques d'auteurs canadiens—Méthodologie (Université Laval—1964)," and "Sociologie de la littérature canadienne (Université d'Ottawa—1965)" were significant because they testified to "l'émergence de démarches où la littérature apparaît moins sous la forme d'un objet de *connaissance* que sous celle d'un objet de *compréhension*" (Fortin 195) (the emergence of approaches in which literature appears less under the form of an object of *knowledge* than one of *comprehension*). This growing belief that Québécois texts were as worthy of study as any other literary texts was, as Fortin rightly points out, due in great part to a changing conception of literature that, through new perspectives such as those offered by structuralist and poststructuralist theory, brought into question aesthetic value as the primary focus of literary study. Emblematic of such an understanding of Québécois literature and of the literary text in general is the fact that when the Université du Québec à Montréal opened in 1969, it had no department of French, only a département d'études littéraires that focused on literary theories or problems and paid less attention on the text's language or nation of origin.

While this departmental structure was undoubtedly a progressive move and remains, even today, a unique experiment in Canada, it also expressed a remarkable confidence—especially for a public institution— as to the ability of Québécois literature to exist on an equal basis with all other literatures studied in the same department. It should not be overlooked, however, that such a confidence allows things to come full circle for the study of the literature of Québec and invokes the very same Romantic nationalist desires that motivated Casgrain and Roy. While the understanding of the literary text certainly changed during this time and the methodology applied to the study of Québécois literature had definitely become more complex, there is no question that there was also a nationalist benefit to disavowing the place of nationalism in research and teaching by scholars of Québécois literature. To do so was to imply that nationalism no longer was an issue because Québécois literature had finally come of age and was mature enough to be considered a true national literature in its own right. As scholars of Québécois literature smartly discovered, believing one's literature to have such a status can be a self-fulfilling prophecy, though only in a social or national context— what one thinks of one's own literature has a limited effect on its international standing. As we will discuss more in the next chapter, just like the social reproductive aspects of the study of French and British literature, the seeming separation of the study of Québécois literature from the *projet national* actually makes it an even more effective contributor to the development of a national identity.

A comparison between courses in littérature canadienne in French universities in Québec during the 1960s and courses on Canadian literature at English-Canadian universities during the same period make it quite apparent that the latter would take much longer to move away from an overtly nationalist approach. Indeed, while the early to mid-sixties saw universities like Laval and the Université de Montréal begin to offer more specialized courses on topics like literary history and the sociology of literature, English-Canadian universities were content with offering usually just single sections of optional courses that surveyed the entire history of Canadian literature or both Canadian and American literature together. During this period, however, there was a growing call for more attention to be paid to the literatures of Canada in the nation's universities. In "Curriculum Crisis," an important 1971 article often overlooked by later critics,[11] Professor Alec Lucas of McGill University reports that the Royal Commission on Bilingualism and Biculturalism surveyed Canadian universities to see how many were teaching courses in Canadian literature in the 1964–65 academic year. From the eight English universities the commission examined, they found only seven undergraduate courses in Canadian Literature (Lucas 58). In the later 1960s, the demand for such courses grew, though Lucas coldly points out that universities were too slow to respond: "By 1967–68, when Canadianism was supposedly in full flower throughout the land, the same universities offered only a total of ten [courses] in Canadian literature and nine combining it with other literatures" (58). To see where things stood in 1971, Lucas surveyed the 1970–71 courses offerings at "twenty-seven Canadian universities from Victoria to Memorial" (58). He notes "some expansion in the number of courses in Canadian literature, but as Dr. Johnson might say, 'The protuberance is scarcely obvious.' Of the 1,119 undergraduate courses given...ninety-four were American literature and fifty-nine Canadian" (58). Lucas goes on to observe that the "score for the eight universities mentioned above now stands at twenty-two American and eighteen Canadian" (58). Lucas's pessimism is reasonable, given that the fifty-nine Canadian literature courses he records represent only 5 per cent of the 1,119 courses offered that year. It is important to note, however, that the number of Canadian literature courses offered in 1970–71 at the eight universities highlighted in the Royal Commission survey marks a 157 per cent increase over their numbers just six years earlier.

This rapid expansion in the number of English courses on "Canadian Literature"—Lucas notes that in 1970 many of these courses ignored French-Canadian literature in translation—occurred in English departments across Canada, particularly in the years immediately following Canada's Centennial. In his article "A Place in the Sun," Robert L. McDougall recalls the situation at Carleton during those years:

> In 1960, [the Department of English] offered one undergraduate and one post-graduate course in Canadian literature to only a handful of students. By the end of the decade it offered four undergraduate and sometimes as many as four postgraduate courses in Canadian literature, with a combined enrolment of more than 450 students. (274)

Although it was not until 1968–69, for instance, that the University of Toronto finally offered an optional fourth-year course on Canadian literature for students in their "English Language and Literature" program, by the early 1970s they too had greatly expanded their offerings in Canadian literature. 1971–72 saw the University of Toronto add not only a 100-level introductory course in Canadian literature but also a number of new 300- and 400-level courses, including "'Canadian Poetry,' 'Canadian Fiction,' and 'Contemporary Canadian Criticism'" (R.S. Harris, *English Studies at Toronto* 158). In 1973, Pacey informally surveyed thirty-eight Canadian departments of English and determined that "there are now at least 90 undergraduate courses in Canadian literature being offered, with a total enrollment of over 6,000 students" ("Study of Canadian Literature" 67). This boom extended to the graduate level as well. Not only were there twenty-two universities that year offering a total of thirty graduate courses in the field, but there were also "162 graduate theses in Canadian literature…being written, 103 at the master's level and 59 at the doctoral level" ("Study of Canadian Literature" 68). Described to me by Clara Thomas as "the Golden Age of Canadian Literature," this expansion of courses during the late 1960s and early 1970s was greatly nourished by the post-Centennial wave of Canadian nationalism. Canadian literature was getting international attention, there was a tremendous increase in scholarly and commercial publishing on Canadian subjects, and more and more students were eager to take courses that related to the people and history of Canada. The universities of English Canada, however, encountered a number of problems in trying to meet this demand.

One of the major problems caused by such a rapid growth of the demand for courses in Canadian literature was the initial lack of professors interested, let alone qualified, to teach them. Most tenured professors had their own areas of specialization and had established courses they were still required to teach. The addition to the curriculum of courses in Canadian literature, therefore, often meant that these courses were given to new or recently hired faculty, whether they were Canadianists or, most often, not. Much like Bridgetower's encounter with the department head in *Leaven of Malice*, in fact, these young faculty were often asked to "retool" and to start focusing on Canadian literature rather than the areas of expertise they had acquired during their years of graduate study. Some of these scholars actually happened to be Canadians who, though interested in Canadian literature early on in their studies, had been unable to pursue these interests due to a great lack in courses in this area before the boom of the late 1960s. Many others, however, were not even Canadian and had read very little if any Canadian literature before being assigned to teach courses in the field.[12] This is not to suggest that such scholars were incapable of teaching Canadian literature or that they should not have been permitted to shift their research and teaching interests to this field—in fact, many of today's senior Canadianists were part of this very group of scholars. What did occur at the very beginning of their careers, however, is that these professors found themselves learning about both Canadian literature and Canada at the same time as they were teaching these early courses. This situation may have then kept such courses tied to the notion of using literature to reach a better understanding Canada and Canadian identity longer than if the instructors been trained Canadianists who might be more likely to focus on the literary aspects of the texts. In other words, unlike in

Québec where the better established courses in littérature canadienne helped to provide the infrastructure necessary for a literature to be studied in more diverse and sophisticated ways, the initial lack of such skills and experience among this new breed of Canadian literature professors undoubtedly pushed the study of Canadian literature in directions it otherwise might not have followed. As Robin S. Harris points out, the lack of training in this area was officially noted as a problem by the University of Toronto's Department of English in a report they submitted to the Ontario Council of Graduate Studies' Advisory Committee on Academic Planning:

> *"Our strength is the remarkable number of scholars accomplished in other fields who have also chosen to contribute to the study of Canadian literature. Our breadth of perspective and lack of parochialism is notable. Our weakness is the absence of scholars who have devoted themselves without distraction to research and criticism in this area."* (English Studies at Toronto *cited in* Harris 184)

An even more significant obstacle was the way in which Canadian literature was incorporated into the curriculum. As Pacey lamented in 1973, "the last two decades have seen a great upsurge in the interest in Canadian literature, but so far this interest has not drawn forth anything like an appropriate scholarly response" ("Study of Canadian Literature" 72). For one thing, almost every department responded to the need for courses in this area primarily by adding courses that surveyed the entire history of Canadian literature. Occasionally, departments would divide this history into more than one survey course, with each addressing more manageable periods of time. When there was an increase in the number of students wanting to study Canadian literature courses, universities often simply added more sections of these survey courses rather than attempting to add more specialized courses in the field. This lack of scope and variety at the undergraduate level also affected the graduate offerings. While, as Pacey discovered, there were in fact around thirty graduate-level Canadian literature courses in 1973, the majority were "still survey courses which would seem to belong more properly to the undergraduate curriculum" ("Study of Canadian Literature" 71). The conflicting evidence at that time of such an expansion in the numbers of Canadian literature courses and such a lack of both specialized courses and the scholarship necessary for the field to advance as it might lead Pacey to warn that "we should be far from complacent. We may have won a battle, but have we really won the war?" ("Study of Canadian Literature" 69). Pacey's ultimate reticence to challenge truly "the traditional study of English literature" again demonstrates how such an attitude hindered the further growth of courses in Canadian literature. Arguing that Canadian literature is most effectively taught as a contemporary literature, he writes,

> The real issue is not whether one should study Chaucer or Carman—Chaucer is a world figure and will always be relevant, Carman was a minor poet and is mainly of historical interest—but whether one should study, say, John Updike or Leonard Cohen, Stephen Spender or Dorothy Livesay, John Braine or Margaret Laurence, Margaret Drabble or Margaret Atwood. ("Study of Canadian Literature" 71)

Evident here is Pacey's unwillingness to envision anything other than aesthetic "excellence" as the chief criteria for a literary work to be studied; the only reason he seems to feel that contemporary Canadian literature is worth studying is because it can now be more justifiably considered to be among "the best that is thought and said" during this period. What he fails to recognize, however, is that by essentially restricting courses in the literatures of Canada to competing with other courses in contemporary literature and not, for instance, other courses on nineteenth-century literature, he marginalizes it to what is, even today, still a relatively minor part of the English curriculum. It was likely a combination of this focus on contemporary Canadian literary works and the disdainful attitude some department members still held towards the literatures of Canada that led to such a relatively few number of courses being offered in the field. This was made worse, no doubt, by the tendency of departments to believe that new courses in the literatures of Canada should in no way affect the quantity of other courses being offered in British and American literature. By envisioning Canadian literature as a supplement to the existing curriculum rather than as an impetus to re-evaluate the entire structure of English programs, department heads and, indeed, Canadianists who supported such policies ensured that Canadian literature could never get much beyond the 8 per cent of total offerings so harshly criticized by the Symons Report in 1975.[13]

During the 1980s and 1990s, scholars and students in both English and French Canada came to understand the literatures of Canada as being more complex than previously portrayed. While the literatures of this country have always been multicultural and yielded works written by many segments of society, the sheer number of literary works being produced in Canada in the last decades of the twentieth century brought these issues to the fore in a way that had never occurred. Debates began over how representative the canon of Canadian literature should be; arguments were made for a greater presence of works by feminist writers, First Nations writers, immigrant writers, gay and lesbian writers, ethnic minority writers, and—though to a far lesser degree, especially in English Canada—linguistic minority writers. Despite this growth of the literatures of Canada and the increasing demands to widen the Canadian canon, the chief mode of transmission of the canon, the curriculum, did not change significantly. As Margery Fee points out in her 1993 article "Canadian Literature and English Studies in the Canadian University," Canadian literature courses at that time still only represented between 5 and 10 per cent of total English course offerings at Canadian universities. David Cameron's book *Taking Stock: Canadian Studies in the Nineties* (1996) reports a somewhat higher figure of 12 per cent of courses with "significant Canadian content" (52), but even these numbers are still too low to respond adequately to the complexity of the literatures of Canada. My own study shows that figures for the years 1997–98 and 2007–08 are closer to those described by Fee, the bottom range of which is no better than the fifty-nine out of 1,119 courses recorded by Lucas back in 1971. Certainly, departments have offered new courses since the 1990s, but these have often been upper-level courses that vary from year to year in topic. Instead, at least in English Canada, the de facto site of contention for these issues of representation remains the lowly and outmoded Canadian literature survey course that, naturally, can only expand to include marginalized groups, genres, and literary styles by neglecting others. In other words, rather than enlarging its presence within the curricula of English departments across the country, the study of "Canadian Literature" has simply tried to reorganize the limited space it eked out in the late 1960s, forcing a much greater number of works and theoretical approaches to compete for a stagnant number of spots in the reading lists of courses that primarily remain organized around genre, period, or, most commonly, the broad multi-genre structure of the survey course.

In her groundbreaking article "L'Entrée en scène de la littérature québécoise," Nicole Fortin notes that during the 1970s and 1980s courses on Québécois literature at Québec's French universities began to incorporate forms of writing not previously considered to be "literary" works, including songs, monologues, and political discourse. Such an infusion of new material to cover, she proposes, can either result in a *redefinition* or a *saturation* of the literary field (206). A redefinition, she argues,

> *signifierait sans doute le changement du statut du littéraire: dégagée de ses genres traditionnels qui ont, depuis les années 1950, servis de base à la structuration des cours, la littérature autorise de plus en plus des formes nouvelles....Cette modification implique à la fois la redéfinition du littéraire et la redéfinition des objectifs et des structures de son enseignement. (206)*[14]

A saturation, on the other hand, indicates "que l'ensemble a atteint un état de stagnation, marqué par l'incapacité, du discours didactique, d'introduire dans le corpus de nouvelles formes 'purement' littéraires" (206) (that the entirety has reached a state of stagnation, marked by the incapacity, of the didactic discourse, to introduce into the corpus new, "purely" literary forms). Fortin argues that her analysis of course descriptions and reading lists from the 1980s points much more to a saturation of the literary field than a redefinition of it. Much like in English survey courses in Canadian literature where "new" or less canonical writers rarely achieve a significant presence, Fortin found that during this period "plus de 75% des nouveaux auteurs apparaissent dans des lieux particularisés, où ils ne côtoieront pas les auteurs 'anciens' déjà inscrits dans l'enseignement" (206) (more than 75 per cent of the new authors appeared in specialized sites, where they are not alongside "old" authors already inscribed in teaching).

As we will see in later chapters, such a "marginalisation de la nouveauté" (207) (marginalization of the new) can occur when there is a lack of specialized courses into which such new or previously neglected works can be inserted. The other possibility, as the data I have collected for 2007–08 reveals to be increasingly common in English Canada, is that in order to accommodate newer works and critical approaches, departments will chose to lessen their focus on older and frequently more canonical texts. By comparing the most recent data from 2007–08 with that collected in 1997–98, we can see how a number of English departments across the country have made attempts to accommodate newer works through the introduction of courses on "Contemporary Canadian Literature." In addition, and this is one of most striking differences between the two data sets, a number of departments have put in place regularly offered courses on writing by Aboriginal peoples. Rather than adding a greater number of courses to their annual offerings, however, in most cases departments have accommodated these new courses by reducing the attention devoted to early Canadian literature and to works that one might ordinarily assume to be the stalwarts of the canon of English-Canadian literature.

There are several examples of university literature departments that revised their curricula in significant ways in the ten years between these two data sets. The Department of English I visited at McMaster University in 1997, for instance, is now the Department of English and Cultural Studies and recently began offering a combined honours BA in cultural studies and critical theory in addition to its regular honours and major degrees in English. The Département des littératures de langue française at the Université de Montréal also launched a significantly revised curriculum. As of the 2006–07 academic year, students in the baccalauréat en littératures de langue française program now choose between three streams or "orientations." The first focuses on literary history, theory, and poetics, the second on dramaturgy, and the third on the *francophonie*. While each orientation includes some of the typical period, genre, nation, or region-based approaches traditionally found in courses on literature, the new curriculum puts more emphasis on some of the larger theoretical issues involved in each area of study. The most dramatic curricular shift between 1997–98 and 2007–08, however, occurred at the University of Alberta, whose Department of English and Film Studies launched a new, innovative curriculum in 2005–06. Like curricula already in place in departments such as Université du Québec à Montréal (UQÀM)'s Département d'études littéraires and, particularly following its own mid-decade redesign, the Université de Montréal's Département des littératures de langue française, the University of Alberta's new English curricula aimed to shift the focus of its curriculum to a more problem-based approach while still maintaining a certain number of the traditional courses structured around period, genre, and nation.

The most innovative aspects of the University of Alberta's new curriculum are found in the first two years of the program. In their first year, students majoring in English would choose one of four different introductory classes: English 111: Language, Literature, and Culture; English 112: English Literature in Historical Perspective; English 113: English Literature in Global Perspective; English 114: Aboriginal Literature and Culture. Each of these courses offers a strikingly different approach and demonstrates a marked commitment by the department to diversify the first-year experiences of their students rather than homogenize them. Unfortunately, as the University of Alberta has recently moved, like many of its counterparts across the country, to eliminate full-year courses in favour of the half-year model, these innovative changes never had the chance to develop fully. Starting in 2009–10, students were required to choose two of the following five half-year courses to make up their six credits of required first-year English: English 121: Literature in Historical Perspective; English 122: Texts and Contexts; English 123: Literature in a Global Perspective; English 124: Literary Analysis; English 125: Aboriginal Writing. While the courses on global and Aboriginal literatures remain part of the first-year option and perhaps even become more appealing to students who want to experience a variety of approaches over their first year, the transformational potential of those courses is lessened somewhat as they no longer have the chance to serve as the full entry point into upper-level English courses. Like the Ontario College of Agriculture that at one time put Canadian literature at the beginning and end of a student's four years in English, imagine how different "English" might begin to look if students began with a solid grounding in Aboriginal or postcolonial literatures before launching into their study of the more canonical British, American, or Canadian texts found in curricula from coast to coast. The second-year or 200-level courses of the revised Alberta curriculum "introduce students to methods and paradigms central to the discipline" through an interesting set of courses with titles such as "Reading Histories," "Reading Politics," and "The Literary Institution" (Department of English and Film Studies). While the third-year and fourth-year courses—period, genre, and nation-based "courses on language and literature from the eighth century to the present" in the case of the former and special topics courses in the case of the latter—resemble, for the most part, the way things have been traditionally done in English departments nationwide, the 100-level and 200-level courses in the University of Alberta's new curriculum offer a carefully considered attempt to sidestep the type of saturation Fortin describes.

How does this new curriculum alter the place of courses on "Canadian literature" at the University of Alberta? If one compares the percentage of courses offered in 1997–98 that were designated as courses on "Canadian Literature," including courses on Aboriginal/indigenous literature, to the same measure in 2007–08, one discovers that they are nearly identical (10.1 per cent vs. 10.8 per cent); Canadian literature, at least in terms of the number of dedicated courses, has fared no better than it did in the previous, more traditional curriculum. While litera-ture departments like those at UQÀM and the Université de Montréal have demonstrated that a theory or problem-oriented curricula does not necessarily temper a department's ability to study in a great level of detail in its own national literature, those universities have also had external structures such as the research centres and grant-funded projects that have long brought students in to assist them with these projects. Although the University of Alberta now has in place a new Canadian Literature Centre directed, significantly, by Marie Carrière, a francophone scholar whose own research looks at questions of minority writing in Canada, the fate of the Canadian Literature courses within this new curriculum implies that the department felt that Canadian literature already had a significant enough place in the overall course offerings. While the department altered some of the course structures for these courses and, as already mentioned, placed an important emphasis on writing by Canada's indigenous peoples, those changes only resulted in a reorganizing of the 10.8 per cent of the overall number of courses offered. If, on some levels, we can view these seemingly major shifts in the curriculum to mark what Fortin would describe as a redefinition of the literary field, a closer examination of the place of Canadian literature says more about the problems of saturation than it does about any fundamental shift in the approach to the study of our country's literature(s).

Ironically, in the case of both courses on Québécois literature and English courses on the literatures of Canada, this resistance to a redefinition of the literary field described by Fortin echoes the original difficulties faced by the literatures of Canada when scholars like Roy and Logan lobbied for their incorporation into the university curriculum. Just as department heads and faculty often opposed the founding of courses on the literatures of Canada on the grounds that, as Henry Kreisel said at the University of Alberta in 1950, the body of work "wasn't yet quite good enough" (Kreisel 38) to be considered at par with British or American literature, so too do some Canadianists of today still voice concern over texts or courses being added to the curriculum for primarily non-literary reasons. What this suggests is that the widespread admission of the literatures of Canada into the curriculum during the 1960s never ultimately resulted in a fundamental redefinition of the purpose of literary studies in Canada. In fact, instead of coming to understand literature in a way that would challenge prior notions of aesthetic "quality" as the fundamental criteria for the study of the text, professors of English-Canadian literature and, to a seemingly lesser degree, professors of littérature québécoise, seem to have aspired all along to consider the literatures of Canada—and particularly works published since the 1960s—from that very same perspective. Especially at English-Canadian universities, where with a few notable exceptions, the study of the Canadian literary institution can still seem to be a somewhat questionable pursuit, the Romantic nationalist dreams of many early scholars appear to have come true: English-Canadian literature seems to have become a literature worthy of study on its own literary merits. In so doing, though, with Canadian texts only occupying a small percentage of those studied in most English departments across the country, was Desmond Pacey not correct to ask, "We may have won a battle, but have we really won the war?" ("Study of Canadian Literature" 69).

How is it, in other words, that English-Canadian literature has still not achieved a greater place in the English curriculum and a status similar to that held today by Québécois literature at the French-language universities in Québec? Is it because the anglophone scholars and students who lobbied in the past for courses in "Canadian Literature" were too easily satisfied with a minor portion of the total number of course offerings or were hesitant to challenge the hegemony any more than they already had? Or have departments of English deliberately worked to keep Canadian literature in its place of secondary or even tertiary importance behind the position accorded to British and American literature? It might be tempting to ascribe the reasons for this, as many of my interview subjects did in 1997–98, to the idiosyncrasies of certain departments and the influence of particular department chairs and instructors. As Professor Max Roy cautioned me in 1997, however, "vous allez voir que c'est très diversifié, c'est très different d'une université à l'autre et la différence masque souvent les régularités. Il ne faut pas se laisser leurrer par ses différences-là" (Personal interview).[15] Although few English-language universities in Canada seem to have taken note of other universities' course offerings when designing and redesigning their curricula, the fact that Canadian literature has a remarkably similar position at nearly every one of these universities implies a much more systematic cause for this phenomenon, one that lies at the heart of the literary institution in English Canada. While the history of the introduction and development of courses on the literatures of Canada can help us to document some of these regularities, the explanation for them can be found in the more theoretical approaches to understanding the literary institution and the role our universities play in it.

"A Prisoner of Its Own Amnesia"

The Role of the University in the Canadian Literary Institution

2

AS DISCUSSED IN CHAPTER ONE, the Arnoldian tenet of superior aesthetic quality as the sole criterion for study was at the centre of
most early refusals to give English-Canadian literature even the smallest
place in the English curriculum of Canadian universities. While the
growing quality of contemporary English-Canadian literature eventually made it more and more difficult for scholars and critics to perceive
it as being of secondary importance to the British and American literature of the same period, its eventual inclusion in the curriculum still
did not bring about the same structural changes that gradually occurred
in literature departments in Québec where, in some cases, the number
of courses in Québécois literature during the 1970s and 1980s rivalled
and even outnumbered those in French literature. This did not occur
strictly because Québécois literature came to be seen as being equal in
literariness or aesthetic quality to the French tradition but was due,
rather, to a growing belief that it was worthy of study for other equally
important reasons and, more importantly, on its own cultural terms.
In English Canada, however, there has never been a similar challenge to
the purpose of literary studies in a system where, despite an influx of
new methodologies and literary theories since the 1970s, literary excellence and the supremacy of the "text" are still the foundation upon
which "English" considers itself to be built. This helps to justify the still

minor presence—at least in terms of the overall number of courses—
of English-Canadian literature in the university English curriculum in
that it is only contemporary Canadian texts that are usually considered
of sufficient quality to be given a similar weight to the other more established national literatures of the United States and England.

Tied to this fairly recent belief that English-Canadian literature is now
part of the English curriculum because it deserves to be so for strictly
literary reasons, is an apparently Arnoldian self-image held by many
of today's English-Canadian critics and teachers that their role should
simply be to indicate, elucidate, and ultimately consecrate "the best that
is known and thought" in (English) Canada (Arnold 38). As Frank Davey
points out so well in *Canadian Literary Power*, to put stock in the objectivity and neutrality of the professor as scholar, critic, and teacher is to
disavow the "power" inherent in such a position, a power that continuously ripples through all levels of the literary institution. In other words,
as critics such as Pierre Bourdieu and Jacques Dubois have illustrated
so effectively in works like the former's "Le Marché des biens symboliques" (1971) and *Homo Academicus* (1984), and the latter's *L'Institution
de la littérature* (1978), there is never an autonomous position in any
field, particularly a field of restricted production such as that of literature. In fact, whatever pretensions of scientific objectivity are held by the
academy, it is clear that the role of professor is one of the least autonomous in the field. Not only is it directly dependent on the production
and distribution of texts, its consecration of texts, in one way or another,
affects all of the other agents in the field. Moreover, "Literature" is not
something to which scholars simply respond to at arm's length; it is,
rather, a notion constructed by the university itself, which, through
the consecrational forces of teaching and criticism, transforms chosen
texts from mere books into works of Literature. In the words of Roland
Barthes, "La littérature, c'est ce qui s'enseigne" (Barthes, "Réflexions"
170) (Literature is what teaches itself).

While Bourdieu and Dubois have made the greatest contributions to
our understanding of the university's fundamental place in the literary
institution, there could nevertheless be a danger of applying their theoretical models too readily to the study of the literary institution in

Canada.[1] The relevant work of both these critics deals solely with the very specific context of the French literary field and, particularly, its highly regimented education system. Canada, with what appear to be two nearly separate literary institutions (English and French), each unique in very different ways from the other, would seem to pose a number of serious challenges to any attempt to articulate fully the complex interactions of the circular processes of literary production, distribution, consumption, and consecration. As we will see through a more detailed discussion of these theories and the specificity of the Canadian context, the work of Bourdieu and Dubois is highly pertinent to a better understanding of the complexities of the literary institution in Canada. In fact, the inter-relation of the study of the literatures of Canada and the rest of the Canadian literary institution may offer some of the best examples of the processes of cultural production and reproduction Bourdieu and Dubois describe. This attempt to map the complexities of the Canadian literary field, then, will provide a theoretical framework for the rest of my argument and, ultimately, will demonstrate how the symbiotic relationship between the Canadian university and the rest of the literary institution ultimately (pre)determines how we conceive of our national literatures rather than vice versa.

Bourdieu, Dubois, and Theories of the Literary Institution

It is only in since the 1970s that critics such as Bourdieu and Dubois have begun to study the "literary institution" and the effect that it has not only on cultural production but also on social and cultural repro-duction. Part of the reason that the role of the literary institution has been neglected until relatively recently is the great difficulty inherent in any attempt to define exactly what the literary institution is and how it works. The complexity of the literary institution, as Dubois's *L'institution de la littérature* (1978) clearly illustrates, lies in the fact that the institu-tion is not a single, coherent, and identifiable entity but, rather, is made up of all the different forces and agents that contribute in various ways to the production, distribution, consumption, and consecration of litera-ture. It is in this way that the literary institution as a whole, while being of tremendous influence, can often be next to invisible: "le dispositif d'institution peut demeurer très peu visible dans la mesure où il n'exerce ses contraintes que de façon implicite sur les pratiques symboliques" (Dubois 26).[2] One of the most important reasons that the study of the literary institution is still a relatively small and unexplored field—particularly in departments of English[3]—is the continuing emphasis on the text as the nearly sole focus of literary studies, a paradigm introduced to university literature departments by the highly influential ideas of New Criticism. Additionally, while theoretical approaches such as poststructuralism, feminism, and postcolonialism reveal the great extent to which the production and reception of the text are influenced by extra-authorial forces, the general public and even many of the agents that make up the literary institution itself continue to envision the author as a solitary and autonomous genius figure whose work is entirely a product of his or her creative mind. Thus, "Literature" is frequently seen as a completely independent product against which the other elements of the literary institution (publishers, readers, critics, booksellers, universities, etc.) react and define themselves. The work of Bourdieu and Dubois, however, explains that this is clearly not the case; for Dubois, the most important aspect of the sociology of literature is its demonstration that there is no such thing as one timeless and universal Literature but, rather, that literature comprises a number of "pratiques spéciales, singulières, opérant à la fois sur le langage et l'imaginaire et dont l'unité ne se réalise qu'à certains niveaux de fonctionnement et d'insertion dans la structure sociale" (11) (special, singular practices operating simultaneously on language and the imaginary, the unity of which is only realized at certain levels of functioning and insertion into the social structure).

In *L'institution de la littérature*, Dubois discusses how Jean-Paul Sartre, Roland Barthes, and Pierre Bourdieu each pinpoint literature's gaining of independence from religious and class ideologies during the nineteenth century as being the formative moment in the development of the literary institution as we know it today. In the nineteenth century, Sartre explains, "la littérature vient de se dégager de l'idéologie religieuse et refuse de servir l'idéologie bourgeoise. Elle se pose donc comme indépendante de toute espèce d'idéologie" (Sartre, *Situations, II* 164).[4] During this period, then, literature comes to be seen as something with no ideological function, something that is to be considered as "pure" art. In *Le Degré zéro de l'écriture*, Barthes too identifies the same time period as the moment when literature gains its autonomy. He explains that, as modern capitalism emerges in France with the beginning of the Second Empire and as the strict class divisions in French society fall apart for good (Dubois 25), "l'écriture" becomes the main focus of literature rather than the expression of a "unité idéologique de la bourgeoisie" (ideological unity of the bourgeoisie): "l'écriture classique a donc éclaté et la Littérature entière, de Flaubert à nos jours, est devenue une problématique du langage" (Barthes *Degré Zéro* 9). At this same moment, Barthes suggests, "la Littérature (le mot est né peu de temps avant) est consacrée définitivement comme un objet" (*Degré Zéro* 9–10).[5] Looking at the history of English studies, Tony Davies points to precisely the same time period for the genesis of "Literature" in England. During the mid-nineteenth century, at around the time Matthew Arnold begins to argue for the study and promotion of only "the best that is known and thought," the use of the term "literature"—initially by critics and then later by all levels of the literary institution—moves away from denoting the totality of written works to signalling a highly specific body of work deemed to be of aesthetic, and thus cultural, value. Such a use of the term "Literature," then, by valuing a very specific set of criteria designated by those agents holding the power of consecration while at the same time deeming these values to be of universal importance, rapidly gained an ideological weight at the same time as it claimed to be above ideology.

As Bourdieu aims for his discussion of "The Market of Symbolic Goods" to apply to all forms of cultural production, he devotes little attention to specific historical events (such as the rise of Second Empire) that contribute to the autonomization of literature. What he does, rather, is point to several key conditions that must be present for any kind of "intellectual or cultural production" to become autonomous (Bourdieu, "Market" 112). The first of these conditions is the presence of a continually growing "public of potential consumers, of increasing social diversity, which guarantee the producers of symbolic goods minimal conditions of economic independence and, also, a competing principle of legitimacy" ("Market" 112). Thus, the great growth in the literacy levels of the working classes and the expansion of the middle class experienced in the West during the nineteenth century combine to create a market for literary works that provides the autonomy needed for a literary institution to develop successfully. The second necessary condition identified by Bourdieu develops in tandem with the increase of "potential consumers" as it is marked by "the constitution of an ever-growing, ever more diversified corps of publishers and merchants of symbolic goods" who fulfill the needs and the desires of the reading public ("Market" 112). The third criteria is met by the "multiplication and diversification of agencies of consecration" who have the power to proffer "cultural legitimacy" on a rare few of the products, producers, merchants, and consumers that make up the rest of the literary institution ("Market" 112). Thus, Bourdieu's theory takes into account not only those cultural products that through sales or ticket purchases achieve material success (the field of large-scale production), it also deals with those works whose success is measured by their ability to earn symbolic or "cultural" capital (the field of restricted production). Unlike the field of large-scale production, in which achievement is measured by market share and the greater financial profit that larger market share ultimately produces, the field of restricted production, in which all its members act in the field as not only producers but also consumers, "tends to develop its own criteria for the evaluation of its own products" ("Market" 115). The "products" that fulfill these criteria are thus accorded an appropriate amount of cultural capital, mostly by those members of the field who act as consecrators of cultural value. As Bourdieu writes, "the degree of autonomy enjoyed by a field of restricted production is measurable by the degree to which it is capable of functioning as a specific market, generating a specifically cultural type of scarcity and value irreducible to the economic scarcity and value of the goods in question" ("Market" 117). Bourdieu's analysis is extremely useful in that, by assigning the cause of the autonomization of cultural production to the development of a field of restricted production and the autonomous symbolic economy that develops along with it rather than to specific historical, political, or economic events, it also provides a framework—as we will see later when we discuss the Canadian literary institution—for examining the same phenomenon in other countries and societies where at least some of the cultural institutions have gained similar independence.

If Dubois's *L'Institution de la littérature* is significant, it is because he addresses *how* the restricted field of literature actually functions. Specifically, Dubois applies Bourdieu's theories of the market of symbolic goods to the literary institution and attempts to trace the roles and interactions of each of its constituent parts. As Dubois demonstrates, the literary institution is a nexus of the field's agents in which not one of them holds a position that does not, in some way, depend on another:

> Il n'y a pas de position autonome dans le champ autonomisé; toute position est toujours et par avance fonction des autres. Aussi l'écrivain est-il toujours, dès le moment où il écrit, quelqu'un qui cherche sa place dans ce jeu de positions, et le statut de ses écrits, il le sait, passera immanquablement par la médiation des instances qui exercent l'autorité symbolique. (87–88)[6]

In *L'Institution de la littérature*, Dubois works through each level of the institution, outlining not only the function of each but also pinpointing some of the complex interactions that necessarily occur, for instance, between "instances de production" and "instances de légitimation" (81). Perhaps the most useful part of his study, for the purposes of this chapter, is his analysis of the role played in the field by the university and, on a broader level, by the entire educational system. The teaching of literature does not only designate and transmit "un code de lecture (voire d'écriture) en forme de catégories stylistiques et thématiques" (98) (a code of reading [indeed, even writing] in the form of stylistic and thematic categories). As Dubois notes,

> À cet égard, [l'école] fait un peu plus que conserver et que célébrer les oeuvres du passé, car elle les introduit dans la logique d'un système qui projette nécessairement ses principes et ses catégories sur les productions du présent— productions que ce système est d'ailleurs toujours prêt à intégrer après sélection. (99)[7]

The university then, by virtue of its function as the most prestigious and powerful consecrator in the literary field, serves to establish and propagate "un 'bon usage,' une 'bonne image' de la littérature" (100), a "good use," a "good image" of literature.

To anyone looking back over the last 150 years of literary studies, it should be evident that the Arnoldian notion of "excellence"—so clearly articulated in his famous phrase "the best that is known and thought"—has played a key role in shaping the discipline as we know it today (Arnold 38). While Arnold's phrase implies that modern literature can be considered equal in many ways to the classics, each representing "the best that [was] known and thought" in a particular period of history, what is most significant about their use is the weight of cultural importance that they place on those texts that are selected for study, and ultimately, for consecration as part of the literary canon. In other words, those texts that are chosen for inclusion in courses on literature (both the first courses ever offered on the subject and, as I will argue later, even those taught today) must, if only to justify the existence of such courses, be those that can be shown to be some of the best—if not *the* best—of their period and genre. Thus, even without any critical commentary, the mere inclusion of certain literary texts in courses of this kind immediately loads those particular texts with symbolic capital. In so doing, the university plays a significant role in maintaining and strengthening of the field of restricted production. As Brian Doyle points out, "[by] legitimizing only the study of 'valuable works,' the discipline manufacture[s] an essential and unbridgeable cultural difference between its own sphere of high art and the general domain of popular fiction and discourse" (*English and Englishness* 6). Bourdieu echoes this idea when he addresses how this type of consecration helps to ensure the restrictedness of the field of restricted production:

> While consumption in the field of large-scale production is more or less independent of the educational level of consumers (which is quite understandable, since this system tends to adjust to the level of demand), works of restricted art owe their specifically cultural rarity, and thus their function as elements

of social distinction, to the rarity of the instruments with which they may be deciphered. (Bourdieu, "Market" 120)

Nevertheless, it is also necessary that there is an adequate enough distribution of these "instruments" to allow the field to survive and even flourish, and that is precisely one of the chief functions of the university in its role as consecrating agent.

The university plays a more complex and multi-faceted role in the literary institution than do other agencies of consecration; while the university usually appears to be the most influential (or at least the most authoritative) bestower of symbolic capital in that it alone "accords that infallible mark of consecration, the elevation of works into 'classics' by their inclusion in curricula" ("Market" 123), it also performs other functions that are of equal importance to the preservation and furthering of the field of restricted production. The first and foremost of these other roles is that—in its aim to transmit those works that it has consecrated, to propagate the canon that it has put in place—the university necessarily must act as a producer of "cultural consumers" ("Market" 123) who it has trained to recognize the qualities that merit those works' acquisition of the amount of symbolic capital required to be considered "the best." In this way, not only does the university assure the continued consecration of those works already part of its canon, but it also establishes the framework necessary to allow for future works (and/ or previously overlooked past works) possessing similar qualities to be included almost seamlessly into that same canon. It should also not be surprising that, since the study of literature first became an integral part of higher education and as the "instruments" for deciphering the restrictedness of the field became more and more dependent on the educational system, that an increasing number of the people who become agents of production (writers, editors, publishers), diffusion (booksellers and publishers), or consecration (critics, academics, teachers, publishers, and editors) are also some of those same cultural consumers produced by the university. This example of the potential (and frequent) interconnectedness of the various levels in the literary field reveals how difficult it can be to study in isolation only one element of any field of restricted production. The typical university literature department is, in fact, a nexus of a varying number of agents in the field. Members of such a department are often more than simply professors of literature (those people who consecrate works and then transmit them to future cultural consumers or, in the very least, those who transmit a previously established canon). They may also be writers (of fiction, non-fiction, drama, and/or poetry), critics, reviewers, editors, and even publishers. Thus, the university serves both to reproduce itself (through its role as producer of future academics) and to reproduce and strengthen that portion of the literary institution composed of the field of restricted production. This, however, is not all that the university literature department serves to reproduce.

In *La reproduction*, Bourdieu contends that the primary function of education is to ensure the continued survival of a society's dominant culture or class by producing agents capable of solidly maintaining and reinforcing the status quo:

> Le travail pédagogique (qu'il soit exercé par l'École, par une Église ou un
> parti) a pour effet de produire des individus durablement et systématique-
> ment modifiés par une action prolongée de transformation tendant à les doter
> d'une même formation durable (habitus), c'est-à-dire de schèmes communs
> de pensée, de perception, d'appréciation et d'action. (La reproduction 233)[8]

When Bourdieu speaks here of a "habitus" he is referring to a key term in his own theory of cultural or social reproduction. The habitus is those common elements of the way we act in society that seem to be second nature to us such as, like Bourdieu mentions in the above quotation, the way we think and perceive the world around us. What Bourdieu points out, however, is that these behaviors are less natural than we think; they are things that we both consciously and unconsciously learn from the time we are born. As summarized by Dubois, Bourdieu's theory sees cultural and social reproduction as being composed of three principal stages: "1° les structures sociales engendrent l'habitus; 2° l'habitus détermine les pratiques (esthétique notamment); 3° les pratiques reproduisent les structures" (Dubois 123).[9] In other words, the social structure is reproduced by creating the habitus required for us to be able to act in the interest of preserving those original structures. Bourdieu also points out that the practices that are determined by the habitus are also unavoidably affected by the circumstances encountered by the individual or group: "la pratique est le produit d'une relation entre une situation et une habitus" (*Esquisse d'une théorie de la pratique*, 172, cited in Dubois 123).[10] Thus, in the case of education, one can see the act of teaching as being one of the practices that helps to pass on the habitus to future students who will in turn reinforce the system as they not only take their place in the society that engenders the habitus but also, as parents and/or *productive* members of society, transmit the habitus along to subsequent generations: "la production en série d'individus identiquement programmés exige et suscite historiquement la production d'agents de programmation eux-mêmes identiquement programmés et d'instruments standardisés de conservation et de transmission" (*La reproduction* 233).[11]

If education serves as a means of facilitating the propagation of the social structure from which it originates, then the study of literature strengthens this function even more. As Dubois points out, any form of discourse (including literature) is itself a transmitter of ideology, a reinforcer of social structures: "l'idéologie de la classe dominante opère insidieusement en se constituant en discours général, en discours de tous, même si les groupes dominés infléchissent et réinterpretent ce discours suivant leurs propres positions. Elle est, comme on la dit, ce qui cimente la formation sociale" (Dubois 63).[12] In this light then, it is not surprising that in any country, the most popular subject of literary studies is often the literature of that country or of the global language group of which that nation is a part. Dubois's statement also suggests that the discipline of comparative literature—which, in its aim to examine "world literature," posits itself as the exact opposite of a nation- or language-based study of literature—can actually be seen to be somewhat of a reinforcement of the dominant ideology rather than a complete subversion of it. Ultimately, however, literature—as both a site of discourse and a discourse in itself—must be read in order for it

to have any significant ideological function. It is not surprising, therefore, that it is the educational system that serves as both a transmitter
and consecrator of literature and thus propagates the existing habitus
or, at the very least, a habitus that undergoes only very minor changes
over an extended period of time. Pointing to the thesis of Bourdieu and
Jean-Claude Passeron in *La reproduction*, John Guillory notes that "institutions of reproduction succeed by taking as their first object not the
reproduction of social relations but the reproduction of the institution
itself" (Guillory 57).

The Canadian Literary Institution

While I will argue that, with their theories of cultural (re)production
and the literary institution, the work of Bourdieu and Dubois is highly
applicable to any study of the Canadian literary institution, there are,
nevertheless, key differences between the cultural context of France and
Canada that must be taken into account. Both a nation formed through
continuous immigration and a land taken from indigenous peoples by
imperial expansion, Canada necessarily injects other unique factors into
the economy of symbolic goods and the transmission of symbolic power
through its education system. The issue of national identity in Canada
is a highly complex one that, as John Ralston Saul argues persuasively
in *Reflections of a Siamese Twin* (1997), is structured around a rejec-
tion of the monolithic model of a nation state in favour of a paradigm
that attempts to accommodate rather than eliminate heterogeneity:
"the assumption of complexity is a search for balance between different
elements; not eradication or domination of one over the others, but a
continuing struggle to develop and maintain some sort of equilibrium"
(223). A geographically and politically decentralized society, Canada has
never had the same singular sense of nation or of national institutions as
does France.

One of the issues at the centre of Bourdieu's analyses of cultural
reproduction in France that differs significantly from the Canadian situation is that of class. Bourdieu's understanding of the "dominant class"
is inevitably tied to the history of social and economic power among
the French elite, though this is somewhat less relevant in France today

compared to issues of immigration and the European Union. In Canada, the power at stake, that consolidated by the dominant class, has always been rooted as much in language and race as in economic and social relations. Further complicating any analysis of these processes is the fact that Canada, both officially and effectively, is a multicultural nation with two official languages. This status, unusual but hardly unique among Western nations, complicates any chance of there ever being a uniform understanding of "Canadian" identity. It has also made Canadians far more conscious of, and frequently insecure, about the fact that we are still in the process of constructing our own identities through the education system, among other channels. As I discussed in Chapter One, this understanding was one of the fundamental forces behind some of the early calls for a "nationalisation de la littérature" (C. Roy 187). In Québec, the important role of literary production and the study of literature in this process of self-identification has been much more overt and has frequently developed in more concrete forms than in English Canada that tangibly affect the literary institution. In English Canada, perhaps because there has not been the same deliberate, psychological break from its status as a British colony, the nature of the national identity is much more amorphous.

The fact that the differences in language, history, and sense of national identity have effectively led to a nation of two solitudes has also meant that there are very few truly national institutions of production, distribution, and consecration in the literary field and only a small number of bilingual readers who can effectively be considered as *national* agents of consumption. Aside from less than a handful of government agencies— Library and Archives Canada and the Canada Council for the Arts being the most prominent—the authors, publishers, distributors, readers, and consecrators of Canadian literature nearly always function solely in either English or French and rarely overlap. Understandably, then, one might be inclined to argue that there are two entirely separate literary institutions in Canada and thus two entirely self-contained literatures. The vast majority of literary criticism in Canada is rooted in precisely such an understanding, one that, importantly, does not conflict with and thus does not challenge the apparent uniformity of the critic's own cultural context. Such a paradigm—which is often expressed by the use of the terms "Canadian literature" and "littérature québécoise" to designate, respectively, English and French-language writing in Canada—is a highly problematic and vastly oversimplified understanding of the Canadian literary institution; in no way can either of these categorizations adequately signify a wholly autonomous and easily definable body of literature.

As Davey has pointed out in regards to English-Canadian literature, the vast size of Canada, combined with the complexity of Canadian identity, has led to a greater focus on regionalism as well as on literature produced by very specific constituencies of writers, such as that written by members of minorities, First Nations, or the gay and lesbian community. Not surprisingly, this fracturing of the literary field echoes and is echoed in other levels of the institution as well, most notably in the growth of regional and specialty presses. Further complicating this field of restricted production in Canada as compared to France, for example, is the fact that at no level does Canada have a nationally controlled system of education. The consecrational power of schools and universities, therefore, is diffused somewhat. More importantly, this heterogeneous system allows for regional and institutional canons to develop in isolation from others while still framing themselves under the rubric of a single "Canadian literature."

As Saul notes, "the solitudes we live with are enormous and essentially healthy, but the concrete cultural interweaving which runs parallel to them is equally complex" (72). Even though, for instance, the Québécois literary institution does not face the same regional diversity and separation that characterize English Canada, it is still not as autonomous as it might like to consider itself. The literary institution in Québec is linked in many ways to institutional forces in the rest of Canada and in France. Aside from the more obvious issue of the not insignificant amount of Canada Council funding received by Québécois writers and publishers, there is also the question of the non-French writing and publishing that occurs in Québec. While some anglophone writers from Québec have had little to do with the predominantly francophone institutional structures there, others such as Gail Scott and publishers like Véhicule Press have benefitted to some degree from the institutional infrastructure that has developed alongside Québécois literature. This may occur simply from a writer or publisher being located in Québec, but they are also often involved with littérature québécoise by translating and publishing translations of Québécois texts, work that, it is important to note, is most often funded with help from the Canada Council translation grants program. As we have increasingly seen happen since the 1990s through new courses and continuing scholarship on *littérature anglo-québécoise*, a solution to this dilemma has been for the institutional structures of Québécois literature to begin to claim anglophone Québec writers as their own, thus positing "Québécois" as a term more inclusive than exclusive. The fact that some of the most successful of these anglophone writers are published by English-language presses outside of Québec and sometimes by multinational presses such as Penguin or Random House, though, would further erode the credibility of any claims to autonomy made by the literary institution in Québec. An additional complication is the fairly vibrant francophone literary scene outside of Québec in provinces such as Manitoba and New Brunswick. Francophone writers and publishers from these regions, too, often depend upon the literary institution in Québec for distribution (via French-language distributors and booksellers who ship to readers outside of Québec) and consecration (via reviews and critical articles in journals and newspapers). As Lucie Robert observes,

> *la frontière géo-politique du Québec n'est elle-même pas très nette: quoi qu'en on dise et quelles que soient nos aspirations collectives ou individuelles, le Québec a des frontières perméables, perméables au Canada et aux communautés francophones hors Québec, à la France, aux États-Unis. Je ne pouvais pas construire une histoire qui soit fondée sur la fiction d'une autonomie politique, économique, et culturelle: celle de l'institution littéraire québécoise.* ("Institution" 18)[13]

For these very reasons, the overly simplistic designations of "Canadian literature" as all literature written in English by Canadians and "Québécois literature" as everything written in French by citizens of

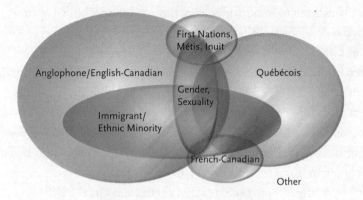

FIGURE 2.1 *The Field of Restricted Production in Canada*

Québec inevitably collapse under any significant scrutiny. To conclude, then, that there are two entirely separate and distinct literary institutions in Canada is highly problematic. One cannot deny that, for the most part, most Québécois agents in the field rarely interact with their counterparts in English Canada and vice versa; this lack of interaction, however, should not be interpreted as proof of two autonomous fields of restricted production in Canada. While they may almost be entirely separate, it is quite clear that they operate within the same overall field of restricted production. A useful way of envisioning the overall shape of this field is as a Venn diagram (Figure 2.1) in which two larger circles, one representing English-Canadian literature and the other Québécois literature, only slightly overlap. The centre area shared by English-Canadian and Québécois literature signifies the institutional structures used by both constituencies and, in terms of literary production, the small body of work translated from one of the official languages into the other. Smaller circles representing First Nations and non-Québécois French-language writing overlap with these two main forces in the literary field but also exist partly outside these circles by means of the lesser known work produced by these communities and only distributed and consumed amongst themselves. Immigrant and ethnic minority writing in French and English occupies a centre position that places it within the two major fields. Finally, the field named "other" represents the Canadian writing produced in languages other than French or English that nearly always relies solely on the institutional structures of countries other than Canada. The field of restricted production in Canada, then, includes all of these aspects of Canadian literature. To look at English-Canadian literature in isolation from Québécois literature and vice versa may perhaps be useful for looking at issues like literary tradition, questions of influence, or literary movements, but it is an inadequate approach when considering issues related to the institution such as publishing or canon formation. As we will see, the similar circumstances of these two primary constituents of the literary field, as well as their occasionally striking differences, reveal a great deal about the particularities of each.

One of the most significant traits of the Canadian literary institution, one that has a major impact on both English-Canadian and Québécois literature, is the extreme restrictedness of the field of restricted production. Unlike in countries with a much larger population—England, France, Germany, and the United States, for instance—the field of restricted production in Canada is so small that rarely can it single-handedly finance its own continuation. The field of restricted production, Bourdieu reminds us, eschews financial gain but nevertheless needs the money achieved through book sales to members of the field in order to maintain the production of symbolic goods. In Canada, due to the small number of these consumers, these material gains are rarely enough to sustain the publishers and authors of these texts. Since the formation of the Canada Council, government funding has, somewhat ironically, helped to provide these agents with the autonomy needed to reinforce their position within the field. Competition for these funds also becomes, in some ways, a quest for cultural capital; those institutions and authors who receive grant money do so only because someone holding this both symbolic and economic power deems them worthy of financial support, thus adding to the symbolic prestige of the new grant holder. With a few notable exceptions, it is only when a book or author gains access to a larger field of restricted production outside of Canada that an author stands to earn enough financial remuneration to allow them to focus solely on their work as agents of production within the field of restricted production. Such success—especially when the author or text is allowed into larger and, to many Canadians, more prestigious, symbolic markets such as Britain, France, or the United States—is most important in terms of the field of restricted production for the symbolic capital it gives to the author or text. Economic success, then, is not questioned, so long as it occurs within and helps to further the field. When such an author or text (both, in a sense, are equally symbolic goods) achieves commercial success and earns a place on the bestseller lists, however, this incursion into the field of large-scale production often brings into question the symbolic worth of that particular author and/or work. As Bourdieu explains,

> [a] negative relationship...as the field increasingly imposes its own logic, is established between symbolic profit and economic profit, whereby discredit increases as the audience grows and its specific competence declines, together with the value of the recognition implied in the act of consumption.
> ("Field of Cultural Production" 48)

The unusually small size of the field of literary production means that there are relatively few solely literary presses in Canada. With such a small market of consumers of symbolic goods, these publishers are only able to publish literary works with financial assistance from govern- ment agencies, most notably the Canada Council. Most Canadian presses primarily publish works for the field of large-scale production, though some still take part in the field of restricted production by publishing a much smaller proportion of literary texts. The most obvious examples of the latter case are the large multinational corporations Random House (which, after itself being acquired by Bertelsmann AG in 1998, went on to purchase McClelland & Stewart and Doubleday and, in 2012, agreed to merge with Penguin Books[14]) and HarperCollins, who have the financial autonomy to enter the field of restricted production through Canadian branch plants and publish a select number of Canadian literary titles in English. A perpetual problem for small literary presses is that these large corporations have the economic capital to provide greater compensation to better-known writers who, usually through the earlier efforts of small literary presses, have already earned a significant amount of symbolic capital. Thus, small literary presses increasingly find themselves devel- oping new authors who, after reaching a certain critical mass of cultural

capital, leave for the greener pastures of larger publishers who, ultimately, are more concerned with acquiring prestige by publishing the
works of writers who have already achieved a certain status within the
field of restricted production. As Davey explains,

> When faced with direct competition for authors by branch-plant publishers,
> all but two or three of the largest Canadian-owned presses are rarely able to
> continue to publish books by the newly established authors whose reputations
> they have developed. Their loss of authors like Brian Fawcett, Audrey Thomas,
> and Mordecai Richler to much better capitalized branch plants which can
> afford large advances and promotional budgets, in turn, limits the possibility
> that the Canadian publisher will ever be able to outgrow its dependence on
> state subsidy. ("(Con)Figuring a 'Canada'" 123)

This need to rely on government subsidy means that, while such grants
do provide some freedom from having to depend on high sales figures
for literary works, literary publishers will never gain the autonomy they
need to function fully within the field of restricted production. What
occurs then is a continual cycle in which Canadian publishers work to
develop literary talent—and thus earn cultural capital—only to lose
that status as soon as the author achieves that type of success and then
signs on with the larger branch-plant publishers.[15] While there is most
certainly a symbolic value to being seen as a press that discovers and
develops important literary talent, the loss of cultural capital that occurs
when the best of that new talent leaves prevents that publisher from
ever reaching the highest ranks in the field. The fact that most of the
publishers to reach that top status are the wealthy multinational corporations further reinforces the popular notion that being published by an
"international" publisher is more worthy of respect than being published
by a Canadian publisher.

Both Québécois and English-Canadian literature have always found
themselves in the shadow of French and British literature, respectively.
One of the chief reasons for this, and the subject of much debate in the
early years of the literary institution in Canada, was whether the literatures of Canada could adequately distinguish themselves from the

literatures of France or Britain without a unique and distinctly national language. Even within Canada, then, these "minor" literatures end up battling for prestige and attention with the "major" literatures written in the same language. The same predicament occurs for minor Canadian literatures. Non-Québécois French-language writing from Manitoba or Acadia, for example, finds itself a further step down the hierarchy, forced to compete for cultural capital with both the literatures of France and Québec, not to mention with English-Canadian literary production by the majority population in those regions. Just as success in foreign markets, especially those of France, Britain, or the United States, guarantees a Canadian author or text a greater amount of cultural capital within Canada than would be earned with a similar level of success solely in Canada, these minority literatures achieve greater symbolic success when they are read and reviewed outside their own immediate cultural contexts. The esteem held by the Canadian literary institution for such outside success is especially true with respect to literary awards. National literary awards such as the Governor General's Awards and awards such as the Giller Prize and the Prix Athanase-David that are devoted to certain segments of the institution are one of the most important means of assigning and distributing cultural capital in Canada. Nevertheless, the institution nearly always pays greater attention to a Canadian book when it is nominated for foreign prizes such as the Booker Prize, the Prix Goncourt, or the American National Book Award. One need look no further for proof of this than the extensive and celebratory media coverage in Canada of Carol Shields winning the Pulitzer Prize in 1995 for *The Stone Diaries* (1993) or Alice Munro's winning of the 2009 Man Booker International Prize.

This notion of a literary hierarchy, of course, is also ever present in the continuing tendency of many of Canada's elite who seem to find a greater "distinction"—to employ Bourdieu's use of the term—in reading foreign literary works, particularly those of the former colonial powers of Britain and France, and to a lesser degree, the United States. For instance, Lucien Bouchard's memoirs, notes John Ralston Saul, "contain dozens of enthusiastic references to European writers and culture" (262). Bouchard—who apparently keeps a complete set of the Pléiade editions of literary classics in his office—mentions a Québécois writer only once, making a "curiously inaccurate reference to Jacques Godbout's *Les Têtes à Papineau*" (523). While one characteristic of elitism in Canada is often a taste for the foreign over the domestic, one could argue that the majority of literature departments at Canadian universities foster this tendency among their students. Perhaps the most obvious manner in which this colonial hierarchy is reinforced, especially in English Canada, is through the weight these departments give to the study of the literatures of Canada.

While the issue of department structures is a significant one— English-Canadian literature often comprises a maximum of 15 per cent of total course offerings in English departments while Québécois literature/non-Québécois French-Canadian literature can sometimes make up nearly 40 per cent of course offerings at some Québec universities— one of the most important sites of the bias in favour of the literatures of England and France has been the mandatory literature courses required in first-year university in English Canada and at the CÉGEP level in Québec. Unlike in the United States where students usually take composition courses and no mandatory courses on literature, most first-year English courses in Canada combine training in writing with literary analysis; using primarily examples from the history of British literature, students frequently learn to analyze novels, poetry, and drama and demonstrate their understanding of the relevant concepts through a series of required writing assignments. While such introductory courses have become increasingly open to texts and genres outside of the British canon, it is still uncommon for Canadian texts to take centre stage in them.

As discussed in Chapter One, the advent of the CÉGEP system in Québec brought about a deliberate increase in the attention paid to Québécois literature. The final level at which students must take required courses in language and literature—university students at Québec universities only take courses in their chosen area of specialization— the CÉGEP literature curriculum during the 1970s and 1980s included a significant proportion of Québécois literature, a great change from the traditional focus of the collèges classiques. Curricular reforms introduced in 1994, however, limited the number and type of courses available and, by returning to a curriculum structured around literary periods and movements rather than genres, shifted the emphasis back towards the French literary tradition.[16] As Max Roy argues, in an observation equally applicable to the place of the literatures of Canada in first-year English courses, the problem with a mandatory curriculum in which a foreign literature is more heavily weighted than an indigenous one is what it implies about the importance of studying the literature(s) of one's own people: "l'enseignement d'une culture différente de la culture ambiante et présentée comme la culture de base implique inévitablement un juge-ment de valeur" (*La littérature québécoise au collège* 103).[17]

Furthermore, there are fundamental problems inherent in trying to posit literatures as naturally complex as those produced in Canada as being part or an offshoot of either the French or British tradition. Any study taking into account *all* literature produced in Canada inevitably reveals "a literary and cultural tradition which has little to do with that suggested by simple linguistics and the false relationships produced by empires" (Saul 430). Nevertheless, the typical structure of English and French departments and the placement of the literatures of Canada therein imply that such unnatural comparisons are, in fact, the most appropriate. As Joseph Melançon argues in his article "La conjoncture universitaire," the somewhat arbitrary division of fields of knowledge into separate university departments, units, and programs "entraîne un fractionnement des savoirs, des disciplines et des compétences. Ces divisions, pourtant inoffensives puisqu'elles ne veulent que faciliter la gestion de l'entreprise universitaire, deviennent des divisions mentales" (67).[18] A prime example of how "le principe de 'division' est également un principe de 'vision'" (67)[19] is that our tendency to see the literatures of Canada as a part of a larger literary tradition in either English or French means that we often overlook even the most striking similarities between the literatures of Canada, not to mention those between our own literatures and those of countries who we may have much more in common with culturally, historically, or geographically than we do with either England or France. "[We] waste a great deal of time comparing our literature with its linear neighbours in English and French," argues John Ralston Saul (426).

> If our fiction resembles any other it is Russian and the other Northern literatures. If our contrasting sophistication and insecurity resembles anyone's, it is that of Central Europe and Latin America. We really have very little in common with two European ex-empires and the United States, all three beneficiaries of temperate, manageable lands, dense populations and centralized mythologies. (426)

The tendency to posit the literatures of Canada as being ineluctably attached to the literary traditions of Britain and France is far more prevalent in the country's English departments, most of which are quite uniform in their curriculum. The requirements for major, specialization, concentration, or honours in English—the terminology varies between institutions—almost always calls for a selection of courses that give the student broad coverage in a variety of periods and genres of British literature combined with a certain number of optional courses, including those in other national literatures such as those of Canada and the United States. Even in those English departments that require students to take a course or two in Canadian literature—I have found no examples of a university requiring more than one full-year course in either Canadian or American literature for a BA in English and several examples of universities without such requirements—the British tradition is still the clear foundation of the literature program. The situation in Québec is significantly different. There is a large variation between the curricula of the Université de Montréal's Département d'études françaises, the Université Laval's Département des littératures, and the Université du Québec à Montréal's Département d'études littéraires. Although, as discussed in the first chapter, there are a significant number of historical reasons for this divergence between the three universities and the vast difference between literary studies at French-language universities in Québec and English-language universities throughout the country, one of the key factors that contributes to the shape of the curriculum in Québec is the presence of the CÉGEP system. Unlike institutions in English Canada, the students entering literature programs at universities in Québec arrive having already taken a considerable number of general courses at the CÉGEP level. This enables the university literature departments to offer much more specialized courses and, seemingly, a wider variety of program choices, although the English-language universities there still seem to have curricula extraordinarily similar to universities outside of the province. The larger presence of Québécois literature in these departments, of course, also makes the university an even greater force within the literary institution as a whole than are their counterparts in English universities.

By their structure alone, then, university literature departments and the courses they offer have a significant impact on how their students conceive of the literatures of Canada. Even more than the equivalent departments in England, France, and the United States, the function of the university literature department in Canada goes beyond being simply the bestower of "that infallible mark of consecration" (Bourdieu, "Market" 123). With Canada's much smaller population—and therefore a smaller constituency of readers of literature—many of the agents within the literary institution become concentrated within the university system. In other words, it is not unusual to find professors or instructors who, in addition to serving as agents of consecration, act as agents of production (as writers of literature and literary criticism) and/or dissemination (as publishers, editors, members of funding bodies, or even booksellers). This multiple agency rarely occurs in the other fields of study housed in university literature departments. One cannot, in other words, be a writer of nineteenth-century French poetry, nor can a scholar of today also be a publisher of, say, new modernist fiction, unless, of course, he or she is attempting to consecrate previously neglected works that have been long out of print. Even scholars of contemporary literature written outside Canada are still one step removed from the literary institution of which those texts are a part; they cannot, therefore, achieve the same level of agency within the field of restricted production that Canadianists Québecistes frequently possess with respect to the literary institution in Canada.

One of the most obvious ways in which Canadian universities affect other levels of the institution is via the symbiotic relationship that forms between publishing and teaching. Naturally, one can only usually teach what has been published and is readily available, but the curriculum can also have a significant effect on the publishing world. Just as changes in the 1890s to the baccalauréat curriculum in France caused more literary histories, anthologies, and textbooks to be published in the first decade of the twentieth century than in the previous fifty years (Melançon, Moisan, and Roy 240), the advent of courses on the literatures of Canada dramatically increased literary publishing in Canada. During the 1920s, for instance, when a surge in Canadian nationalism prompted the offering of a number of courses on Canadian literature at both English and French universities, there was a great output of critical works on the subject. These included Ray Palmer Baker's *A History of English-Canadian Literature to the Confederation* (1920), three new editions (1920, 1923, 1925) of Camille Roy's *Manuel d'histoire de la littérature canadienne-française* (1918), J.D. Logan and Donald French's *Highways of Canadian Literature* (1924), Archibald MacMechan's *Headwaters of Canadian Literature* (1924), Lionel Stevenson's *Appraisals of Canadian Literature* (1926), and Lorne Pierce's *An Outline of Canadian Literature (French and English)* (1927). Later, as the study of the literatures of Canada became more common and, more importantly, as literary studies moved away from a historical approach to a methodology oriented towards textual analysis, it became increasingly important that affordable and complete editions of literary texts were made available for students of literatures of Canada. Responding to this need, McClelland & Stewart founded the New Canadian Library series in 1957 under the direction of Malcolm Ross, then a professor of English at Queen's University. Conversely, once the New Canadian Library series began, the choice of titles to be included had a tremendous effect on what was taught in these Canadian literature courses. Academics, though hardly lazy in their scholarship or teaching, are understandably more inclined to teach readily available texts than they are to search out forgotten classics and endeavour to distribute them to students in the form of photocopies or used editions tracked down through the local antiquarian bookseller.

A text's availability at an affordable price also contributes to its inclusion on a course. Yet, the relationship between publishing and the university in very often far more complex than there simply being two autonomous organizations, each of which benefits by responding to the needs of the other. In many instances, professors themselves are directly involved in the editorial decisions made by publishers and sometimes even in their day-to-day operations. As editors, academics not only serve as experts in the field apparently capable of judging the quality of a given work but also as signs of prestige that imbue that text with a certain authority, an endorsement from the chief consecrators of the literary field. With the New Canadian Library, for example, the long-time general editor is David Staines, a professor of English and the former dean of Arts at the University of Ottawa. A well-known critic and commentator on Canadian literature, Staines is responsible for calling together the advisory panel—made up of writers Alice Munro, Guy Vanderhaeghe, and UBC English Professor Emeritus W.H. New—to decide upon which books should be added to the series and which writer and/or critic should be asked to write the book's afterword, a further mark of consecration that is highlighted on the book's cover. Publishers also often choose academics to edit literature anthologies that, not coincidentally, are nearly always oriented towards the classroom. Aside from making these selections on the basis of who will compile an interesting and worthwhile collection of literary work, the publishers also intend for the name of the editor to confer a symbolic value upon the anthology, not only because he or she is an expert researcher but also, presumably, an expert teacher in the field. In a few notable cases, these literary publishers are themselves professors of literature. Two of the most important English-language presses in which academics play or have played a fundamental role are ECW Press, of which McGill English Professor Robert Lecker was a co-founder and, for many years, a co-director, and NeWest Press, founded by a number of academics and writers including Rudy Wiebe, Diane Bessai, and Douglas Barbour. There are numerous other examples of professors who have founded their own presses or literary journals. Frank Davey, for instance, owns and edits *Open Letter*, and *Voix et Images* and *Canadian Literature* are published under the aegis of the

Université du Québec à Montréal's Département d'études littéraires and the University of British Columbia's Department of English respectively. These cases clearly reveal that, in the context of the Canadian literary field, it is rarely easy to separate academia from publishing.

Adding to the complexity of the field of restricted production in Canada is the number of professors who are also writers of fiction, poetry, and, to a lesser extent, drama. One need only look at past winners of the Governor General's Awards to see how intertwined the worlds of academia and creative writing can be. Of the ten winners of the awards for fiction in English and French between 1993 and 1998, for instance, eight are or have been employed as professors of literature and/ or creative writing at either the university or college level: Carol Shields (1993), Don Coles (1993), Rudy Wiebe (1994), Greg Hollingshead (1995), Guy Vanderhaeghe (1996), Aude (1997), Diane Schomeperlen (1998), and Christiane Frenette (1998). In the poetry categories for the same years, a total of three winners are or have been employed as professors of literature and/or creative writing at either the university or college level: Denise Desautels (1993), E.D. Blodgett (1996), and Pierre Nepveu (1997). One decade later, the five year period between 2003 and 2008 reveals a smaller percentage of winners who were also professors at the university or college level, indicating perhaps, though not necessarily, a slight increase in the separation between publishing and academia. Winners who are or were part of academia during this period included: Michael Ondaatje (2007), John Pass (2006), Jean-Marc Desgent (2005), Anne Compton (2005), André Brochu (2004), Douglas Glover (2003), Tim Lilburn (2003), Élise Turcotte (2003), and Pierre Nepveu (2003). The list of writers and poets who teach or have taught in universities as professors of literature and/or creative writing includes many of Canada's most important writers, such as Lorna Crozier, Frank Davey, Kristjana Gunnars, Thomas King, Robert Kroetsch, Alistair MacLeod, Anne Michaels, W.O. Mitchell, and Guy Vanderhaeghe. An even greater roster of Canadian writers have benefitted from writers-in-residence programs at universities across the country. One need only look at the biographies of writers such as Margaret Laurence, Timothy Findley, Margaret Atwood, Nicole Brossard, Austin Clarke, Alice Munro, Eden Robinson, and Dionne Brand to see how such programs have affected the history of the literatures of Canada. In some cases, writer-in-residence positions allowed emerging writers to hone their craft without needing to resort to finding day jobs that would distract them from their work; in other cases, such positions allowed writers the time to begin or complete works that would become major landmarks in Canadian literature. Additionally, the placement of such writers in term positions at Canadian universities gave young aspiring writers access to the experience and advice of writers who had already achieved some literary success.

The place of creative writing programs at Canadian universities further reinforces the enmeshment of the university in the Canadian literary institution. Many successful Canadian writers have emerged from master's programs in creative writing such as those at the University of British Columbia, the University of Calgary, and the University of Guelph. It is not unusual, in the data I gathered, to find instances of writers' work being taught at the institutions from which they graduated. The example of NeWest Press is again relevant here. Their Nunatak First Fiction Series publishes fiction by young and emerging Canadian writers. The two most successful novels of this series have been Thomas Wharton's *Icefields* and Hiromi Goto's *Chorus of Mushrooms*. Both authors are graduates of the Creative Writing Program at the University of Alberta, where Rudy Wiebe, general editor of the Nunatak series, and Douglas Barbour, president of NeWest, were long employed as professors. Wharton's novel, in fact, was begun as a project for a creative writing course taught by Wiebe. This is not to suggest that there was any nepotism involved in the publication of Wharton's book. On the contrary, *Icefields* is a stellar debut novel that received critical acclaim nationally and internationally—Wiebe's position merely gave him the fortune of discovering it. Nonetheless, the circumstances surrounding the novel's production and the fact that it has subsequently been taught in courses at the University of Alberta and that the department later hired Wharton as a professor of creative writing serves to demonstrate further the potential complexities of the university's role in such a small and insular field of restricted production. In other words, in the case of *Icefields*, the University of Alberta and several of its staff were intimately involved in its production, dissemination, and consecration. The model of the field as envisioned by Bourdieu and later echoed by Dubois, however, only positions the university as being directly involved in the process of consecration. In the cases of the literatures of Canada, but especially English-Canadian literature and Québécois literature, the university is tightly enmeshed in nearly all levels of the literary institution.

The Canadian university's effect on publishing goes beyond the multiple agencies of many academics in that departmental structures and curricula also have a major impact on what gets published. Books and especially anthologies are often published primarily to fill specific niches or gaps in the school or university courses. Anthologies in particular are nearly always designed with teaching in mind and, thus, can have a limited audience outside the classroom. While ostensibly aiming to respond to perceived curricular needs, texts published with the classroom in mind notably shape the curriculum into which they are integrated. As Malcolm Ross, the editor of the original New Canadian Library Series noted about convincing Jack McClelland about the potential market for inexpensive works of Canadian literature that could be used in the classroom, "I seemed to convince him...that such a series would *create* a market in the universities and schools of the country" (MacSkimming 127). Ross was absolutely correct in his projections for the potential usefulness of the New Canadian Library series. The same theory of interdependence applies even more so to the fate of general anthologies of "Canadian Literature."

The most frequent use for Canadian literature anthologies is in survey courses where it would be unrealistic and impractical to use only individual texts to cover a literary history of several hundred years. Survey courses, which are based on a principle of coverage of various periods, genres, and movements rather than in-depth analysis of individual texts, require anthologies that possess a similar range of content. When an anthology is chosen for a course, though, the choices made by its editors will often play a significant role in what texts a student will read in the course. Obviously, an instructor will choose to cover only a relatively small portion of the selections for his or her students to read—

anthologies are often large enough to accommodate a wide range of instructor preferences. Given the limited time and resources available to an instructor, it is often difficult and impractical for him or her to address adequately what has been left out of the anthology, those texts the editors deemed unworthy of inclusion given the limited space available for any one author, text, or period. Relegated to focusing on those texts chosen by the editors, the instructor often unhappily allows the anthology, at least partially, to shape his or her syllabus.

The popular Oxford anthology *A New Anthology of Canadian Literature in English* (2002, revised in 2010), edited by University of Toronto professors Donna Bennett and Russell Brown,[20] offers an excellent example of how the contents of an anthology can influence the content of a course. One of the most frequently included books on Canadian Literature courses in both 1997–98 and 2007–08, the anthology is oriented towards the type of full-year survey courses offered at the University of Toronto, and, as such, it aims to cover English-Canadian literature from its origins to the present day. Bennett and Brown make several key choices, though, which reflect a very specific notion of "Canadian literature." The first and most obvious choice any editor must make is where to begin. This is an especially important decision when, as in the case of the Bennett and Brown anthology, the editors are arranging the selections chronologically and therefore are establishing a de facto literary history, whether they intend to or not. Unlike literary histories like W.H. New's *A History of Canadian Literature* that take into account Native oral tradition and early exploration literature, Brown and Bennett's 1990 anthology situates the beginning point more conservatively with excerpts from Frances Brooke's *The History of Emily Montague* (1769). Their *New Anthology of Canadian Literature in English* amends this slightly, by including one eighteenth-century oral text by Saukamapee, as transcribed by the explorer David Thompson, in which he describes "Life among the Peigans" (Bennett and Brown 2). In their introductory note, Bennett and Brown describe the challenges caused by transcribed narratives such as this one, as much, it seems, to explain the absence of such material in their earlier anthology as to justify its inclusion in the new version: "Because most transcriptions of these early oral materials are the product of European pens such as Thompson's, they have been regarded with suspicion by scholars of Native culture as unintentionally distorting, if not explicitly falsifying. More recently, scholars have begun to feel such records, if used carefully, can provide valuable accounts that might otherwise be unavailable" (Bennett and Brown 1). As my 1997–98 interviews with professors who use Brown and Bennett's earlier anthology revealed, the difficulty of asking students to purchase separate texts dedicated to Native oral literature and exploration literature, combined with the fact that these topics would only be a small part of the survey course, led professors to begin their courses with one of the other early texts in the anthology, even if they would have otherwise welcomed the chance to use an earlier historic moment as the starting point for their course.

One of the other most obvious editorial choices, which may actually have been decided for the editors by Oxford itself, was to focus solely on English-Canadian literature—in other words, Canadian literature written originally in English. While an anthology that would cover all of the literatures of Canada would be larger, far more difficult to compile, and partially outside the editors' areas of expertise, the decision to focus solely on English-Canadian literature also reflects the practice of a great number of English departments in Canada, most notably that of the University of Toronto, where Bennett and Brown spent the majority of their academic careers. Such a decision, likely prompted by the realities of some departments that do not include French-Canadian literature as part of their "Canadian literature" courses, therefore limits the ability of other universities that do not have such policies or practices to offer an introduction to French-language literature in any meaningful way. At best, professors relying on the anthology plus a selection of individual novels might be able to include one or two French-language novels in translation. The vast majority, or so my 1997–98 interviews and the collected data from 2007–08 indicate, do not make the effort and resolve to follow the less complicated path of dealing only with English-Canadian literature. Each of these cases demonstrates the perfect circularity of the process in which decisions made by academics prompt decisions made by publishers that then lead to further decisions made by academics.

While some might argue that this exclusion of work in translation is simply the case of the preferences of a particular publisher or the editors of an individual anthology, two recent anthologies, published in great part to compete with the ubiquitous Bennett and Brown anthology, demonstrate that this is emblematic of a broader approach to the literatures of Canada. Robert Lecker's *Open Country: Canadian Literature in English* (which comes in one longer comprehensive edition or a variety of shorter editions oriented to a particular period or genre) and Cynthia Sugars and Laura Moss's two-volume *Canadian Literature in English: Texts and Contexts* each go to great lengths to position themselves as being a better choice for the classroom than the Bennett and Brown. According to its publisher's website, the Sugars and Moss anthology, which, not incidentally, starts with early exploration narratives from Jacques Cartier and Samuel de Champlain,

> *differs from other anthologies of Canadian literature in its inclusion of substantial contextual material; its historical emphasis on the production of Canadian literature; its interdisciplinary approach; its emphasis on intertextual dialogue between selections; its inclusion of popular culture texts, such as song lyrics; and its inclusion of a substantial representation of Canadian First Nations writing within a general Canadian Literature anthology.* ("Canadian Literature in English: Texts and Contexts, Vol. 1")

Lecker's publisher, on the other hand, highlights that the anthology offers an "excellent collection of contemporary fiction including unexpected stories from established authors with varied themes, such as ethnicity and race, gender, sexuality and the gay and lesbian experience" ("Open Country"). Like with the Sugars and Moss anthology, the publisher makes a point to mention the "fair representation...of aboriginal authors" and also the textbook's "comprehensive footnotes" and "companion website" ("Open Country"). Unlike both the teams of Moss and Sugars and Brown and Bennett, Lecker decides to commence his anthology with a text that falls under our more traditional understandings of what is literature: Oliver Goldsmith's "The Rising Village." As I will discuss in greater detail in the final chapter of this book, the fact that neither Lecker nor Moss and Sugars see the inclusion of texts in translation to be a worthwhile way of differentiating their anthologies from previous ones is very telling; it is a foregone conclusion to them that professors and students of "Canadian Literature" (the term "Canadian Literature in English" quickly gets dropped once one gets past the title of both books) will not be well served by the inclusion of even a few works in translation.

There is, as we have already discussed and will see in great detail in the coming chapters, an unavoidable connection between publishing, teaching, and the reception or consumption of texts in the field of restricted production. The continual inclusion of certain texts in curricula of courses on the literatures of Canada assures regular sales and a continually renewed body of readers. Equally critical to the survival of the field is the potential that these readers may go on to read other works by the authors they have studied and may also assist in the dissemination of the chosen authors or texts by recommending them to other readers outside those courses or even outside of the academy. The mere inclusion of texts on course reading lists, then, imbues those works and their authors with a symbolic value not easily acquired by those that are not chosen to be part of the curriculum. In other words, it is highly unlikely that works or authors in the latter circumstance will ever be widely diffused over an extended period of time. As David Arnason contends,

> A Canadian writer who does not end up being taught is unlikely ever to prove
> more than an historical footnote. Any writer who is dead and whose work
> is not part of the canon, that is to say not studied in schools by a sufficient
> number of students to make the reprinting of his or her work worthwhile, will
> simply vanish into the dustheap of Canadian literary history. (Arnason 60)

A look at sales figures for the New Canadian Library series from its inception to 1999 reveals to what degree the frequent teaching of a text can affect both sales and readership. Perhaps the most frequently taught Canadian novel of the last forty years is Margaret Laurence's *The Stone Angel*. Its habitual presence on high school and university courses—what

Arnason labels "the biggest market we have for Canadian literature" (60)—has undoubtedly affected its sales and readership tremendously; at the time of the 1999 sales figures, *The Stone Angel* remained the all-time bestselling title of the New Canadian Library series, outselling its nearest competitor, Laurence's *The Diviners*, by more than two to one. Two important novels that appeared in the New Canadian Library series around the same time as *The Stone Angel* are Sheila Watson's *The Double Hook* and Mordecai Richler's *The Apprenticeship of Duddy Kravitz*.[21] Although these two novels are reasonably canonical, neither has ever been taught as habitually as *The Stone Angel*. New Canadian Library sales figures for up to January 1999 indicate that while Laurence's novel had sold around 212,000 copies in that edition, *The Double Hook* had only sold approximately 23,000 copies (about 11 per cent of Laurence's sales) and *The Apprenticeship of Duddy Kravitz* had sold just over 41,000 copies in its New Canadian Library edition (just over 19 per cent of Laurence's sales). Thus, the inexpensive editions of the New Canadian Library series helped make English-Canadian literature far easier to teach, but the choices made by professors also helped to keep these books in print and, more importantly, shaped a definite canon of which texts should be taught and/or are the most "teachable." As Jack McClelland revealed in a letter to Allan Weiss, McClelland & Stewart relied as much on the efforts of professors of Canadian literature as the professors relied on the New Canadian Library: "From the late fifties to the seventies the Canadian literature market grew very rapidly because of a handful of dedicated people—spread across the country in fact—at universities and high-schools who were nationalistic and who pushed Canlit very actively" (Weiss 175–76). As the sales figures indicate, however, there is no doubt that certain writers were "pushed" more than others.

While it is difficult to argue that *The Stone Angel* is not one of the more significant novels ever written in Canada, its popularity is clearly linked to the frequency with which it is taught. Although a prominent place in university and high school curriculum is far from the sole factor to earn *The Stone Angel* such a prominent place in Canadian literary history, it is highly unlikely that it would still be cited as one of the great Canadian novels of the twentieth century without that continuous introduction of new readers to the text. As Max Roy argues in the introduction to his 1998 study *La littérature québécoise au collège (1990–1996)*, the teaching of works by authors from Canada in literature courses has a profound effect on all levels of the literary institution:

> *Son influence se mésure éventuellement dans les habitudes de lecture et de fréquentation du théâtre qui signifie de multiples répercussions. Dans cette perspective, la situation de l'enseignement littéraire or théatral au collégial mérite toute l'attention des personnnes intéressées par les arts et les lettres, qu'il s'agisse des auteurs, des distributeurs, des libraires, des producteurs, ou des enseignants eux-mêmes.*[22] *(*La littérature québécoise au collège *12)*

Roy, of course, refers here to a very specific context, that of the mandatory language and literature courses for CÉGEP students, to which the nearest equivalent at universities in English Canada is the compulsory first-year English courses for arts students. By including these comments in his introduction, Roy clearly aims to make his readers recognize that by instituting a new curriculum that lessens the proportion of Québécois literature studied in these courses, those responsible for this decision have set in motion a gradual but inevitable reshaping of the entire field of restricted production. Roy's observation is perfectly applicable to the place of the literatures of Canada in both English and French universities. When university literature departments choose or are obliged to provide only limited coverage of the literatures of Canada, they also necessarily limit the number and scope of works that will ever be consecrated as "classic" or important Canadian books. This, in turn, affects the production, sales, and legitimation of the literatures of Canada, thus lessening the probability that any future great Canadian novels will be recognized and consecrated as such. In his 1971 article on Canadian literature's "Curriculum Crisis," Alec Lucas observed how crucial these interconnections are between the different levels of the literary institution:

> *Yet what is to be studied is inseparable from issues such as personnel policy, Canadian publishing, even arrangements for guest speakers and poetry*

readings, and most obviously inseparable from the general question of the
well-being of our culture, the bedrock of our national identity. All are inextri-
cably united, and, as in a gestalt, no one component shifts without affecting
all others. (Lucas 58)

While the role of universities today are difficult to define fully, it is
clear, as Joseph Melançon remarks, that

[leur] raison d'être, toutefois est la transmission du savoir. Non par une
transmission empirique, au gré des circonstances et des individus, mais une
transmission autorisée, officiellement reconnue, qui conduit à une sanction,
sous forme de diplôme.[23] *(63)*

Consequently, the knowledge that the university and its professors deem
worthy of being transmitted is inevitably loaded with a symbolic
authority. As people who produce works of literary criticism, occasional
reviews, and lectures oriented to the general populace, and, more importantly, teach works of literature to future "cultural consumers," professors
of literature invariably and intentionally accord certain titles and authors
a privileged place within the field of restricted production; bestowed with
this symbolic value, what were once mere books become works of Literature
worthy of being passed on to future generations and a few authors are
deemed to be representative of a national literary tradition. At first, the
writing of criticism and reviews may seem to be the most long-lasting
form of consecration, but the effect of teaching reaches much further. As
Carole Gerson persuasively demonstrates in "Cultural Darwinism:
Publishing and the Canon of Early Canadian Literature in English,"
although curricula may initially be affected by what books are available,
what gets taught even further affects what gets published. The case of the
teaching of early English-Canadian literature, an area of English-Canadian
literature most frequently represented by one or two texts on a survey
course, perfectly demonstrates how a limited place on the curriculum
leads to fewer titles being available to fill that slot. This limited choice
inevitably works to narrow the field of consecrated texts, resulting in
professors being forced to choose always those same titles as course texts.

What Bourdieu describes as the "almost perfect circularity and revers-
ibility of the relations of cultural production and consumption resulting
from the objectively closed nature of the field of restricted production"
("Market" 118) also extends to the world of scholarly publishing. As
Gerson points out, "we tend to research and write about the authors and
texts that we teach in our more specialized courses" (26). While such
upper-level courses are often designed around a professor's own research
interests, it is important to note that for these authors or texts truly to be
consecrated, there usually must be a mutually reinforcing interplay
between teaching and research and, as we have already seen, publishing.

The decision as to what to teach or write about is never apolitical and
never based solely on "excellence," despite the Canadian universities'
apparently ongoing faith in the ideals of Arnoldian humanism; while the
political agenda of pedagogy may be more difficult to determine than in
literary criticism, it is certainly, as Heather Murray contends, "as 'political' as scholarship, despite a persistent ivory-towerism that sees literary
studies as a haven in a heartless university" (161). No matter how neutral
or objective some professors of the literatures of Canada may like to see
themselves, it is impossible for them to escape the multiple forms of
"literary power" they hold. Aware of their own agency and that of their
colleagues, they cannot overlook the far-reaching effects of their decisions in matters of curriculum, teaching practices, and research. There
is also, at the same time, a huge pressure for professors of literature to
appear to others and even themselves as objective, dispassionate scholars
who, as the primary consecrators of this particular field of restricted
production, base their decisions on a single criteria: literary "excellence."
For consecration to occur, it seems essential for scholars to deny rather
than declare their own self-interest in the literary institution; the more
professors are seen as having nothing to gain by their deliberations over
the symbolic worth of a given text or author, the more their opinion
appears to other levels of the field as being credible and authoritative.
"Paradoxalement," notes Mélançon about the role of professor and critic,
"le désintéressement est rémunéré en 'distinction,' dans la conjuncture
scientifique. Plus spécifiquement, la forme impersonelle de son exposé
devient l'argument souverain de sa crédibilité" (68).[24]

The even greater paradox here is that this denial of self-interest is motivated entirely by self-interest—more precisely, every professor's own quest for symbolic capital. Given their often multiple interests in the literary field and, additionally, that their work as consecrators through publishing works of criticism is the activity Canadian research universities rewards most heavily, professors nearly always have a great deal of personal investment in the consecration of particular works or the oeuvres of certain writers. These texts and authors, it is worth noting, have usually achieved some degree of symbolic legitimacy in the field or are already part of the canon. As Gerson observes, this tendency ties in to the continuing pursuit of symbolic profit by these supposedly neutral agents of consecration: "research performed on an unavailable text by an obscure author may be accorded little recognition for career advancement" (28). There can be, however, some additional distinction to be earned by working on writers or texts from just outside the mainstream but that still have been received the legitimation bestowed by previous critical attention—a difference Bourdieu pinpoints by distinguishing the true avant-garde from the "consecrated avant-garde" (Bourdieu, "Production of Belief" 86). There are, in other words, many factors that may motivate the teaching, research, and eventual consecration of a particular text or writer by the field's primary agents of consecration: professors of literature.

Legitimation, let alone consecration, does not occur simply because of the preferences of individual university literature departments and the professors who work (in) them. The inclusion of a text in a single course or in several courses taught by the same professor or within the same institution functions within the field of restricted production as merely an anomalous event that, while perhaps pointing to a certain legitimacy of the cultural product, can in no way represent the judgement of the field as a whole. To be truly consecrated and receive the full symbolic profit accorded in this process, a single work or the oeuvre of an author needs to be taught far more than once or twice and must appear on the curricula at a good number of universities. What makes writers such as Anne Hébert and Margaret Atwood and texts such as *Roughing it in the Bush* and *Maria Chapdelaine* so canonical, then, is that they are

on the curricula at practically every Canadian university and have likely
been taught at least once by nearly every professor in the field. Once
these authors and works earn a major place in the canon, their canonicity generates a greater amount of literary criticism about them. For as
Dubois points out, the university's role is not only one of consecration,
but also one of conservation (87). The goal is to conserve the hegemony
of the canon, of course, but also for the university to preserve itself and
its role in the literary field.

The primary means by which Canadian university literature departments preserve themselves is by producing agents who will recognize,
value, and perpetuate the aesthetic qualities deemed important by
the field and, particularly, the scholars in university literature departments. The continual production of graduates well versed in these
criteria allows the field to conserve the privileged position of already
canonized works, but also to admit into the fold new works that live up
to the same criteria. These agents produced by the university are not
simply the few graduates who will continue on to eventually teach literature at the post-secondary education level or even at the primary or
secondary education level. More crucial to the field's survival and self-
reproduction are the "cultural consumers" generated by the university,
for they act as a knowledgeable audience for the products in the field of
literary production. While in Canada they are rarely numerous enough
to bring great economic reward to cultural producers, their support and
consumption of symbolic goods is of fundamental importance to the
symbolic economy, bringing cultural capital to the most successful agents
of production and symbolic bankruptcy to the least. In addition, the
existence of an active symbolic economy further justifies the need for
departments of literature that serve as the most authoritative consecrators and, thus, distributors of symbolic capital. Part of the reason, then,
that the models proposed by Bourdieu and further addressed by Dubois
are so appropriate to the context of the Canadian literary institution is
the degree to which the field of restricted production relies so heavily on
an economy of purely symbolic goods.

Unlike the markets in countries with larger populations, there is
usually not a consumer base large enough to allow Canadian agents

of production (writers, publishers, distributors) to survive, let alone prosper, purely from the economic profits derived from the consumption of symbolic goods. In fact, a great number of Canadian publishers, if not the majority, get a significant amount of their operating revenue from government grants, which give them the funds necessary to publish and keep in print literary works by Canadian authors. In this way, the symbolic economy in Canada is propped up to a considerable degree by public funds that facilitate the competition between works, publishers, and authors for the limited degree of symbolic capital available in such a closed system. It is not insignificant to note that the Québec government provides a vastly higher level of funding to its publishers and the book industry than any other provincial government,[25] for they understand particularly well the crucial role played by the symbolic economy in terms of the strengthening of national identity and the process of cultural reproduction. Just as governments fund publishers and give grants to writers and translators, the parts of the literary institution responsible for the production of the goods that will enter into the symbolic economy, they also subsidize the education system, which looks after both the dissemination of those works (through the students who are obligated to buy and read them) and their consecration. Clearly, the universities' role in this process is essential because it provides the outlet for the symbolic goods the government has already helped to produce.

The magnitude of the university's role in the Canadian literary institution, then, is necessarily much greater than in the larger markets such as Britain or France, where products might be able to acquire enough capital from other agents of consecrations (reviews, academies, literary prizes) to maintain a considerable status. In Canada, however, there is a heavy reliance on the role of the university in the study of the literatures of Canada, though it may not be as significant in the early twenty-first century as it was in the 1970s. Once overly dependent on the university for legitimation and consecration, the growing symbolic economy in Canada, fuelled partly by an increasing global interest in the literatures of Canada, seems to be leading to a day where some Canadian writers and publishers may be able to achieve and, more importantly, maintain a high level of symbolic capital without a major acceptance by the university literature departments. This growing diversification and apparent independence of agents of production—many of whom, it is important to remember, are still directly involved in the university—plays directly into the ambition of Canadianists to increase their own symbolic worth. Once heavily criticized for their supposedly unscientific encouragement and patronage of literary production in Canada, professors of the literatures of Canada are now more able to assume a position of disinterest and claim that the literatures no longer need their help to survive. As we have seen, though, such claims of scientific objectivity are not only disingenuous, but completely erroneous; they seek only to perpetuate an Arnoldian vision of the function of departments of literature in which scholars objectively and dispassionately determine and pass on to future generations the "best that is thought and said in the world" (Arnold 38). In reality, though, there is much more at work in such deliberations.

As Bourdieu notes in *La reproduction*, one of the essential functions of the educational process is to "reproduire, autant que le lui permet son autonomie relative, les conditions dans lesquelles ont été produits les reproducteurs, i.e., les conditions de sa reproduction" (*La reproduction* 47) (reproduce, as much as its relative autonomy permits, the conditions in which the reproducers were produced, i.e., the conditions of its own reproduction). In the context of the study of the literatures of Canada, it is clear that Canadian university literature departments have done exactly this and used this new area of study as a means of perpetuating themselves. Specifically, these departments have encouraged the study of literatures of Canada to develop in ways that subtly reinforce the primary role of the English and French studies in Canada rather than actively bringing them into question.[26] A prime example, as I will discuss more thoroughly in Chapter Four, is that of the place of the literatures of Canada within monolingual department structures. Initially, the study of French-language literature from Québec in French departments or programs and the study of English-Canadian literature in English departments or programs made practical sense as these were the only sites for the study of contemporary literature. Rather than eventually growing beyond the confines of these department structures,[25] the study of the literatures of Canada has settled into what is most often a minority role in these departments. In the process of doing so, the tendency among professors has been more and more to consider the body of literature produced in Canada as being divided into two separate and monolingual entities: English-Canadian literature (more frequently referred to as simply Canadian literature) and Québécois literature. While there are obviously political and culturally reproductive reasons to envision literary production in Canada as a case of "two solitudes," the traditional department structures of English and French also have much to gain from perpetuating such a simplistic notion of the literatures of Canada. By finding ways to mask the unsuitability and inability of such monolingual and monocultural department structures to deal with what can potentially be understood as a multilingual and multicultural body of work, departments such as these have been able to make it seem as if they are progressive and incorporating new literary voices while actually reinforcing the traditional hegemony of English and French literature.

Like the entire process of education, literature departments are able to create this illusion by successfully creating a setting in which students, and even faculty, first accept and then come to forget "l'univers de présupposés, de censures et de lacunes" (Bourdieu, *Leçon sur la leçon* 10) (the universe of presuppositions, censures, and lacunae). In this way, the educational system, which, as Bourdieu contends, always serves to reproduce cultural relations, effectively imposes "la vérité partielle d'un groupe comme la vérité des relations entre les groupes" (*Leçon sur la leçon* 23) (the partial truth of a group as the truth of the relations between groups). With the case of the literatures of Canada, it is clear that this is precisely what happens; by (re)producing certain understandings of the literatures of Canada—principally those that concentrate on the English and French literary production and posit each as being entirely separate and uncomplementary to the other—courses in the literatures of Canada also work to perpetuate a similar understanding of Canada itself. As the circularity of Bourdieu's model suggests, this cultural reproduction occurs on many levels. Courses in either English-Canadian literature or Québécois literature that promote a monolingual vision of that particular body of literature inevitably affect the demand for Canadian literature in translation. Not only do such courses not employ translated works as course texts, they also make it less likely that any of the cultural consumers they produce will read much work from the "other" main body of Canadian writing. The example of literature in translation is only one example of how those "présupposés, de censures et de lacunes" (Bourdieu, *Leçon sur la leçon* 10) work their way into other levels of the institution, thus making those gaps perpetuated by literature departments seem even more natural and appropriate.

A careful look at the interactions between all of these levels of the literary field in Canada makes it abundantly clear that the literary institution (pre)determines the parameters of our understanding of the Canadian literatures. In a 1998 interview on CBC *Newsworld*, John Ralston Saul remarked, "What you think the country is, determines entirely what you are able to do." As Bourdieu and Dubois reveal in seminal texts like the former's *La reproduction* and "Le marché des biens symboliques" and the latter's *L'institution de la littérature*, the inverse is equally true: practice affects perception in every possible way. The synechdocal constructions of "Canadian literature" (as English-language literature only) and, to a much lesser degree, "Québécois literature" (as French-language literature from Québec), are prime instances of how universities frequently employ what Bourdieu describes as their "monopoly of legitimate symbolic violence" (*Manet and the Insitutionalization of Anomie* 250). By accepting such a completely arbitrary construction as natural or, at least, logical, university literature departments across Canada have perpetuated an oversimplified understanding of the national literatures that, conveniently, does not truly threaten their own stockpiles of symbolic capital. At the same time, of course, they also project a very specific vision of English-Canadian and Québécois society that reinforces the hegemony of the dominant class in each constituency. As we will see in Chapter Three, while these conceptions of the literatures of Canada are firmly rooted in issues of institutional self-reproduction, they have also been influenced by the forces of cultural nationalism.

Field Notes

Assessing the State of Canadian Literary Studies in 1997–98

3

AS ITS HISTORY REVEALS, the teaching of the literatures of Canada has been significantly influenced by both cultural nationalism and institutional structures and interactions. One of the chief shortfalls of the previous research done in this area—particularly that concerned with Canadian literature in English—is that there has been little attempt to document precisely *how* current institutional practices and curricula are affected by the history of the field. To begin to fill this void in our understanding of the contemporary Canadian literary institution, I decided in 1997 that it would be necessary to gather as detailed a body of information as possible about the teaching of the literatures of Canada. It was clear from my 1993 study of the subject entitled "Which Canadian Literature(s) Do You Teach?" that collecting course descriptions from afar can only provide a partial picture of the teaching of the literatures of Canada; such data is a reasonably effective demonstration of *what* gets taught, but can fail to address the far more important questions of *why* it gets taught and in which contexts. By travelling to twenty-seven Canadian universities to interview professors, survey students, and collect course descriptions and department calendars, I was able to assess the place of the literatures of Canada in the relevant departments more thoroughly than had I tried to do so from a distance. More important, perhaps, my experiences visiting each of these departments allowed me to gain a much better understanding of the university's role in the Canadian literary institution. This chapter details my fieldwork of 1997–98 and then analyzes, for that year, the situation of courses on the literatures of Canada in Canadian university literature departments, the types of courses used to teach this material, and finally the content of these courses. Ultimately, this chapter also lays the groundwork for Chapter Five, which will address the implications of what the instructors told me about the complex set of issues that influence how they construct their curricula and lead them to choose certain texts and authors over others.

Methodology

A cross-Canada journey through all ten provinces and to twenty-seven universities in just under seven weeks is an enormous undertaking. During the course of this initial research, I cast my net widely; I interviewed every professor and instructor of courses on English-Canadian, Canadian, comparative Canadian, and Québécois literature who would talk to me, and I gathered course descriptions and department and university calendars, material that, unlike today, was nearly impossible to obtain online. Aiming to learn everything I could about the teaching of the literatures of Canada at these particular institutions, I intended my research to set the exact direction for my book. Naturally, I had some definite topics that I wished to explore, such as canon formation and perpetuation, cultural nationalism, representation of the diversity of literary production in Canada, and the effect of course and department structures on each of these processes. While I certainly learned a great deal about all of these topics, I also gained a wealth of knowledge I had not initially anticipated. The more than one hundred hours of interviews I conducted helped me gain a greater appreciation of the history of the field and the significant challenges faced by some of the pioneers of Canadian literary studies. Moreover, my experiences during this research trip revealed to me that the field is far more complex than I had ever anticipated; each department has its own culture, history, structure, rationale for its overall curriculum, and, most significantly, vision of the literatures of Canada. I will not directly discuss much of this type of knowledge that I acquired—that would be an altogether different book that I hope will eventually follow this one—but this information nonetheless informs all of the interpretations and conclusions I have made from the data I collected.

Data Collection

Fieldwork

The first stage of my research trip for this book began on October 5, 1997. Flying to Toronto, I spent until November 8 travelling by train, plane, and automobile from Toronto to St. John's and then back to Edmonton, visiting twenty-one English and French universities in five weeks. From Edmonton, I visited the remaining six in short side trips to Saskatchewan, Calgary, and British Columbia and wrapped up the last of my interviews with professors at the University of Alberta in the spring of 1998. My decision to visit so many universities and every province in the country in such a relatively short period of time necessarily imposed a certain number of parameters on my research. First, to get a sense of the broad scope of university-level courses on the literatures of Canada and how this is affected by issues of region, language, and the size of individual departments and universities, I elected to visit universities in every province, ensuring that I looked at Canada's largest research institutions, but also some of its smallest regional universities. My plan to visit institutions in every province during my relatively limited timeframe meant that I was forced to overlook some medium-sized institutions, such as the University of Waterloo and Trent University. While these institutions may have had a more significant impact on the data that I went on to analyze than smaller institutions like the University of New Brunswick or the University of Prince Edward Island, I felt it was important to have representation from every province in Canada. Second, and more importantly, my plan to study as many universities as possible meant that my time at each institution was very limited. With more time, one could easily write a lengthy article or book chapter about the history each of our country's literature departments and the entry of the literatures of Canada into their curricula.[1]

Ultimately, the research plan I had set out for myself proved, in a number of important ways, to be unworkable in Québec. There was such a number and variety of courses, so many faculty members working at least partially in Québécois literature, and such an array of research institutes or research groups in the field—such as the Centre de recherche en littérature québécoise (CRELIQ)[2]—that I would have needed to spend additional weeks there analyzing curricula and course structures to provide an adequate study, at least on the micro level, of *how* Québécois literature is taught in Québec and which factors affect that process. With these challenges in mind, I elected to focus my energies on interviewing as many of the key scholars in the field as I could and in looking more generally at the course and department structures themselves, approaching the latter less as a subject of detailed study than as an important point of comparison with their counterparts in English Canada. What I found in so doing is that while there are some key similarities between French-language and English-language universities in Canada in terms of the study of our national literatures, the most dramatic differences help to reveal just how arbitrary the English course and department structures really are.

Interviews

Over the course of my travels in 1997–98, I managed to interview ninety-four professors and instructors of courses on the literatures of Canada. Naturally, this number was not split evenly between the various universities; at some institutions, there were only one or two people teaching Canadian literature, while at others there were easily more than a half dozen. Although I had initially planned to interview only those instructors teaching Canadian literature courses in the first term of the 1997–98 academic year, I abandoned this approach when I realized I would be missing the opportunity to speak with a number of important people in the field who were either on sabbatical, on administrative assignments, or retired. Subjects to whom I spoke who would have otherwise been excluded from my research included Malcolm Ross, Clara Thomas, Roy Miki, Stan Dragland, W.H. New, Denis Saint-Jacques, and E.D. Blodgett. Interviews were arranged as much in advance as possible—though the difficulty of reaching some subjects in advance caused me to conduct some interviews with little prior warning to the subject—and all were recorded on cassette tape. Given the potentially sensitive nature of some aspects of my topic, I requested and received permission from each subject to record and utilize our conversations in my research and the final book. In addition, each subject was guaranteed complete anonymity should he or she request it.

Like my approach to the research trip overall, the initial interviews I conducted were exploratory in nature. Even though I utilized a set series of questions that dealt with the various factors that affect their particular approaches to teaching Canadian literature, I deliberately avoided checking any tendencies among the subjects to digress from the topic at hand. This open-ended approach to my interviews led many of the subjects to provide me with what is essentially an oral history of their involvement and experiences in the field. The somewhat surprising enthusiasm with which nearly everyone I interviewed spoke about themselves, their teaching, and the field in general points, at least in part, to a perceived lack of opportunity for members of the field to discuss these issues amongst themselves in any detail. More important to the final shape of my research, though, is how this open approach to the interviews brought to my attention many other significant factors that influence the teaching of the literatures of Canada that I might not otherwise have discovered had I stuck solely to my initial array of questions.

Data Processing

From my research trip and my follow-up requests to departments and instructors for further information, I accumulated a half dozen boxes of data that can be divided into several primary types: interview tapes; course descriptions and syllabi; department and university calendars; and student surveys. To facilitate the analysis of this data, I created relational databases for each of these first three categories.[3] This series of connected databases has allowed me to compile data and perceive connections between all levels of this information that I would not have seen otherwise.

Interview tapes

Because I had over one hundred hours of interview tapes in both French and English, I recognized that it would be more useful to listen to the tapes and to extract all the most important information and quotations than it would be to transcribe each tape in its entirety. To do so, I set up a database, "Instructors," that included for each subject some limited biographical information, a list of the courses they were teaching, and spaces in which I could enter their responses to each of the set questions I asked in my interviews (see Figure 3.1). By organizing the database in this fashion, I could easily compare the responses of different instructors to questions relating to the place of Native literature in their courses, for instance. The ability to perform searches or to sort records according to the data in any of the database fields meant that I could also compare the answers of all the subjects who, for example, were male or who received their PHDs at a particular institution. Aside from creating one of these records for every instructor I interviewed, I also created records for those instructors to whom I did not have the opportunity to speak but who were teaching Canadian literature courses in 1997–98 at any of the universities included in my study. In this way, I was able to link as much as possible the records of the courses taught that year with even some limited information about the people who taught them.

Course descriptions and syllabi

To get a good sense of not only the diversity of the structures of Canadian literature courses taught by these instructors but also the texts and types of texts taught in them, Lu Ziola and I designed a database, "Courses," that, for each course, listed the instructor's name, the books required, the type of course it was, and, when possible, the number of students enrolled (see Figure 3.2). I also allowed space to record my observations about each course's content and objectives. Again, some of these records are more complete than others. Of the 207 course sections offered in 1997–98 in the twenty-eight departments I visited, there were 132 for which I was able to obtain complete syllabi. For each of the seventy-five remaining course sections, I was still often able to determine the type of course, what types of texts would have

Instructors' Information

Name	Gender	Date interviewed	Tape #	DataSetYear
DeFalco, Amelia	☐ M ☒ F			☐ 1997/98
				☐ 2006/2007

Department	University		Province	☒ 2007/2008
Dept. of English and Cultural Studies	McMaster University		Ontario	

e-mail address defalcai@mcmaster.ca   **telephone**

Area of specialization   **Documents obtained**
Sessional lecturer

Courses taught   **Documents still needed**
English 4ID3: [Canadian Writings: Immigration

Education Information

Degree	University	Thesis Topic	Cdn?	Comments
B.A.				
M.A.			☐ Yes ☐ No	
Ph.D.	University of Toronto		☐ Yes ☐ No	

Post-doc

Other comments

FIGURE 3.1 *Sample Data Entry Page from "Instructors" Database*

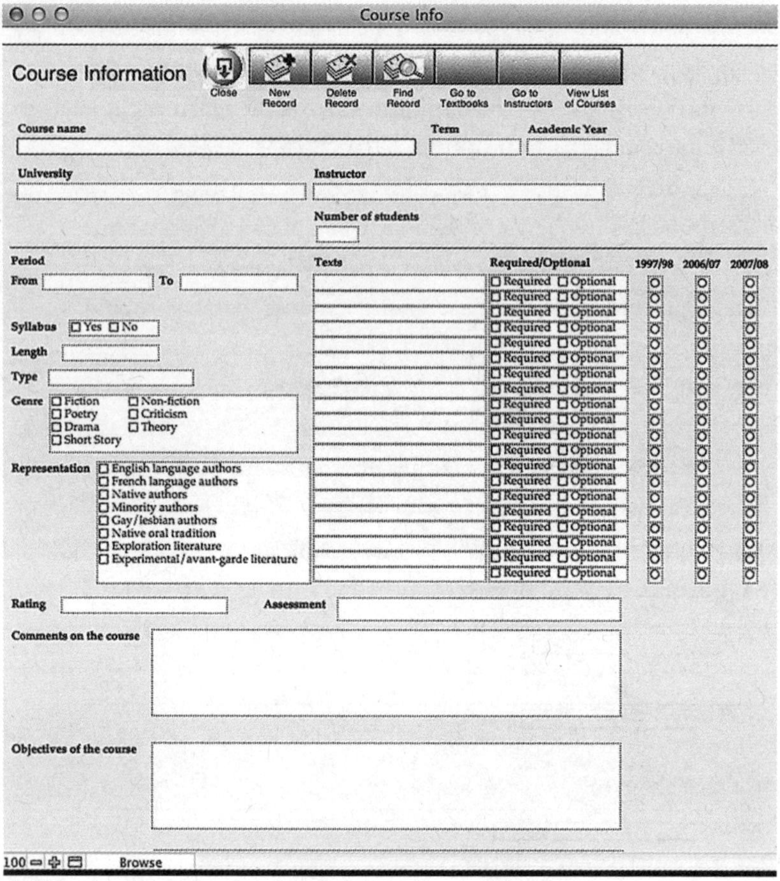

FIGURE 3.2 *Sample Data Entry Page from "Courses" Database*

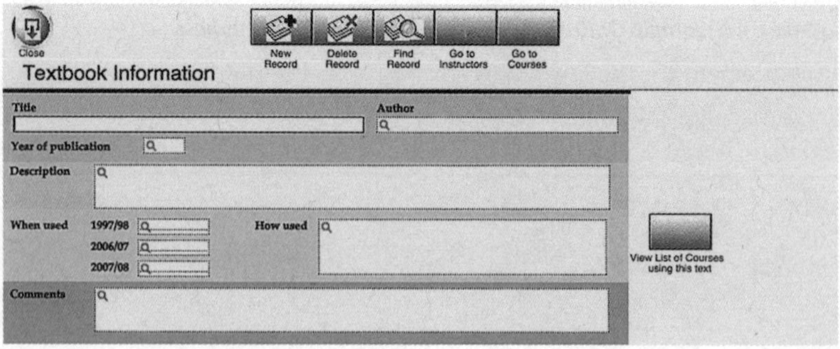

FIGURE 3.3 *Sample Data Entry Page from "Texts" Database*

been included, and, in many cases, a full or partial list of the texts on the course syllabus. As we will see in the following chapter, the availability of current course and department information on the Internet allows us an even more complete picture of the courses taught in 2007–08.

To document and analyze the variety of texts taught across the country and the frequency of their inclusion in Canadian literature courses, it was necessary to create a separate database of texts taught ("Texts"), to which the text fields in the "Courses" database would be linked (see Figure 3.3). In this way, I was able to create a master list of texts that had been taught in courses on Canadian literature in the 1997–98 academic year. Because of the limited information I was able to obtain about the specifics of many Québécois literature courses offered that year at French-language universities, I elected to include only English texts in this database. Thus, some of the analysis I perform later in this book with regard to which texts and authors are taught is limited to data from English and comparative literature courses on the subject.

Department and university calendars

I created the fourth and final database, "Universities," when it became clear that there needed to be some way to get an overall sense of department structures and the place of Canadian literature within them. For each university, then, I set up a record detailing the name of the department I visited, the instructors I spoke to there, the names and numbers of the Canadian literature courses taught that year, the number of courses taught in that department and the number of which were devoted to Canadian literature, and finally whether a Canadian literature course was a requirement for the English major degree and, if there was one, for the honours degree in English (see Figure 3.4).

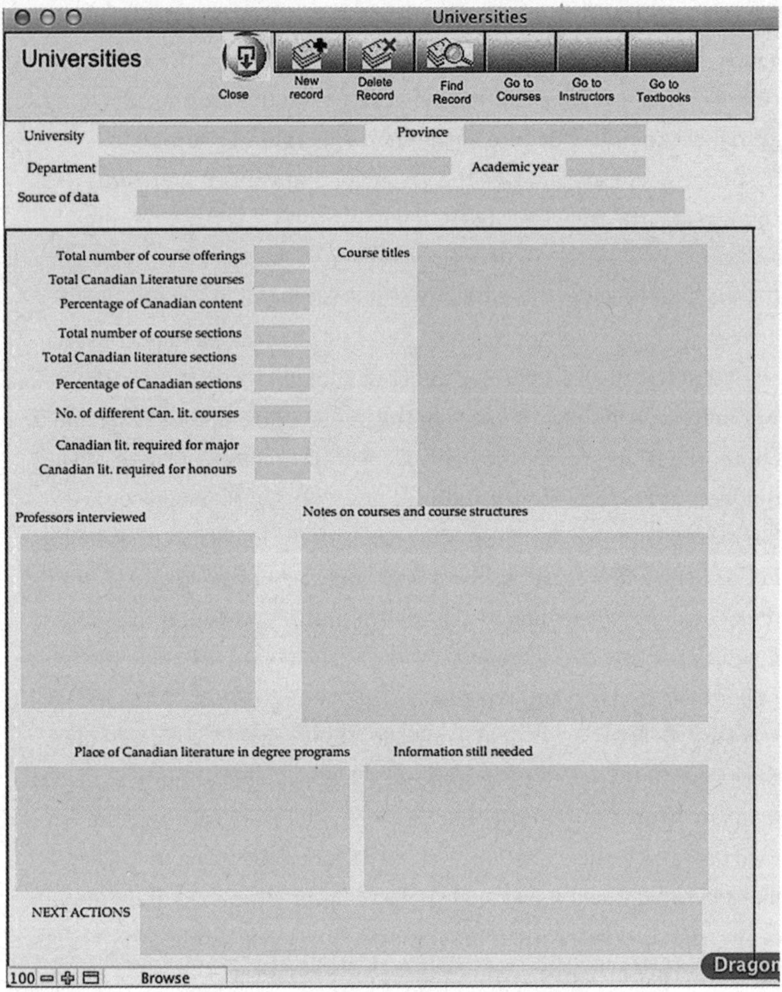

FIGURE 3.4 *Sample Data Entry Page from "Universities" Database*

Analysis

Universities and departments

The wide variation between the post-secondary education systems in Québec and English Canada make it difficult to examine simultaneously the functions of literature departments in English-language and French-language universities. When I commenced my research for this project, however, I assumed otherwise. My trip to Québec and the interviews I conducted with professors at the four French-language universities I visited were a revelation to me, for they revealed the true arbitrariness of the structures of literature departments at English-language universities. Not only does Québécois literature have a greater place in the literature departments of the French universities, there is also a much wider variety of courses on the subject than any English department has in Canadian literature. Why is this? While some might try to argue that the English-speaking world is larger and has produced a greater amount of literature than the French, the traditions are comparable in their richness. Moreover, both disciplines are expanding in similar ways; for instance, while postcolonial literature courses are one of the greatest areas of growth during the early twenty-first century in departments of English literature, there are also a growing number of courses at French-language universities on the literatures of the Francophonie. Nevertheless, the literature of Québec still retains a more prominent role in the literature departments of Canada's French-language universities. The reasons for this are as much tied to the history of the study of the literatures of Canada in Canadian universities as they are to any current valuation of the literatures themselves. What seems clear, however, is that the *projet national* of fostering the growth and, more importantly, the understanding of a national literature has ultimately been of greater import in Québec than in the rest of Canada. In English universities, the place of Canadian literature in English departments has not markedly improved since the 1970s. While there is today, at the beginning of the twenty-first century, undoubtedly, a presence of Canadian content in introductory or genre-based English courses where there may have been none before, the number and variety of Canadian literature courses has remained nearly the same since its period of rapid growth in the late 1960s and early 1970s. In fact, during the 1990s and 2000s, the number of Canadian literature courses has declined at many universities. The lack of variety in the types of Canadian literature courses offered, a predicament caused primarily by the reluctance of many departments to depart in any way from the model of the all-inclusive survey course they have relied on since introducing their first courses on Canadian literature, is even more troubling.

The rest of this section attempts to offer a brief summary of what I was able to determine about the place of the literatures of Canada in each of the universities I visited in 1997–98. My focus here has been on departments where language acquisition is not one of the primary or secondary goals in any of the literature courses they offer. For each of the departments I address here, I have indicated, whenever possible, the number of courses and course sections and the percentage of these devoted to Canadian literature. In some cases, I have had the necessary information to determine this percentage in terms of full-course-equivalents, a more precise means of examining the relative position of Canadian literature courses within the curriculum than in cases where the course listings I obtained did not distinguish between full-year and half-year courses. In a few other cases, I have been hampered by a lack of precise information—my figures for Memorial University, for instance, incude only courses offered in the fall term as they were unable to provide me with data for the winter term. Nevertheless, the data that follows offers the best possible snapshot of the place of courses on the literatures of Canada at nearly every one of the universities I visited on my research trip. Before revealing the data broken down by university and province, it will be helpful to look first at what we can learn from the data as a whole. (See Appendix 1 for a complete list of each university, their relevant course offerings, and a list of instructors interviewed.)

One of the most obvious indicators of the importance given to the teaching of the literatures of Canada at these universities is the percentage of offered courses devoted to the subject. There are several possible approaches to organizing this data: by the percentage of a

TABLE 3.1 *Universities Ranked by Percentage of Courses Offered on the Literatures of Canada (1997–98)*[4]

University	Department	Cdn. Courses
Université de Moncton	Département d'études françaises	38.89%
Université de Montréal	Département d'études françaises	25.00%
Université Laval	Département des littératures	22.86%
McGill University	Department of English	22.22%
University of Alberta	Department of Modern Languages and Comparative Studies	19.05%
Université du Québec à Montréal	Département d'études littéraires	18.42%
University of Manitoba	Department of English	18.42%
Carleton University	Department of English Language and Literature	15.79%
University of Victoria	Department of English	15.07%
Memorial University	Department of English Language and Literature	14.71%
University of Winnipeg	Department of English	13.33%
University of Western Ontario	Department of English	12.50%
University of Saskatchewan	Department of English	12.50%
York University	Department of English	12.20%
University of Alberta	Department of English	10.78%
University of Toronto	Department of English	10.45%
University of Ottawa	Department of English	10.42%
University of British Columbia	Department of English	9.89%
McMaster University	Department of English	9.26%
Acadia University	Department of English	9.09%
Simon Fraser University	Department of English	8.90%
University of Calgary	Department of English	8.16%
Concordia University	Department of English	8.11%
Dalhousie University	Department of English	7.69%
Queen's University	Department of English Language and Literature	5.13%
University of Prince Edward Island	Department of English	4.88%
University of New Brunswick—Fredericton	Department of English	2.86%

department's courses devoted to the literatures of Canada; by the percentage of course sections devoted to the literatures of Canada (departments routinely offer multiple sections of popular classes); and by the number of different courses offered on the literatures of Canada. Each of these approaches can reveal something that the others do not. As Table 3.1 demonstrates, when ranked by the percentage of a department's courses devoted to any of the literatures of Canada, francophone universities fill the top three positions and comprise four of the top six departments. Equally striking, some of the country's oldest and most prestigious departments of English fare poorly in these standings, with the University of Toronto (10.45 per cent), the University of British Columbia (9.89 per cent), and Queen's University (5.13 per cent) occupying sixteenth, eighteenth, and twenty-fifth position, respectively. Indeed, in the top five positions, there is only one department of English— that of McGill University (22.22 per cent) in fourth position, with fifth spot being occupied by the University of Alberta's Comparative Literature Program in what was, at that time, the Department of Modern Languages and Comparative Studies.

Of course, because the way I have calculated the above figures counts each multi-section course as only one course offering, universities that offer a smaller variety of courses but teach several sections of those courses sometime do not fare as well as when we consider the percentage of total course sections devoted to the literatures of Canada. Table 3.2 reveals how the rankings of some departments change significantly when we take into account the number of sections offered. The University of Saskatchewan, for instance, shifts from thirteenth to ninth spot, while the position of the University of Ottawa's Department of English changes dramatically, moving from seventeenth to seventh place. On the other hand, although the University of British Columbia and the University of Toronto both rely quite heavily on multiple sections of their survey courses on Canadian literature, they offer multiple sections of other non-Canadian literature courses as well. Thus, when ranked by percentage of sections rather than by the percentage of courses, the University of British Columbia only moves from eighteenth to fifteenth

TABLE 3.2 *Universities Ranked by Percentage of Course Sections Offered on the Literatures of Canada (1997–98)*[5]

University	Department	Cdn. Sections
Université de Moncton	Département d'études françaises	38.89%
Université de Montréal	Département d'études françaises	25.00%
Université Laval	Département des littératures	22.86%
McGill University	Department of English	20.00%
Université du Québec à Montréal	Département d'études littéraires	18.42%
University of Alberta	Department of Modern Languages and Comparative Studies	16.00%
University of Ottawa	Department of English	15.38%
Carleton University	Department of English Language and Literature	14.06%
University of Saskatchewan	Department of English	13.95%
University of Winnipeg	Department of English	12.77%
Memorial University	Department of English Language and Literature	11.90%
McMaster University	Department of English	11.11%
York University	Department of English	10.70%
University of Victoria	Department of English	10.19%
University of British Columbia	Department of English	9.45%
University of Manitoba	Department of English	8.60%
Acadia University	Department of English	8.33%
Simon Fraser University	Department of English	8.25%
Dalhousie University	Department of English	7.69%
University of Toronto	Department of English	7.03%
Concordia University	Department of English	6.70%
University of Calgary	Department of English	5.56%
Queen's University	Department of English Language and Literature	5.36%

place, while the University of Toronto actually drops four spots to twentieth position.

Department rankings of this kind also shift significantly when we take into account simply the raw number of courses offered on the literatures of Canada. While such figures may not accurately represent the relative weight given to the study of the national literatures in these departments, they demonstrate the quantity and variety of courses available to students. As we might expect, the larger literature departments fare better in these standings than do those of much smaller universities like the University of Prince Edward Island or Acadia University. Table 3.3 suggests that, when we look at the number of different courses offered in a department (which does not include different sections of the same course), the larger French-language institutions retain their dominant positions for the most part. Institutions with large English departments, such as the University of Victoria, York University, and the University of Western Ontario, find themselves substantially higher in the rankings than when we consider the percentage of course offerings in the literatures of Canada.

When we consider the raw number of course sections devoted to the literatures of Canada, the shift in results becomes even more dramatic (see Table 3.4). The country's largest universities move to the top of the rankings, led by the University of British Columbia, which offered eighteen sections of courses in Canadian literature in 1997–98. Equally striking is the fact that while French-language universities such as the Université du Québec à Montréal and the Université de Montréal maintain their positions quite well, the Université Laval drops to fourteenth place and the Université de Moncton to sixteenth. Again, these results are somewhat flawed because they do not take into account whether these courses are half-year or full-year courses—though it should be noted that the vast majority of Canadian literature courses I examined were only half-year courses. What these figures do provide, however, is a sense of the variety of course offerings available to students at larger universities, as even when there are multiple sections taught of what is ostensibly the same course, students are able to make their enrolment choices based upon which instructor is teaching the course and which books are being taught. Naturally, such options are not available to students taking courses in much smaller literature departments.

TABLE 3.3 *Universities Ranked by Number of Different Courses Offered on the Literatures of Canada (1997–98)*

University	Department	Different Cdn. Courses
Université du Québec à Montréal	Département d'études littéraires	14
Université de Montréal	Département d'études françaises	12
University of Victoria	Department of English	9
York University	Department of English	9
University of Alberta	Department of English	9
Université Laval	Département des littératures	8
McGill University	Department of English	8
University of Western Ontario	Department of English	8
University of Toronto	Department of English	8
University of British Columbia	Department of English	8
Université de Moncton	Département d'études françaises	7
Carleton University	Department of English Language and Literature	6
University of Manitoba	Department of English	5
Memorial University	Department of English Language and Literature	5
University of Saskatchewan	Department of English	5
University of Ottawa	Department of English	5
McMaster University	Department of English	5
Concordia University	Department of English	5
Simon Fraser University	Department of English	5
University of Alberta	Department of Modern Languages and Comparative Studies	4
University of Winnipeg	Department of English	4
University of Calgary	Department of English	4
Acadia University	Department of English	3
Dalhousie University	Department of English	2
Queen's University	Department of English Language and Literature	2
University of Prince Edward Island	Department of English	2
University of New Brunswick—Fredericton	Department of English	1

TABLE 3.4 *Universities Ranked by Number of Course Sections Offered on the Literatures of Canada (1997–98)*

University	Department	Cdn. Sections
University of British Columbia	Department of English	18
Université du Québec à Montréal	Département d'études littéraires	14
University of Toronto	Department of English	12
University of Alberta	Department of English	12
Université de Montréal	Département d'études françaises	12
University of Western Ontario	Department of English	11
University of Ottawa	Department of English	10
York University	Department of English	9
Carleton University	Department of English Language and Literature	9
Concordia University	Department of English	9
University of Victoria	Department of English	9
McGill University	Department of English	8
Simon Fraser University	Department of English	8
Université Laval	Département des littératures	8
McMaster University	Department of English	7
Université de Moncton	Département d'études françaises	7
University of Saskatchewan	Department of English	6
University of Manitoba	Department of English	6
Memorial University	Department of English Language and Literature	5
University of Winnipeg	Department of English	4
University of Calgary	Department of English	4
University of Alberta	Department of Modern Languages and Comparative Studies	4
Queen's University	Department of English Language and Literature	3
Acadia University	Department of English	3
University of Prince Edward Island	Department of English	2
Dalhousie University	Department of English	2
University of New Brunswick—Fredericton	Department of English	1

It is important to remember that these rankings are only applicable to the 1997–98 academic year. The fortunes of a number of departments depicted in this data are partly a reflection of their staffing situations in that particular year. For instance, McGill University's excellent ranking—they are the highest English-language university on the list in terms of the percentage of Canadian literature courses and sections offered—is due in great part to the three courses taught in the department that year by Dr. Roxanne Rimstead (currently a professor at the Université de Sherbrooke) whose limited-term position was funded by the McGill Institute for the Study of Canada. Conversely, although the University of New Brunswick in Fredericton has a long history of teaching and scholarship in Canadian literature and several faculty members at the time who specialized in the subject, sabbaticals, retirements, and administrative leave meant that there was only one Canadian literature course that year and it was taught by a recently retired professor from another university who had never before taught a course on Canadian literature.

Statistics such as these are sometimes also unable to provide the full context for the place of Canadian literature in a given department. While these figures portray quite well the tendency of some departments to place less emphasis on Canadian literature than they might, the departments to which this research does not do complete justice are, generally speaking, those that already fare quite well in the above rankings. An excellent example of this, and perhaps the most fascinating department I visited, is the Département d'études littéraires at the Université du Québec à Montréal. As a department that is not oriented around any single national literature or language, the Département d'études littéraires offers many courses focused on questions of genre or theory in which Québécois literature still tends to play a prominent role. Strikingly, if we subtract all the literature courses taught in UQÀM's Département d'études littéraires that do not focus on literature from a particular linguistic, cultural, or national formation, the percentage of courses that focus primarily on Québécois literature would be far greater than the 18.4 per cent of Table 3.1. There were, to be exact, seventy-six courses in total, of which fourteen focused on Québécois or Canadian literature. However, only twenty-seven of the total number of courses were based on a national literature, with eleven focusing on the literature of France. Thus, one could actually consider the "Canadian" content in that department to fill 52 per cent of the literature courses not based solely around questions of genre, theory, or theme.

Another university worth mentioning for its attention to the literatures of Canada is the University of Victoria. While their English department's overall percentage of courses and sections devoted to Canadian literature is good, its offering of nine different courses on Canadian literature in 1997–98 is greater than the number of courses offered that year at nearly every other English-language university, with the exception of York University and the University of Alberta's Department of English, each of which also offered nine unique courses that year. The most important fact about the University of Victoria, perhaps, is that they offer undergraduates the ability to do a combined major in English and French focused on Canadian literature. After taking a number of courses in both languages, the students have to take an upper-level course (English 458/French 487) that introduces them to the comparative study of Canadian literature in their third or fourth year. Founded in 1988 and under the direction of Professor Marie Vautier since 1989, the Canadian literature major, remarkably, remains the only one of its kind in the world. Such a program can only be offered, however, when there are a wide variety of courses on the literatures of Canada to take from both the departments of French and English. Even at the University of Victoria, students sometimes have difficulty fulfilling the program's requirements due to a lack of courses in French-Canadian or Québécois literature in a given year caused by faculty leave of various forms. This issue causes some students to leave the program, which otherwise is highly successful and very much appreciated by the students.

The course availability problems encountered in the University of Victoria's Canadian literature program points to another key factor in determining the place of the literatures of Canada in any department in a given year: the interests, experience, and availability of faculty. At the University of Victoria, for instance, it is unlikely the program would have remained in place without the continued presence and perseverance of Marie Vautier, a specialist in comparative Canadian literature teaching in the French Department. As we have already seen in the case of the University of New Brunswick, factors such as retirements, sick leave, maternity leave, or administrative appointments can have a tremendous effect on the course offerings of smaller universities where there may only be one or two faculty qualified and/or willing to teach Canadian literature. Similarly, other large departments such as the University of British Columbia's Department of English or the Université de Montréal's Département des littératures de langue française have a large number of faculty capable of teaching in these areas, which gives them far more flexibility in offering a variety of courses on the literatures of Canada. Even more important, of course, is how the research and teaching interests and experience of these faculty can help to shape the current and future Canadian literature curriculum in a department. Again, without someone like Marie Vautier at the University of Victoria or E.D. Blodgett in the University of Alberta's former Department of Comparative Literature (an internationally recognized department which, in the years following Blodgett's retirement, has sadly faded into one of seven programs joined together in the university's Office of Interdisciplinary Studies), it is unlikely that there would be any courses on comparative Canadian literature in either of these programs. For the University of Victoria, this would most likely mean the complete collapse of the country's only undergraduate major in Canadian literature.

At nearly every other university I visited in 1997–98, students were unable to receive a degree so highly focused on the any or all of the literatures of Canada—the Université de Montréal, the Université Laval, and, to a certain degree, the Université du Québec à Montréal being the only exceptions. When students pursuing an English or French major, specialization, or honours degree are required to take a majority of their courses in the subjects of French, British, or American literature, they are rarely left with the opportunity to take more than a few courses on the literatures of Canada. Thus, department structures, and the program requirements or curricula those departments devise, have an immeasurably strong effect on the amount and type of literary knowledge that they produce in their students. To reiterate Max Roy's observation, the positioning of one's own national literature(s) in a distinctly minority role in the overall literature course offerings "implique inéviablement un jugement de valeur" (*La littérature québécoise au collège* 103) (inevitably implies a value judgement). Moreover, once such a precedent is set, this limited number of courses will never grow on its own, nor will this implied valuation of the literatures of Canada likely ever change dramatically. The fundamental aim of any institution, Bourdieu reminds us, is to reproduce itself; the average university literature department serves as a perfect illustration of this process in action. So long as literature departments continue to produce students with a limited amount of knowledge about the literatures and literary histories of Canada, there will be no need for expanded and specialized course offerings at either the undergraduate or graduate levels, as the situation of French-language universities has already demonstrated. By choosing relatively early on to devote a significant number of courses and a major amount of research funding to the study of Québécois literature, these universities have been able to offer regular courses (as opposed to an occasional upper-level seminar) on highly specific aspects of the subject. In 1997–98, for instance, the Université Laval offered an undergraduate course on the twentieth-century Québécois song and in 2007–08 a course on "la littérature intime québécoise du XIXe siècle."[6] By the time students in Québec who specialize in Québécois literature enter graduate studies they have already had the opportunity to take a vastly greater number and variety of courses in their field than their counterparts in English Canada. If one accepts the premise that research and teaching frequently develop out of what one studies or teaches, it is fair to assume that a system such as this is capable of producing a greater amount and depth of literary knowledge in this field than one in which departments offer their future graduate students (and the faculty who teach them) a limited number and scope of courses.

Again, for a rich and diverse body of knowledge to be produced, there need to be an adequate number and wide variety of courses available to students. My look at courses across the country revealed a great deal about how different departments appear to envision the study of the literatures of Canada. Joseph Melançon's comments about how universities somewhat arbitrarily separate the study of knowledge into the various disciplines and domains of faculties, departments, and programs—what he calls "un fractionnement des savoirs, des disciplines et des compétences" (a splitting of knowledge, disciplines, and competencies)—are equally applicable to understanding the significance of the ways in which Canadian universities choose to structure their courses on the literatures of Canada (67). "[Le] principe de 'division,'" he reminds us, "est également un principe de 'vision'" (67).[7] In other words, the way a university decides to divide or structure the way in which the student is able to study a subject such as the literatures of Canada invariably reveals a certain "vision" of that subject. We have already discussed several departments that offer a distinct vision of the importance of the literatures of Canada. Simply allowing students to specialize in that field, for instance, says a great deal about the importance placed by the Université de Montréal, Université Laval, and the University of Victoria on the literary production and history of Canada. We can also learn a great deal simply by examining the types of courses on the literatures of Canada offered at other universities.

Courses

While the number of courses offered has a tremendous effect on the shape of students' understanding of the literatures of Canada, the types and structures of those courses are even more influential in this regard. When deciding how best to assess the great number of courses I was cataloguing from 1997–98, I realized it would be essential to assess the types of courses as much as the texts that were taught. To do so, I divided the possible configurations of any literature course into six categories: courses structured around a historical period; courses focusing on a single genre of writing; courses that deal solely with the oeuvre of a particular author; "special topics" courses where the content is always variable and thus changes dramatically from year to year; courses offered regularly that address the writing done by people of a particular region; and, finally, "survey" courses that cover a variety of genres, eras, and movements in order to present a larger picture of a fairly substantial span of literary history. The survey courses remain the most frequently offered type of course on the literatures of Canada and therefore have a tremendous influence on the types of texts and authors who are studied. Though I did not collect any precise data on enrolment figures, it was also clear from my interviews that the survey courses are frequently designed for classes with a greater number of students than the typical special topics or author-centred course.

Of the 207 Canadian or Québécois literature course sections from 1997–98 for which I have data, a mere eighteen were structured mainly around a particular era. More surprising, perhaps, is that there were only five courses (2.4 per cent of the total number of course sections) that were devoted to early Canadian literature. The vast majority of courses structured around period were fiction courses such as the University of Manitoba's English 4.289: Canadian Literature Post-1967: "The Postmodern Novel in Canada" or Concordia University's English 372: Contemporary Canadian Fiction. The issue of time periods, especially when they are described with such ambiguous terms as "early" or "contemporary," is that there are varying opinions as to what such terms mean. Some courses on "early" Canadian writing, for instance, focus mainly on texts published in the late nineteenth and the early twentieth centuries. Conversely, one section of Concordia's 1997–98 course on "Contemporary Canadian Fiction" contained primarily works written in the 1970s, with the most recent work on the course being Joy Kogawa's *Obasan* (1981).

Of the fifty-nine courses from 1997–98 (28.5 per cent of total Canadian literature courses) I determined to be oriented primarily around genre, there were ten courses on drama (4.8 per cent), fifteen courses on poetry (7.2 per cent) with five of these being taught at French-language universities, six on Canadian children's literature (2.9 per cent), eight on the short story (3.9 per cent), and fourteen on fiction in general or the novel (6.8 per cent). Interestingly, only French-language universities offered any genre-oriented courses in 1997–98 that focused on other genres. Included in the eight remaining courses of the fifty-three devoted to a specific genre were courses on the Québécois essay at the Université du Québec à Montréal, the Université de Moncton, and Université Laval, the Québécois song at the Université du Québec à Montréal and the Université Laval, courses on Acadian folklore at the Université de Moncton, and on nineteenth-century literary life in

Québec ("La littérature intime au XIXe siècle") at the Université Laval. What this reveals, of course, is that while English departments in English Canada in 1997–98 were starting to look beyond the boundaries of what we traditionally consider to be "Literature," the aforementioned departments in French Canada had already been doing so for some time. One only needs to look at the broader list of courses not offered every year at the Université Laval and similar lists at English-language universities to see the difference. While the University of Toronto, for example, did have a course on Canadian poetry in its complete course listings in 1997–98, it was rarely offered at the time because, as one professor there told me, "students just are not interested in poetry. When it's offered almost no one will take it." The Université Laval, on the other hand, had in their overall list of courses two courses on "Poésie et chanson du Québec (XIXe siècle)" and four on the "Poésie et chanson du Québec (XXe siècle)." It appears that the content of these courses varied each year and focused on special topics (the one poetry course offered in 1997–98, for instance, focused on the poets of the "génération de l'Hexagone"). The significance of there being six courses in poetry and the song listed in the calendar, even if only one or two are offered in a given year, is that, over the course of a student's degree, he or she may take several of these without having to worry about not getting credit for taking "the same course" twice, as one would if there was but a single poetry course in the calendar. Again, such a difference is the perfect illustration of how a "principe de 'division' est également un principe de 'vision'" (Melançon 67); it is assumed at the Université Laval, in other words, that a student should be allowed to take more than one course on Québécois poetry.

Even if some universities, whether French or English, rarely offer regular courses on certain periods or genres, nearly every department offers, on a semi-regular basis, senior courses of variable content that focus on what are often referred to in course calendars as "Special Topics." In some cases, these courses are structured around the study of a particular author and in others they offer students the opportunity to examine a particular theme, movement, or theoretical approach in detail. For the 1997–98 academic year, I found a total of seventeen special topics courses (8.2 per cent of all courses) devoted entirely to the work of a single author, more than one third of which were at French-language universities. While many of these courses dealt with canonical authors such as Margaret Laurence (three courses), Robertson Davies (two courses), or Réjean Ducharme (one course), the focus of others were less predictable and included authors like Constance Beresford-Howe (one course), Jane Rule (one course), and Jacques Brault (one course at the Université du Québec à Montréal plus another at the Université de Montréal that looked at Brault and his relation to other poets). The other forty-three courses (20.7 per cent) that I labelled as being focused on special topics included regularly or occasionally offered courses on topics such as Native or First Nations writing (five courses or 2.4 per cent of all courses), postcolonial or minority writing in Canada (five courses or 2.4 per cent), or Canadian women writers (two courses or 1.2 per cent). Other courses focused on more specific topics, often tied directly to the research interests of the professors teaching them. Courses on topics like the Canadian gothic, Québécois science fiction, French-language Jewish writing in Montréal, and on orality and literacy in Canadian cultural studies, were among the most interesting of this type. Because such courses often reflect the specializations of particular faculty members, they do seem to get offered more than once, perhaps reappearing on the curriculum every two or three years. While their existence does appear to demonstrate a diversity in course offerings, we must remember that such courses are, for the most part, outliers whose influence is very limited. The faculty members responsible teach them sporadically and these courses, for the most part, do not spread to other institutions.

There were also a small number of regularly offered courses oriented around questions of region. In the 1997–98 academic year, the University of Alberta, the University of Manitoba, and the University of Saskatchewan each offered a course on Western Canadian writing, with the courses at the latter two institutions being courses offered on a regular, if not annual basis. In that same year, Simon Fraser University offered two sections of their regularly offered English 359: The Literature of British Columbia. While there seem to be few, if any, regional Canadian literature courses offered at any of the universities I visited in Ontario and Québec (one professor at a university in Toronto told me there was "no such thing" as an Ontario or Québec regionalism), there are a number of such courses offered quite regularly at universities located in Eastern Canada. In 1997–98, however, only Memorial University offered a course of this type, English 3155: Newfoundland Literature. Acadia University and the University of Prince Edward Island offer courses in Atlantic Canadian literature on a regular basis but were unable to offer them in 1997–98. The courses offered by the Université de Moncton on Acadian literature and folklore might also be considered regional courses, but, more often, they are focused on the literature of a people and culture rather than a region, like courses on Québécois literature.

Survey courses were the most numerous type of course I examined. I concluded that sixty-two (30 per cent) of the 207 courses could be considered survey courses; that is to say, they included works from more than one genre and covered a reasonably wide period of Canadian literary history. The historical, generic, regional, cultural, and linguistic scope of a survey course can differ tremendously between institutions and even at times between faculty members at the same institution, but such variations can reveal a great deal about an institution's or an instructor's vision of the literatures of Canada. Many introductory survey courses at the time, such as English 202 at the University of British Columbia or English 252Y at the University of Toronto, covered the entire history of English-Canadian literature over the course of two semesters. With so much material to cover in such a short time, instructors frequently spend little time looking at early English-Canadian literature, in part so they can try to cover the twentieth century in some depth. Moreover, relatively few instructors actually begin such courses with exploration narratives or any reference at all to the Native oral tradition and instead begin their studies of English-Canadian literature with writers such as Susanna Moodie.

Other universities, however, chose different approaches, such as making the introductory survey course simply focus on twentieth-century Canadian fiction, or dividing the survey course into half-year courses that each cover a different period of Canadian literary history. A few universities from this first data set, notably the University of Alberta and Memorial University, tried to create intermediate level courses that broke the history of the literatures of Canada down even further to avoid, or at least to compensate for, the inherent problems of the traditional survey course. At the University of Alberta, for instance, while students at the time could take English 271, a full-year survey entitled Canadian Literature: Major Writers and Movements covering the entire history of English-language literature in Canada, they could also choose from two full-year courses that divided Canadian literature into that written before and after 1925 or from three half-year courses that focused on Canadian literature before 1925, from 1925–1960, and then from 1960 to the present. Memorial University did something quite similar, except they broke the history of Canadian literature into four more period-oriented half courses: English 3152: Canadian Literature to 1918; English 3153: Canadian Literature, 1918–1945; English 3157: Canadian Literature 1945–1970; and English 3158: Canadian Literature 1970 to the Present, all of which remained part of the curriculum in 2007–08. These courses are, however, quite significant exceptions to the typical practices of English departments in Canada.

The question of whether a university relies on multiple sections of a single survey course or offers a wider variety of courses but with fewer sections can have a tremendous impact on the production of literary knowledge. The rationale, it would seem, behind having students choosing primarily between multiple sections of a Canadian literature survey course is the same behind the requirement for most arts students to take a common English course in their first year of study. Such practices aim to produce a relatively standard experience, or a more homogenous base of knowledge than if there were a huge variety of courses from which students could choose freely. Indeed, many of the universities that rely heavily on these multi-section courses take clear steps to normalize the student experience. While some universities set generic descriptions of the courses in their calendars that outline the types of works and authors that one should find in the individual course sections, other universities take these guidelines a step further. The University of Toronto and the University of Western Ontario, for instance, have for years regulated some of the content that will be chosen by instructors of these multi-section courses. Specifically, they outline how many books will be taught and mandate that a certain number of texts be chosen from a prescribed list. The 1997–98 course description of the University of Toronto's Canadian literature survey (English 252Y) reads:

> An introductory survey of Canadian poetry, prose and drama, consisting of the work of at least twelve writers, at least one of them of Native Canadian origin. At least one third of the works date from before 1950, but attention is also given to very recent works. The course includes works by at least eight of the following: Moodie, Lampman, Leacock, Pratt, Klein, Ross, Birney, Davies, Laurence, Reaney, Munro, Atwood.

Interestingly, however, in both cases these lists are based around authors and not texts. This, of course, gives the instructors a somewhat greater degree of personal choice when designing their curricula. More importantly, these lists make a significant statement about these universities'—and many of their instructors'—vision of the Canadian canon: it is the author who is canonical and not the text.

Texts

This section considers which books were taught in the 169 English or comparative literature courses on the literatures of Canada I surveyed from the 1997–98 academic year. Unfortunately, it was impossible to obtain the relevant text data for every one of these courses. Thus, the data presented here is derived from 128 course sections for which I was able to obtain full or partial lists of the books taught. Instead of listing every text taught in 1997–98 here (see Appendix 2 for the full list), I summarize some of the most important findings. If anything, the list of texts and the frequency with which each text is taught proves the limiting effect of most current course and department structures at English-language universities.

Although we might expect the text data to demonstrate how the same texts are taught over and over again, especially with the preponderance of Canadian literature survey courses, this is clearly not the case. By

TABLE 3.5 *The Twenty-one Most Frequently Taught Texts (1997–98)*

Title	Author	Occurrences
Anthology of Canadian Literature in English (1 vol.) (1990)	Brown, Russell, Donna Bennett, and Nathalie Cooke (eds.)	20
As For Me and My House (1941)	Ross, Sinclair	20
Sunshine Sketches of a Little Town (1912)	Leacock, Stephen	20
Green Grass, Running Water (1993)	King, Thomas	16
Wacousta (1832)	Richardson, John	16
In the Skin of a Lion (1987)	Ondaatje, Michael	15
Obasan (1981)	Kogawa, Joy	15
Roughing it in the Bush (1852)	Moodie, Susanna	15
The Diviners (1974)	Laurence, Margaret	14
15 Canadian Poets x 2 (1988)	Geddes, Gary (ed.)	14
The Imperialist (1904)	Duncan, Sara Jeannette	14
The English Patient (1992)	Ondaatje, Michael	13
The Double Hook (1959)	Watson, Sheila	12
Fifth Business (1970)	Davies, Robertson	11
Dry Lips Oughta Move to Kapuskasing (1989)	Highway, Tomson	10
The Handmaid's Tale (1985)	Atwood, Margaret	10
The Mountain and the Valley (1952)	Buckler, Ernest	10
Lives of Girls and Women (1971)	Munro, Alice	9
The Stone Angel (1964)	Laurence, Margaret	9
Surfacing (1972)	Atwood, Margaret	9
Tay John (1939)	O'Hagan, Howard	9

recording the text lists from the 128 course sections for which I was able to find this information, I determined that there were 407 different texts taught in 1997–98.[8] Nevertheless, by examining this fairly extensive list of texts, we can still find evidence of a number of tendencies or practices that significantly influence the overall shape of the body of work privileged by its inclusion in course curricula. The most obvious place to start, perhaps, is to look at the twenty-one most frequently taught texts in 1997–98 (see Table 3.5). Granted, twenty-one is an unusual number, but with so many works with the same number of occurrences, creating a list of the top ten or twenty would necessarily leave some out that should be included.[9]

For anyone who thinks they have a definite idea of what the "Canadian canon" might have looked like in the late 1990s, the list of the most frequently taught texts in 1997–98 may be somewhat of a surprise. Most striking about the list is the fact that the top ten does not include works by many of the country's most canonical English-language writers, including Margaret Atwood, Alice Munro, Robertson Davies, or Timothy Findley. While most of these writers do show up in or around the top twenty (Findley first appears near thirtieth spot with three works each taught seven times), their most frequently taught works are hardly fighting for the top position. The two exceptions to this pattern are Michael Ondaatje's *In the Skin of a Lion*, which, in sixth position (fifteen occurrences), is actually one of the three works tied as the third most frequently taught, and Margaret Laurence's *The Diviners*, which, in ninth position (fourteen occurrences), is one of the fourth most frequently taught works. The relatively weak showing in these figures by most of Canada's most prominent authors is due primarily to the fact that these authors are seen as more canonical than any one or two of their texts. This is proven dramatically when one examines the list of the top twenty most frequently taught authors (see Table 3.6). (See Appendix 3 for the full list of authors ranked by frequency of course inclusions.)

Table 3.6 shows that the list of most frequently taught authors in 1997–98 bears little relation to that year's list of most frequently taught books. The only exception to this pattern occurs when very few different works by a particular author are taught and those that are included on courses are taught a great number of times. Two authors whose status exemplifies this situation are Sinclair Ross and Stephen Leacock; *As For Me and My House* and *Sunshine Sketches of a Little Town* top the list of most frequently taught texts in 1997–98, but the authors have few other texts taught on a regular basis. Conversely, in the case of Margaret Atwood, instructors in both sets of data seem to have little preference as to which of her works they include on their courses; given Atwood's easy domination of the 1997–98 rankings by author, it is surprising to

TABLE 3.6 *The Twenty Most Frequently Taught Authors (1997–98)*

Author	Occurrences
Atwood, Margaret	51
Laurence, Margaret	44
Ondaatje, Michael	42
Davies, Robertson	33
Findley, Timothy	26
Leacock, Stephen	26
Ross, Sinclair	23
King, Thomas	21
Munro, Alice	21
Brown, Russell, Donna Bennett, and Nathalie Cooke (eds.)	20
Highway, Tomson	18
Moodie, Susanna	17
Richardson, John	17
Richler, Mordecai	14
Duncan, Sara Jeannette	14
Geddes, Gary (ed.)	14
MacLennan, Hugh	13
Montgomery, L.M.	12
Watson, Sheila	12
Grove, Frederick Philip	11

note that her most frequently taught work that year, *The Handmaid's Tale* (ten occurrences), does not enter the text rankings until sixteenth spot (one of the three eighth most frequently taught works) and has only two other works, *Surfacing* (nine occurrences) and *The Journals of Susanna Moodie* (eight occurrences) in the top thirty. Much like many of the top-ranked authors in this study, and particularly those who are still alive, there seems to be little consensus about her literary works, except that her body of work is of importance and should be represented in suitable Canadian literature courses.

The 1997–98 rankings of texts and authors reveal several important facts. The first is the relative scarcity of works of poetry, drama, and non-fiction and their authors. Atwood's *The Journals of Susanna Moodie* is the first individual collection of poetry on the list that is not an anthology; it has an impressive eight occurrences, more than any poetry collection that year. The next most frequently taught collection is Ondaatje's *The Collected Works of Billy the Kid* (five occurrences) in forty-fourth spot, followed by the Canadian Poetry Press' edition of Isabella Valancy Crawford's *Malcolm's Katie* (four occurrences), which does not appear until sixty-fifth position on the list. The other poetry books to be found in the top one hundred are Louise Bernice Halfe's *Bear Bones and Feathers* at seventy-ninth spot and Marlene Nourbese Philip's *Looking for Livingstone* in ninety-second spot, each with three occurrences. In terms of anthologies, however, there are five in the top one hundred texts that are either partly or wholly devoted to poetry: in first position, Brown, Bennett, and Cooke's *Anthology of Canadian Literature in English* (twenty occurrences); in ninth place on the list, Gary Geddes's anthology *15 Canadian Poets x 2* (fourteen occurrences); in twenty-third spot, *Canadian Poetry From the Beginnings through the First World War* (eight occurrences), edited by Carole Gerson and Gwendolyn Davies; in fifty-seventh spot Robert Lecker and Jack David's two-volume anthology of *Canadian Poetry* (four occurrences); and finally, in seventy-third position, the Oxford *Anthology of Canadian Native Literature in English* (three occurrences), edited by Daniel David Moses and Terry Goldie.[10]

The fact that, in terms of the frequency of occurrences, these five anthologies outnumber the four individual collections of poetry by a margin of slightly more than two to one says a tremendous amount about how poetry is taught in Canada's English-language universities. Because poetry is almost always only a part of a larger course on Canadian literature, instructors choose the larger scope that a single anthology can provide rather than choosing to teach one or more individual volumes of poetry. Returning to Bourdieu's theories of the market of symbolic goods, we can see how the tendency to rely on anthologies has an enormous impact on the place of poetry in this country's literary landscape. When we see how many times anthologies such as Oxford's *An Anthology of Canadian Literature in English* are taught, often in course sections containing upwards of one hundred students at a time, it is clear how the economic and symbolic health of Canadian poetry publishing would be affected by a move away from the use of anthologies in literature courses to the inclusion of individual volumes by Canadian poets. Obviously, students can get a broader sense of the field by looking at the work of a greater number of poets, but this again implies and reproduces a certain value judgement about poetry. If a student is taught or takes with them the impression that one reads poems one by one, outside of the context of the larger collection or sequence from which the anthologist extracts them, it is less likely that the student will ever opt to read (and perhaps purchase) a collection of poetry by a single author. The bias of such courses towards novels—instructors would likely never consider teaching fiction primarily from an anthology that just included selected chapters from a wide variety of Canadian novels—and away from individual volumes of poetry can also be seen in the list of texts taught with relation to drama and short fiction.

Drama, too, is often taught from anthologies, but usually only in courses that focus specifically on that genre. Other times, when drama is included in part of a broader course on Canadian literature (which happened thirty-eight times in 1997–98), instructors include one or two texts of plays that their students purchase in separate editions. This leads such works to take a more prominent place than poetry in the list of texts taught in 1997–98. For instance, Tomson Highway's *Dry Lips Oughta Move to Kapuskasing* occupies fifteenth spot (ten occurrences) and is one of the three eighth most frequently taught texts. The next play on the list, in twenty-sixth place and one of the tenth most frequently taught books, is Highway's *The Rez Sisters* (eight occurrences). The frequency with which these two plays are taught combines to make Highway the playwright whose works are most often taught in non-genre-specific English or comparative literature courses on the Canadian literatures. The next most frequently taught play, *The Book of Jessica* by Linda Griffiths and Maria Campbell, was taught four times in 1997–98 and does not occur on the list until fifty-sixth position. The plays found in the one hundred most frequently taught texts are rounded out by three plays that each occur on courses three times: Michel Tremblay's *Les Belles Soeurs* in eightieth position, Sharon Pollock's play *Blood Relations* in eighty-first position, and Ann-Marie MacDonald's *Goodnight Desdemona (Good Morning Juliet)* in eighty-sixth position.

Short fiction fares much better than drama in the 1997–98 list in part because there was a tendency among many instructors I surveyed to include at least one collection of short stories in their non-genre-specific courses on Canadian literature. The most prominent example of the popularity of a collection of short fiction is Stephen Leacock's *Sunshine Sketches of a Little Town*, which, with twenty occurrences, is one of only three texts taught that many times in 1997–98. A full 11 per cent of the top one hundred most frequently taught books are works of short fiction. This list includes: two works by Alice Munro, *Lives of Girls and Women* (nine occurrences) and *Who Do You Think You Are?* (seven occurrences); two by Morley Callaghan, *Such is My Beloved* (four occurrences) and *The Loved and the Lost* (three occurrences); and collections by other important authors of short fiction including Jack Hodgins, Margaret Atwood, and Sinclair Ross. Of course, short stories also make their way into course syllabi through their inclusion in anthologies like the popular Brown, Bennett, and Cooke anthology and W.H. New's anthology *Canadian Short Fiction*, the latter of which appeared four times among the courses I surveyed.

Also worth noting is the fact that only one original work in the top five and four of the top ten of 1997–98 were written after 1970. This data contradicts the observation made by many professors that courses in Canadian literature are more heavily weighted to literature written after the mid-1960s. This contradiction is easily explained, however. More recent works do not overly dominate the 1997–98 top ten only because instructors were able to choose from a much wider variety of texts and authors than they could when choosing, say, texts from the 1910s or 1920s, let alone the nineteenth century. In addition, the vast majority of courses on Canadian literature that I examined define "Literature" as only fiction, poetry, and drama. While there were a variety of volumes of essays, criticism, and theory taught in Canadian literature courses during the academic year in question, none were taught frequently enough to appear in the first one hundred texts on the list (see Appendix 2). The two most frequently taught works of non-fiction were Marshall McLuhan's

The Medium is the Massage and Arthur Kroker's *Technology and the Canadian Mind*, each of which was taught twice in comparative literature courses at the University of Alberta and wind up in 138th and 153rd position, respectively. There are, nevertheless, a fair number of non-fiction texts that occur only once and are often part of upper-level special topics courses offered that year. These include everything from Northrop Frye's *Anatomy of Criticism* and Germaine Warkentin's anthology of *Canadian Exploration Literature* to Linda Hutcheon's *The Canadian Postmodern* and the anthology *New Contexts of Canadian Criticism* edited by Ajay Heble, Donna Palmateer Penee, and J.R. Struthers. It is also likely that some critical or theoretical essays are included in the curriculum through "coursepacks" of photocopied readings. The number of courses that include such pre-packaged sets of additional material is significant—in 1997–98, there were thirteen courses that used coursepacks—and many professors I interviewed suggested that this practice would continue to grow. Their predictions proved to be absolutely correct. By 2007–08, the use of coursepacks more than tripled, with forty-one different courses using them to supplement the assigned books and anthologies.

The most interesting question raised by these lists of texts included in English and comparative literature courses on the literatures of Canada, of course, may not be which texts were taught but rather *how* instructors chose which texts to teach. Course and department structures directly, and perhaps unavoidably, influence many of these decisions. What is most striking about the beliefs and practices of the instructors I spoke with is that nearly everyone took these structures as a fait accompli around which they needed to work when designing their syllabi. This uncritical acceptance of "the way things are" is a textbook example of Bourdieu's theory of how the habitus shapes the practices of those immersed in it. There were very few instructors that I interviewed who saw any need or had any desire to lobby for Canadian literature to assume a more substantive place in the course offerings of their department. With the only exceptions in English Canada being the relatively recent BA program in Canadian literature at the University of Victoria and the occasional course restructuring or new course development at other universities, the place of the literatures of Canada in

English departments today seems to have changed very little since the Symons Report, *To Know Ourselves* (1975) criticized Canadian universities for not studying and teaching Canadian subjects more broadly. On the other hand, the flourishing of the study of Québécois literature at Québec's French-language universities demonstrates this need not be the case. My interviews with professors in both English and French Canada clearly suggests that, without new approaches and revised course and department structures in English-language universities, the effect of the cultural reproduction and institutional self-reproduction in which departments of literature engage will continue to hinder any attempts we make to further our understanding of the literatures of Canada in any truly significant way.

Mind the Gaps
4

Professors, "Coverage," and the Canadian Literature Curriculum

*Confined to the study of one representational complex, literary critics accept
and paradoxically ignore the lines drawn around what they do.*

—EDWARD SAID, "Opponents, Audiences, Constituencies, and Community"

*To choose this or that is to affirm at the same time the value of what
we choose.*

—JEAN-PAUL SARTRE, *Existentialism and Human Emotions*

THE MANY DEPARTMENT CALENDARS, course outlines, and book-
lists I gathered on my research trip provide a very detailed snapshot
of a single year in the life of Canadian literature as it was taught in the
207 literature courses I catalogued from that year. While that data can
reveal much to us about *what* was taught, it tells us less about *why* it was
taught. For this reason, I chose to do a significant amount of my research
in the field, so to speak, rather than from within the physical and meta-
phorical walls of the University of Alberta. The importance of getting a
sense of individual practices and attitudes towards the teaching of the
literatures of Canada was particularly reinforced for me by Professor

Larry McDonald of Carleton University, who suggested to me that "far too much attention is paid to which texts we select to teach, as if that itself were the canon. The canon is not what texts we teach; the canon is the way we teach texts" (McDonald). Noting how, for instance, many anthologies and critical works downplay the political views and activism of the works and lives of writers like Earle Birney or F.R. Scott, something he emphasizes in his own teaching and writing, McDonald added, "I can teach exactly the same texts as other people, but my canon is totally different." While I deliberately chose not to focus on questions of instructor's positions in relation to important factors such as aesthetics, theory, literary history, politics, or pedagogy, these issues did come up regularly in my interviews, proving McDonald's point that one cannot entirely determine *how* a particular work is taught simply by gauging its presence on a course and its placement vis-à-vis the other texts on the syllabus. Nevertheless, I will argue, and this was borne out in many of the interviews I conducted, many instructors tend to overestimate the role those factors play in shaping their courses and underestimate the effect on knowledge production of the departmental and curricular boundaries that are "imposed" on them as instructors and designers of course syllabi.

When I initially planned this first stage of my research and then began interviewing subjects, I believed I would learn most about the process of canon formation from understanding how professors' own conceptions of the literatures of Canada—which are, of course, thoroughly influenced by the habitus of their current department and those where they studied, the discipline, and their respective histories—helped them to determine which texts to teach. If there is one thing the results from my interviews demonstrate, however, it is that professors and instructors—in their roles as both critics and teachers—do not make enough of a connection between their vision of the canon and the curriculum at their own institutions. An overwhelming majority of the people with whom I spoke envision the composition of the individual course syllabus as the primary shaping force of the canon—or at least of the smaller canon of those books that are taught—and vice versa. Although several suggested to me that there was no such thing as a Canadian canon, many other professors expressed feeling a need and/or an obligation to represent the canon in their courses. A number of my interview subjects also felt that they could take action against some of the canon's apparent exclusions by integrating the occasional "neglected" work or author into their courses. That said, there was rarely any clear consensus as to the boundaries and shape of the canon. Indeed, the canon, as it is constructed by literature courses, often looks somewhat different depending on which institution one is examining or in which region of the country one finds oneself.

Defining the canon, whether we seek to defend or attack it, is ultimately an impossible task, for the literary canon is always in transition; it is a cultural stock exchange, or, in Bourdieu's terms, "a market of symbolic goods" in which works are in a constant state of gaining or losing cultural capital. The canon, as John Guillory argues so persuasively in *Cultural Capital*, is "never other than an imaginary list" (Guillory 30). In his essay "Contingencies of Canonicity," Paul Trout suggests, appropriately, that "the canon should be envisioned as a series of concentric circles, like those on a target, in which canonical works have varying degrees of canonicity. In other words, it is not a simple case of a text being either in or out of the canon, or even of canonical works having the same degree of canonicity" (3). In the innermost circle, Trout places those works that are "the *least* vulnerable to displacement by hostile re-assessment or by changing cultural, political, or intellectual fashions" (4). As one moves outwards, the degree of a work's canonicity becomes less stable; it may be acquiring a greater degree of canonicity or cultural capital, or it may in fact be slowly drifting away from the centre as it begins to lose its apparent relevance.

While, as Bourdieu and Dubois have shown us, the degree of a work's canonicity is the result of continuous and complex interactions among all the levels of the literary institution, such as criticism, publishing, and bookselling, perhaps the most influential force in determining a work's status is the education system. Guillory points out that "what does have a concrete location as a list...is not the canon but the syllabus, the list of works one reads in a given class, or the curriculum, the list of works one reads in a program of study" (30). The syllabus, then, is usually the place where the canon is most visible. While the teaching of a text, and more importantly the continued teaching of a text, is one of the greatest influences on its canonical status, that status does not have an equivalent effect on which texts will or will not be taught. In other words, the curriculum of any department of English or French and the structure of the courses that make up that curriculum, while obviously reflecting a certain vision of the canon, inevitably obliges instructors to choose to teach certain texts or types of texts over others for reasons unrelated to the canon. These kinds of choices are especially pertinent when an instructor is trying to create a syllabus for a survey course in which the aim of representing different time periods, regions, styles, or genres frequently supersedes considerations of canonicity. The curriculum, then, not only affects which works or types of works get taught but also continually works to shape the canon, that "imaginary list" from which those course texts are chosen.

Not only is the teaching of the literatures of Canada frequently an excellent illustration of how this interaction between canon and curriculum occurs, in the case of English-Canadian literature it also demonstrates remarkably well the fundamental problems with the current Canadian literature curriculum found in nearly every English department in the country. Unfortunately, aside from the work of a few scholars, including Margery Fee and Sarah King, there have been few, if any, sustained looks at the Canadian literature curriculum. This has not been the case in Québec where scholars have been paying serious attention to questions of the university's role in the literary institution since the 1970s. This frequent neglect of the curriculum has been one of the major shortcomings of much of what has been written in English Canada about the literary canon. This particular lack of self-reflexivity on the part of many anglophone scholars of the literatures of Canada, Gerald Graff would undoubtedly agree, is one of the fundamental effects of what he calls the "field coverage principle" (6) around which nearly every literature department in the country is organized. One of the seemingly innocuous, but remarkably insidious aspects of the field coverage model is that it permits departments to incorporate new literary voices or address challenges to the curriculum simply by adding new (and nearly always optional) courses to the current list of courses offered. While this allows the department to seem open and responsive to such challenges, it also quietly reinforces the hegemony in that such changes rarely, if ever, disrupt or threaten the way in which the rest of the department has always done things. Many of the professors' responses to the questions I asked clearly reveal these very consequences of the field coverage model and illustrate the process of cultural reproduction in action. Moreover, they demonstrate some of the ways in which the curriculum has shaped and continues to shape the knowledge we have of our own literatures.

Aiming to learn more about how professors design syllabi for courses in the literatures of Canada and why they choose certain texts over others, I asked many questions that were directly focused on these issues. As my ultimate goal, however, was to develop a greater under-standing of the type of knowledge produced by these courses, the broader questions I asked each professor were oriented towards his or her goals for the course(s) in question and how those goals related to issues such as the relationship between literature and nation, a concern that ties into the origins of departments of English and French but also to the early rationale behind the inclusion of the literatures of Canada in the curriculum. The rest of this chapter is structured around the following groups of questions I asked during each interview:

1. *At which institutions did you receive your post-secondary education? How did you wind up teaching at this particular university?*

2. *Which Canadian literature course(s) are you teaching this year? When you planned this/these course(s), what were your objectives? What kind of influence do your past personal, academic, and/or teaching experiences play in this process?*

3. *Which factors helped you to determine which texts to teach? Did price and/or availability of texts have an effect on that decision? Did department regulations or guidelines shape the course(s) in any way?*

4. *Do you feel the need or a pressure to represent various cultural, ethnic, or language groups in your syllabus? Have you included Native literature on your course? Have you included any French texts in translation?*

5. *Do you think it is possible to develop in your students a greater sense of*
    Canada (or Québec) through teaching them about its literature? If so,
    do you structure your course in such a way so as to facilitate this? [1]

From every interview I received a wealth of information, so much so,
in fact, that I could have likely written an entire book on the responses
I received for each of the different questions I asked. What follows in
my discussion of each of these issues, then, is a general summary of the
responses I received for each question with a number of representative or
otherwise noteworthy responses from the professors to whom I spoke.
As one would expect to come from this type of exploratory research,
this chapter will perhaps raise more questions than it answers. My hope,
however, is that the result still sheds a great deal of light on our relation
to "the lines drawn around what [we] do" (Said 153).

Origins

I began every interview by asking my subjects to recount briefly their
academic history and what led them to teach courses on the literatures
of Canada at their current institution. I hoped by gathering this information to be able to make some observations as to the lineage of Canadian
literary studies. I was curious to know, for instance, if professors who did
their PHD at a certain institution or with a particular supervisor would
carry with them a distinctive conception of the literatures of Canada,
and if that type of influence would dissipate as they began teaching at a
different institution, with at least a somewhat different curriculum, and
a new set of colleagues. Obviously, an instructor's training in the field
(or lack thereof) is very likely to have a profound effect on one's perspective of it, even twenty or thirty years after making the transition from
student to faculty.

What particularly caught me off guard, however, was the eagerness with which the professors I interviewed offered detailed accounts
of their academic and professional histories. While I first envisioned
this part of my questioning as simply yielding some basic biographical
data, it became clear from the first day I conducted interviews that in
fact I was gathering personal and disciplinary oral histories. Although

a significant amount of what people told me was not directly relevant to the specific nature of this study, I also began to see in the stories some distinct patterns of experience that helped to provide some useful contexts for understanding the data I was collecting. Because I tried to speak to everyone who was currently teaching courses in the literatures of Canada at the institutions I visited, my subjects ranged from people like Christopher Bracken at the University of Alberta and Glenn Willmott at Queen's University who were then at the beginning stages of their careers to professors such as Stan Dragland at the University of Western Ontario and Donna Smyth at Acadia University who were, as it turned out, on the verge of retiring from their positions as professors. The disparity between the different generations of professors I interviewed, however, is something that extends far beyond differences in age and what were sometimes quite divergent attitudes towards theory, aesthetics, and the canon. Specifically, the experiences of those who started teaching the literatures of Canada in the 1960s and 1970s have given them a markedly different sense of the field than the professors who were hired over the last thirty years and, particularly, the relatively small number who were hired in the 1990s.

When we look at the academic history of those professors teaching courses on the literatures of Canada in 1997, their demographics strikingly illustrate the history of the field since the late 1960s. The fact that the majority of the professors with whom I spoke had been hired in the late 1960s or early 1970s reminds us not only of the longevity of academic careers, but also of how the developments in the study of the literatures of Canada at that time continue, in some form, to influence the field today. What would likely surprise anyone without a knowledge of the history of the field is that the majority of the people hired during the late 1960s and early 1970s who now teach—in some cases exclusively—courses in the literatures of Canada had no formal training, let alone a PHD, in the field and were, in fact, initially hired to teach in other areas such as Romanticism or Old English literature. The same cannot be said of the professors I interviewed who were under the age of forty-five, of whom there were only one or two who did not do graduate work and a PHD dissertation in the field. This demographic divide is reflected clearly in the still quite dramatic figures that I was able to gather.

Of the 104 professors and instructors I interviewed in 1997, only fifty-two (50 per cent) had written a PHD thesis on a topic related to Canadian literatures. Forty-four (42 per cent) had written their doctoral theses on non-Canadian topics, while six (5.8 per cent) had no PHD. Two (1.9 per cent) professors had PHDs in creative writing. There are, of course, many historical reasons for these statistics, as was illustrated by the anecdotes most of the older scholars told me about their academic history. Many of the interview subjects who had no graduate specialization in the literatures of Canada were of a generation for whom there was almost no possibility of taking advanced courses in the field and, more importantly, the idea of writing a PHD on a Canadian topic was frowned upon by departments and, indeed, fellow graduate students. With the post-Centennial surge in Canadian nationalism and the resultant boom in interest in the national literatures, the few scholars I spoke to who at one time had wanted to study the literatures of Canada were later given the opportunity to teach some of the new courses that were developed to meet this growing need.

The cases of at least thirty of the professors I interviewed were quite different. Some were foreigners who discovered the literatures of Canada when they emigrated here, while others were Canadians who, while studying abroad, developed a profound interest in the literature of the country they had left behind. The late 1960s and early 1970s saw a significant number of academics emigrating primarily from the United States to take positions at Canadian universities. While they too were hired to teach in other areas, many found themselves attracted to Canadian literature as they tried to learn more about the country to which they had come. As Russell Brown, a University of Toronto professor of English originally from the United States, explained to me about his own discovery of Canadian literature, "it made sense to be reading contemporary Canadian stuff because I was interested in contemporary lit in general but also I had this terrific sense that it was telling me something about the place to which I'd come" (Brown). Ironically, it was this same desire to make a deeper connection with the country through its literature that prompted another group of new or future professors to move away from or expand upon the areas in which they had pursued their graduate research.

Although this bias has lessened considerably since the 1960s, in Canada scholars still acquire a greater amount of prestige or cultural capital from the pursuit of a graduate degree at a major British, American, or French university than if they do the same work at a Canadian institution. A number of the professors I interviewed left Canada to pursue their graduate work at foreign universities but ultimately found that their immersion in a different culture made them much more curious about their own. As University of Western Ontario professor Tom Tausky put it, "I had gradually become aware of the need to know something about my own country when I went away" (Tausky). In reading more Canadian literature, the scholars I spoke to who, like Tausky, left Canada temporarily, described becoming more and more engaged with the sense of recognition they found in a literature rooted in their own place and (sometimes) time. In this respect, Donna Smyth, who has since retired from her position as a professor of English at Acadia University, recounted returning home from her studies in England and reading *The Stone Angel* in a hotel room in Saskatoon, where she had just accepted her first academic position at the University of Saskatchewan: "It was just complete recognition, of a kind I hadn't discovered anywhere else....I remember thinking 'this is it!' It was like a revelation. This is what I want to do. This is what I want to teach" (Smyth).

By focusing momentarily on the significant number of professors of the literatures of Canada with no formal training in the field, I do not mean to suggest that those who never studied the literature are, as a result, less capable of teaching that body of work than those who studied it as undergraduate and graduate students. The professors who began teaching the new courses in the literatures of Canada as they sprouted up across the country in the 1960s and early 1970s were, in many cases, true pioneers. Though they may not have been among the first to view the terrain, as were figures such as J.D. Logan, Carlyle King, or Camille Roy, it was these professors who helped to clear the land and began to work "the field." Because the materials (course texts, library holdings, works of criticism and theory) with which these scholars and teachers had to work were rudimentary and limited in number, they needed to fashion new tools—not to mention their own knowledge of the subject—from scratch. Prompted to "retool" by their own burgeoning interest in the field, the sentiment of Canadian and Québécois nationalism of the 1960s and 1970s, and student demand for courses on their national literatures, these professors essentially found themselves exploring the literatures of Canada at the same time as their students.

Though an obvious point to make, it is important to remember just how different the experience of those who began teaching courses in the literatures of Canada during this period is from those who completed their graduate work in the field and began teaching from the 1980s on. The professors who have entered the field since the 1980s or who are poised to do so in the near future did not encounter the same degree of resistance from their own departments and individual colleagues to the offering of courses on the literatures of Canada. Those generations may have still encountered others who consider Canadian works to be the lesser cousins of those written in Britain or France, but from the 1970s on students had the option of taking one or more courses on the subject and graduate students found themselves free and even encouraged to write their dissertations on Canadian topics, partly because there were now teachers and supervisors who could offer such courses and super-vise such research. The growing wealth of new and recovered primary and secondary sources, not to mention the explosion of international attention to the literatures of Canada, also brought a greater credibility to the field and led to increasingly specialized and sophisticated types of research. The legitimacy that the teaching and research of the literatures of Canada has accrued means that those working in the field today are now seen to be on par with the rest of their colleagues. As Russell Brown said in my interview with him, "In some ways, if we are more 'post-national' right now, I think it is true in the same way that young women right now are 'post-feminist.' That is to say, the work got done" (Brown).

If the experiences of the younger generation(s) of professors in 1997–98 were fundamentally different from those of their older colleagues, the former nevertheless continued to be shaped profoundly by the latter. For instance, many belonging to the earlier generations of academics with whom I spoke, whose initial enthusiasm for one or all of the literatures of Canada was influenced by the surges in Canadian and Québécois nationalism, not only believed that it was possible to gain a better understanding of Canada through studying its literatures but also affirmed that this was one of the pedagogical goals in their courses—something one cannot imagine hearing with respect to courses on Shakespeare or the Romantic poets, for instance. While a few of the older professors I interviewed objected to the concept of there being such a close and unproblematic connection between literature and the nation, it was typically the younger generation of professors who balked at any attempts to see the teaching of the literatures of Canada as a sort of nationalistic project in which one is teaching the students about the country as much as the body or bodies of literature it continues to produce. Nevertheless, even instructors who discussed trying to problematize the notions of Canada as being a simple, knowable, and uncontested space admitted that they too were still promoting ways in which one can read the country through its literature. As University of Western Ontario professor Frank Davey explained to me,

> I see myself as teaching a course in the literary construction and articulation of cultural conflict. I assume that for many, because these conflicts occur all around them, because this literature is set within the conflicts in which they have a personal stake, or [in which] their families have had personal stakes because they live in this country, that this was much more meaningful for them and they will read perhaps more attentively and more perceptively than they would read the literature of a culture in which they had no stake. (Davey, Personal interview)

The most significant difference I found in 1997–98 between anglophone professors who came to the literatures of Canada at a later point in their career and those who studied and wrote dissertations on the subject was that members of the former group frequently defended the minor place of the literatures of Canada in their department's curriculum, arguing that one should view "Canadian Literature" (by which they obviously meant only that which is written in English) as an extension of the British tradition. For this reason, therefore, they viewed it to be quite important that students have a solid grounding in the history of British literature in order to understand English-Canadian literature. "I thoroughly agree with that," said one professor, "and I still think that one cannot really know Canadian literature without knowing British literature and American literature. Because they are the ones that are closest to us, they are the context within which we are working.... There are just all sorts of things that one can't fully know within Canadian literature if you don't know those other things." Regardless of our stand on the issue, it is clear that the curriculum at nearly every department of English in the country reflects and indeed promotes this very paradigm. No Canadian university student can earn a bachelor of arts degree with an honours, major, or specialization in English unless the vast majority of the courses she or he has taken is centred on British literature. The sole alternative that provides a greater space for under-graduate English courses in Canadian literature is the bilingual program in comparative Canadian literature offered the University of Victoria. Conversely, as we have already seen, there are a variety of curricular formations at the French universities in Québec; while a student can specialize in French literature, she or he also has the option of focusing her or his studies on Québécois literature. Furthermore, by the time most students graduate from the CÉGEP system to the university level, they have already been exposed to more Québécois literature than many English majors, honours students, or "specialists" will ever see of English-Canadian literature in their entire undergraduate programs.

It is evident that any study of how the literatures of Canada are taught must examine the effect of the personal and academic experiences of the professors teaching courses in the subject, for these have left and continue to leave an indelible impression on the shape of the field. The traditional trajectory of academic employment—where tenured professors usually remain in their positions and in the same departments that first hired them for upwards of thirty years—and the increasing reli-ance on sessional/adjunct faculty who have little or no power to bring about far-reaching curricular reform contribute significantly to the seemingly glacial pace of institutional change. If anything, the dearth of new tenure-track jobs means that there is even less opportunity than there was in the 1970s or 1980s for new writers and texts to find an entrenched place in the curriculum. Institutional and cultural reproduction, then, occurs both through the habitus the department continually creates, maintains, and reproduces and the cultural agents (undergraduate and graduate students) it produces and sends out into the world. Again, the experiences of those agents who go on to become teachers and researchers in the field aid especially in spreading and furthering the influence of the habitus in which they did their training. For instance, one of the most common factors cited by professors for excluding from their courses texts in translation and/or First Nations literatures was that they had little, if any, experience or training in those areas. This is just one of the most apparent examples of how one's initial experiences in any field can go on to affect how one perceives and transmits that body of knowledge from that point on.

In terms of the teaching of the literatures of Canada, one can begin to document this chain of influence in a number of ways. For instance, one way to look at the cause for the prevalence of excluding translated works in English courses is to consider the number of current professors in the field who received their PHD from institutions such as the University of Toronto's Department of English where, as I have already discussed, there remains not only a policy against teaching works in translation but also some very definite guidelines as to which authors should be taught in the survey course in Canadian literature. From the fact that thirteen of the ninety-four English professors I interviewed (14 per cent) had a PHD in English from Toronto, one can assume that most, if not all, of those thirteen will not teach works in translation, not only because of their lack of experience with it but also because it is excluded from the vision of "Canadian literature" that they have likely inherited. This tendency, logically, then trickles down to the students they teach and so this view of the literatures of Canada is not only perpetuated but, in fact, continues to grow. This same process of cultural reproduction is visible in instructors' selections of authors and texts to teach, as those choices wind up both reflecting and affecting their perceptions of the literary canon.

One of the more fascinating aspects of the literature curriculum at the French-language universities in Québec both in 1997–98 and 2007–08 is that, unlike the continuing state of English departments in English Canada, the departments that teach Québécois literature at the three major universities diverge substantially in their approaches to their curricula. The Université du Québec à Montréal's Département d'études littéraires, for instance, by its very structure advocates a vision of literature that sees past national and linguistic boundaries and focuses instead on the more aesthetic concerns of genre, theme, and style, not to mention literary theory. Conversely, the Université de Montréal seems to offer a more traditional approach to the study of literature, in part because, as one of my subjects speculated, historically many of its faculty were either French or Québécois in origin who had done their graduate work in France. They also, in 2007–08, seem the most interested of the three in focusing on literature in French as a global phenomenon. Traditionally, as then Laval professor and director of the Centre de recherche en littérature québécoise (CRELIQ) Denis Saint-Jacques suggested to me, the Université Laval's Département des littératures has had a greater number of faculty born and educated in Québec and has placed a greater emphasis on the teaching and research of Québécois literature (Saint-Jacques). The Université Laval's status as the most important of the three in terms of the study of Québécois literature is partly due to the subject's strong place in the curriculum today, but also because of the department's long history of promoting research and teaching in the field, which led it to hire, whenever possible, those scholars who could best contribute to furthering this vision.

CRELIQ existed at the Université Laval between 1981 and 2002, at which point CRELIQ joined together with the Université de Montréal's Centre d'études québébcoises (CÉTUQ) and researchers from UQÀM to form the Centre de recherche interuniversitaire sur la littérature et la culture québécoises (CRILCQ). The long presence of CRELIQ and now CRILCQ at Laval has played an instrumental role in the process of both expanding knowledge in the field and further cementing and then reproducing a habitus hospitable to the study of Québécois literature. In other words, by fostering further research into, for instance, literary history with its epic *La vie littéraire au Québec* series, the centre not only provides faculty with a means of publishing their research but also helps to expand our understanding of the field. This ultimately filters into the classroom, where professors' teaching interests often mirror their research whenever possible.

Objectives

The question of a professor's pedagogical objectives when designing a course is a complex one. In order to assess such objectives fully, we would need to examine in detail each professor's academic history, research interests, and teaching philosophy, particularly as it pertains to what he or she envisions to be the purpose of studying literature. Moreover, there is also the question of how successful he or she is in meeting those objectives; in other words, we would need to try to measure the degree to which the students' retention of content corresponds with the professor's goals. Nevertheless, having a sense of what the professor aims to accomplish in a course is an essential component of trying to understand the choices of texts he or she has made. For this reason, it is worth examining in some detail the types of responses I received when I asked my subjects about their specific objectives for the courses they were teaching on the literatures of Canada. In many cases, professors described aims that seemed to have little direct correlation to the use of specific texts in the classroom, such as the goal of helping students to be more proficient at textual analysis or more enthusiastic about reading the literature of their own country. Others emphasized that their primary aim is to give the students a sense of the literary history of Canada or a better understanding of the themes and issues they believed to be central to the literatures of Canada. In each case, however, the curriculum has a more important impact on the shape of the course than any of the professors' objectives.

What is most surprising about the responses I received in 1997–98 when I asked professors about their main objectives when designing and teaching their courses on the literatures of Canada is that around

40 per cent of them focused initially on broader goals of general education and skill development rather than on historical, regional, or thematic coverage of the body of the literary traditions. This can be explained in part by the number of introductory courses to Canadian literature that I looked at. People who taught more specialized courses on a particular author, time period, or movement were, naturally, less likely to offer such explanations. Among those who did, however, several important themes emerged, the most prominent of which were the objectives of making students more aware of and enthused about their national literature(s) and increasing their skills of close reading and textual analysis. Many professors who were teaching introductory courses spoke of how it was their goal not only to expose their students to the literature but to make them lifelong readers of it. Given that a fair proportion of students of such courses are not literature majors and may never take another literature course in their lives, this is an understandable and noble objective. Anyone who teaches literature, in fact, can find inspiration in some of the practices described to me by subjects such as John O'Connor, a professor of English at the University of Toronto:

> I've said to [my students] at the end of my courses that the real test of the course is not whether they read the books—because I'll find that out when I read the final test—but whether they read a book again. I say: "If you don't, and this is the last Canadian book you'll ever read, then you may not fail the course, but I would have to say that the course has failed you. The whole point of this ought to be to hook you, to commit you in some sense to a knowledge of the literature of your own time and place." (O'Connor)

For others, however, making students enthusiastic about the literatures of their own country and about reading literature in general is, at best, a secondary or tertiary objective. Many of the professors of introductory courses posited the greater development in their students of skills of analysis and writing to be their primary goal, a sign, perhaps, that they view themselves as teachers of literary studies as much as teachers of a particular national literature. One response from Lorraine

York, a professor of English at McMaster University, illustrated this perspective quite well, though it is not completely representative of her more comprehensive approach to the teaching of Canadian literature. She describes her primary pedagogical goal as

> teaching method, teaching interpretation, teaching a habit of thinking about how texts are formed. It has shifted much more to that and away from a content base. I never really had much taste for that idea of, you know, you give people the content and it's the content that they need...I think my inclination has always been to shift much more to teaching a method of thinking, teaching approaches, teaching reading, in effect. Or teaching texts as part of a culture instead of very separate entities, which of course is the way I was taught. (York)

Not surprisingly, this is a view that I heard in both English and French Canada from many of the younger professors in the field who seem to have moved to more of a "post-national" approach to the literature. For some, this is a sign that the literatures of Canada have "grown up" and occupy a place alongside the other major literatures studied in departments of English, French, literary studies, or comparative literature; that is to say, the reasons for studying them are no different than for any other body of work. What is most striking, of course, about placing method and skills at the centre of the course objectives is that the coverage of "content" becomes to some degree a vehicle to achieve the latter rather than vice versa.

Yet, although a number of professors seem to be moving more towards a skills-based approach to literary studies and numerous critics advocate such a paradigm as the ideal replacement for the outmoded and stagnant field coverage model, the Canadian literature(s) curriculum, particularly in so far as introductory-level English courses are concerned, remains focused on covering the histories and traditions of the literatures of Canada as well as representing their major authors and works. It should not be surprising, therefore, that many of my subjects suggested that such "coverage" was their primary aim when constructing their courses. The ineluctable weight of the curriculum inevitably leads most, if not all, professors, regardless of their teaching philosophy, to work to meet the demands of the course structure(s) the department provides for them. These constraints are frequently laid out very clearly in department calendars, which function in a subtle but highly effective manner to ensure institutional and, ultimately, cultural reproduction. Take, for instance, the description of English 202: Introduction to Canadian Literature from the University of British Columbia's 1997–98 Department of English guide:

> English 202 provides an introduction to major authors, themes and forms in Canadian literature. While the approach to this material varies from section to section, all sections teach works published in the genres of poetry, fiction, drama and prose (critical, exploration, etc.), and all sections seek to represent varieties of cultural experiences within Canadian literature.

Although this generic description for the survey course, of which the department offered eight sections in 1997–98, is very general in nature, it still sets out some definite parameters for the instructor teaching the course and provides students with a number of significant expectations before they even enter the classroom. Stating that the course is centred around "major authors, themes and forms in Canadian literature" immediately lends a canonical weight to the works and ideas covered in the course, implying, in other words, that if a work is covered in class, it is because that work is important. The same emphasis on the significance of the works chosen for study is found in the description of the Université du Québec à Montréal's 1997–98 survey course, LIT 1605: Panorama de la littérature québécoise:

> L'objectif de ce cours est d'identifier les courants et les pratiques littéraires dominants et de prendre connaissance des oeuvres marquantes du corpus littéraire québécois. L'approche sera davantage historique et on couvrira l'ensemble du corpus, depuis les écrits de la Nouvelle-France jusqu'à l'écriture contemporaine.[2]

At the same time as it denotes an emphasis on "les courants et les pratiques littéraires dominants" and those works deemed to be "marquantes," the description also delineates certain elements of the course structure—namely, a historical focus that aims to cover all of the major movements and works since the founding of New France. Similarly, the final clause of the description for English 202, which indicates an attempt to "represent varieties of cultural experiences," makes it clear that the department (and the student) expects that the instructor will endeavour to include texts by writers from a wide variety of regional, ethnic, and/or cultural groups.

Other types of course descriptions direct the instructor's work in even more specific ways. In some cases, such as that of the 1997–98 description for the University of Alberta's English 271: Canadian Literature: Major Writers and Movements, these texts lay out a vision of the literatures and literary histories of Canada, which the instructor is then obliged to either follow or subvert:

> A study of the growth of English-Canadian literature in its historical and cultural context from the colonial period to the present, with an emphasis on major writers and movements. The course examines the development of a literary culture in the decades prior to Confederation; the rise of Canadian imperialism and of a "national" literature in the period between Confederation and the outbreak of WWI; the emergence and consolidation of literary modernism following WWI; and its eclipse in the closing decades of this century by postmodernism.

We can see from this description how it posits an narrative of growth that begins with the immature seeds of the "colonial period" when the description suggests there was no "literary culture" to the rise and fall of Canadian "literary modernism"—the mere existence of which is not an uncontroversial topic in Canadian literary criticism—to a new point of maturity as illustrated by the prevalence of postmodernism. Whether the instructor agrees with such a narrative or not, it becomes the de facto starting point for the course. In some cases, the stock course descriptions even include lists of authors whose work will or might be included in the course. The description for a University of Prince Edward Island course on English-Canadian poetry (English 322) effectively illustrates this process. It reads:

> This course examines English-Canadian poetry from the Nineteenth Century to the present, focusing on poets of the Confederation era, major figures of 1930–1970 such as Pratt, Livesay, Birney, Page, Avison, Layton, Purdy, Cohen and Atwood, and the important new voices and poetic developments of the 1970s and 1980s.

Again, the inclusion of such names and the exclusion of others—in this case, all poets who first published after 1930 or before 1970—is an explicit indication of the department's valuation of certain writers in comparison to others. Every one of these examples is a reminder of the degree to which, in creating the syllabus, each instructor has to negotiate the array of boundaries or "guidelines" established by the curriculum and expressed in department publications. The fact that many instructors frequently see themselves as the source or originators of the primary objectives in any course they teach is an indication of just how much professors deliberately or unconsciously accept and/or forget the "lines drawn around what they do" (Said 20).

Selection of Texts

In any literature course, the primary vehicle used by an instructor to achieve his or her pedagogical goals is the selection of texts. I deliberately spent much of each interview asking my subjects questions about which texts they had chosen to teach and why they had chosen them. One of my first questions was if issues of price and availability—a factor almost always ignored in discussions of the canon—ever affected which texts they chose to include on the course. Although nearly everyone I spoke to had at least one or two examples of a text they were unable to teach because it had fallen out of print, many suggested that, ultimately, availability was not a critical issue. As one professor put it to me, "if you're teaching a survey course and one text you want is out of print, don't tell me that's the only text that fulfills the reason that you're teaching it." Although we could take the prevalence of this opinion to be a sign of the wide availability and diversity of Canadian literary works currently in print, we can also see it as an indication of the effectiveness of the market of symbolic goods and cultural reproduction. In other words, the reason that so few people have major complaints about the choice of texts they have at their disposal is that they primarily teach the texts that are almost always in print. Those texts then remain in print precisely because they are taught so frequently, further augmenting their symbolic value. That increased status, in return, increases the chances the text will be taught. It should be noted that there were some professors such as John O'Connor who recognized the danger of making assumptions about those texts that are available versus those that are not: "On the whole, we tend to feel—maybe because we preconceive it— that what's there is the best. Because if it weren't the best, it wouldn't be there. I think we have to resist that a little bit to say 'what has fallen away?'" (O'Connor). These same professors also often discussed having strategically supported texts that they feared might disappear from print if they were not taught on a regular basis.

The price of texts is also a significant issue that ultimately has a tremendous effect on the shape of students' knowledge of the literatures of Canada. Despite the fact—or perhaps because of the fact—that most undergraduate students routinely pay hundreds of dollars for textbooks for a single computing science or biology course, there is a strong feeling among literature professors that it is unfair to burden students with having to spend a lot of money on books for their courses in literature. Some professors keep close tabs on the total cost of the books they have ordered for the course; a number told me they always ensure the total cost never exceed a set dollar amount for a full-year course. The more common means of keeping down the cost in a survey course, however, is for the professor to use a combination of inexpensive books and an anthology that allows students to buy a single book that will be used at a number of points throughout the course. The use in 1997–98 of anthologies such as Brown, Bennett, and Cooke's *An Anthology of Canadian Literature in English* or Geddes's *15 Canadian Poets x 2*—the latest, revised editions of which are both still used extensively—has numerous repercussions on the choice of texts to be covered in a course. Most obviously, instructors find themselves using poems or short stories from an anthology they likely would have not taught had they not been part of that volume. The choices made by the editors of such anthologies, however, can also direct the instructor's choice of the other books for the course. For instance, the instructor might choose texts that help fill what he or she feels to be gaps in the anthology, such as the lack of much early Canadian literature in the Brown, Bennett, and Cooke anthology. While the gaps in anthologies may boost the likelihood that some other texts will be chosen as a supplement, they can also cannibalize the sales of other titles, especially individual collections of poetry or short stories. By reducing the potential course adoptions of such texts, anthologies can help to drive them out of print, thus reinforcing the seemingly valuable status of the anthologies themselves, for they then become the only in-print source for certain stories and poems.

The price of anthologies, of course, can also have a profound effect on the shape of a course's book list. With anthologies increasingly being priced at over fifty dollars, many instructors who use anthologies told me they also deliberately try to assign inexpensive texts such as those from, as one professor put it, the "cheap and cheerful" New Canadian Library series or, in the case of courses in Québécois literature, the Bibliothèque Québécoise. In the case of the teaching of English-Canadian literature in 1997–98, we need only look at the statistics from Table 3.5 in Chapter Three, which outlines the twenty-one most frequently taught texts, to realize that titles from the New Canadian Library series make up eleven of those top spots with two others being occupied by the previously mentioned anthologies published by Oxford University Press. Of the eight remaining titles, *Green Grass, Running Water; In the Skin of a Lion; Obasan; The English Patient; Fifth Business; The Handmaid's Tale; Dry Lips Oughta Move to Kapuskasing;* and *Lives of Girls and Women*, all were priced at the time below twenty dollars. The low cost of series like the New Canadian Library and the Bibliothèque Québécoise give them a ubiquity in course reading lists that is hard, if not impossible, for any other Canadian publisher to achieve.[3] Moreover, their omnipresence and the seemingly official and inclusive titles of each series immediately bestow on their constituent texts an increased level of cultural capital and imply that those works have been chosen for the series because of their importance and not, as is so often the case, because the rights happened to be available. The price and cultural status of these texts, then, make them attractive choices for professors trying to assemble an ensemble of texts that is readily available, inexpensive, and helps them to achieve their own pedagogical objectives as well as those of the curriculum.

While I was initially quite interested in how the price of texts and their availability affected these choices, what became most intriguing to me with each interview were the strategies employed by professors as they tried to choose a group of texts that together would assist them in achieving their goals for the course. For those I interviewed, the most important challenge they described facing when designing a curriculum for nearly any type of course was to achieve the widest coverage possible of the body of literature(s) they were teaching, whether it be the entirety of Canada's written and oral literatures produced since before first contact between Natives and Europeans or the Canadian novel in English published since 1970. The question of coverage, however, is not the same when designing special topics courses or those organized around the oeuvre of a particular author. It is far more difficult, in other words, to design either a broad introductory survey course that incorporates works from multiple genres, regions, and historical periods or even a course focusing on a specific genre or around a narrower historical period. In many cases, when professors are trying to achieve this balance of coverage, they are first trying to respond to the parameters of the course as they have been established in the department curriculum. As many professors described to me, the richness and diversity of the literatures of Canada make such guidelines impossible to meet in any meaningful way.

One the one hand, choosing which texts to teach is a very personal matter, and the final selection does reflect on the interests and enthusiasms of the professor. Burke Cullen, who taught the University of Toronto's broad Canadian Literature survey course (English 252Y) in 1997–98, argues that decisions about coverage are still secondary to one's own aesthetic and political biases: "It does come down to a kind of personal choice based as much on one's own personal ideology and sensibility as, perhaps to a lesser degree, on one's moral sense on whether they're getting enough coverage of region, period, and male, female, and Native [writers] and things like that" (Cullen). This very concern over coverage was echoed by many people I spoke to who, while lamenting sometimes the limitations it imposed upon their choices, felt strongly about the need to represent the diversity of Canadian literature. In many cases, professors view the issue of coverage as primarily one that relates to region, though with many English departments disallowing the study of works in translation, courses in "Canadian literature" frequently do not include Québec. As one professor from the University of Western Ontario told me, "I try to think in terms of regions and makes sure that I cover the Atlantic provinces....Then Quebec just gets left out of this, of course. Then Ontario, the Prairies, and BC. I try to represent each of those regions and at least introduce the students to some of those regional differences." The situation at French universities in Québec, of course, is somewhat different because equivalent courses in Québec deal solely with French texts written there, thus enabling them to avoid, for the most part, any significant concern over regional representation. Instead, they tend to focus more on, as we have seen with the description of the Université du Québec à Montréal's "Panorama de la littérature québécoise" course, the most important works, movements, and developments throughout their literary history.

In fact, most professors, whether anglophone or francophone, who spoke to me about trying to achieve historical and regional coverage in their syllabi reminded me that they also find it important to choose what they feel to be the great and/or most important works of the literatures of Canada. This type of focus on "the canon," as is demonstrated by the previous chapter's statistics on the most frequently taught books and authors, often privileges the significance of an author's oeuvre over the importance of a single text. While certain professors may prefer one author over another, it was clear from most of the subjects I interviewed, as it was as well from many department calendar descriptions of courses in the literatures of Canada, that they feel strongly about representing certain authors but are less particular about which works by that author they teach. We can clearly see this pattern in action in this statement from one of my interview subjects: "So, I [teach] a Davies, a Laurence, a Munro, an Atwood. It would just be unthinkable, in a sense, to leave those people out. To other people, it's equally unthinkable to leave out Gallant, Findley, Ondaatje, and the list could go on." As is highly visible from the list of the most frequently taught titles, the books whose authors have not yet reached a status of having their works referred to as "a Thomas King" or "a Sinclair Ross" are sometimes included on courses because they have been recognized as being "canonical" in that they are singularly important works from an author's oeuvre or because they may have been the only title written by that author. More frequently, however, they are included because they fill very well one of the niches a professor is trying to represent, such as "the prairie novel" or "feminist writing." In this way, as I suggested earlier, while a text's canonical status is bolstered significantly by its presence on the reading lists for such courses, it does not necessarily get taught simply because it is (or is becoming) a canonical text.

The Politics of Representation

Perhaps the most provocative question I asked of professors was whether they felt "the need or a pressure to represent various cultural, ethnic, or language groups in [their] syllabus." While many argued that there was no external pressure to do so, the majority of them also suggested that they tried to achieve such "coverage" in their syllabus. One of the reasons cited for this was the desire to respond to the diversity of the campus. As York University professor John Lennox told me, "This campus is a United Nations. This campus is Canada present and Canada future and we need to pay attention to that" (Lennox). Some were more successful in meeting these objectives than others, but most saw the curriculum and course structures as interfering with any way of covering works by many different constituencies. Citing the fact that, in the broader survey courses, they needed to cover the entire history of Canadian literature, professors suggested time and again that there was little minority writing available to choose from that was not written quite recently and so that, by the time they got to that point in the course, there was only the possibility of adding a single text by a minority writer. The list of texts most frequently taught in 1997–98 points very clearly to the fact that single texts are often used to fill this niche, with Joy Kogawa's *Obasan* being one of the prime examples. Tied with Moodie's *Roughing it in the Bush* and Ondaatje's *In the Skin of a Lion*—another text singled by professors as an example of their efforts at making a more multicultural syllabus—as the third most frequently taught text in the English courses on Canadian literature that I surveyed, *Obasan* frequently served in these courses to represent the entirety of literature by writers of colour in Canada. One response to my question about representing various cultural groups that I received from a professor with no such writers represented on his survey course supports this notion even further: "I probably don't feel that [pressure] as much as I should…In terms of ethnic diversity, no, I probably don't do enough of that. I know that there is some pressure to do that so I should be teaching Kogawa and…who else….Sorry, my mind is a blank at the moment. I haven't done that."

The place of Native literature in such courses is equally revealing. In Québec, when I asked this question in 1997, I was told by everyone I interviewed that there is no significant body of written literature by Natives in Québec, partly because of the small number who speak or write in French. "Il n'y pratiquement pas de littérature des autochtones écrite en français," said Denis Saint-Jacques. "Pour le peu qui sont francophones, il n'y a presque personne qui écrivent" (Saint-Jacques).[4] Given that Diane Boudreau's *Histoire de la littérature amérindienne au Québec: Oralité et écriture* (1993) and Maurizio Gatti's *Littérature amérindienne du Québec* (2004) prove that this is not entirely the case, one might argue that the prevalence of this opinion in 1997 stemmed partly from the attachment of the field in Québec to the notion of there being a single tradition of *Québécois* literature. One need only look at the *Histoire de la littérature québécoise* (2007) and its inclusion of sections on "littérature anglo-québécoise" and "l'imaginaire anglo-montréalais" to see that this perception is changing in Québec (Biron, Dumont, and Nardout-Lafarge). It is clear, however, that the desire to uncover a single and unifying tradition has, historically, led to the exclusion of the Native oral literatures and anlgophone Québec writers from what could be a much broader understanding of the literature(s) of Québec. In English Canada, there is also a widespread attachment to the idea of a single tradition that has its origins in Britain and not North America. For this reason, the vast majority of survey courses and anthologies exclude any consideration of the oral tradition of Native peoples. This position was summarized for me very well by a senior professor of the University of Toronto. Asked whether he includes oral literature in his survey course, he responded,

> No. That's a hard one. If you're talking about tradition, you're talking about continuity rather than simple contiguity. And also linguistic continuity...So, it's not a question of ignoring that heritage but seeing where it is part of the English or French traditions in literature. I don't see any point in historical overview of starting with English translations of Inuit and Aboriginal legends. They seem to me to be part of anthropology or ethnography. What I'm doing is a history of Canadian literature. So Thomas King, in a way, is part of that, whereas the legends—to which, in fact, he has no access in the original because he doesn't read it—aren't.

The mention here of Thomas King is also important because in 1997–98 he and Tomson Highway were the most frequently taught Native writers, as one can see from the places occupied on the list of most frequently taught texts by *Green Grass, Running Water* (tied, ironically enough, with Richardson's *Wacousta* as the second most frequently taught text) and Highway's plays *Dry Lips Oughta Move to Kapuskasing* (one of the three eighth most frequently taught texts), and *The Rez Sisters* (one of the tenth most frequently taught texts). With a few exceptions, these texts dominated the single place frequently allotted to Native writers in the English survey courses of Canadian literature. King's text is problematic for a number of reasons. The humour of the book, its constant theme of the collision between Native and non-Native cultures, its vast network of intertextual references, and the ease with which instructors and critics can (mistakenly, in my opinion) discuss it as a postmodern novel, make it a highly "teachable" Native text for white students and professors alike. One professor, for instance, described this very fact by saying that "Tom King's been the great gift to all of us," while another put it more bluntly: "I am so glad that Thomas King wrote *Green Grass, Running Water* because now there's finally a Native book I can teach."

The above examples illustrate the myriad problems inherent in this type of "coverage" in any type of literature course. It is inevitable that any text chosen to stand for the literature of a particular region, culture, or language group, literary movement, or even an individual author will be a misrepresentation of the referent. In a passage from *Cultural Capital* that is equally applicable to this notion of coverage, John Guillory reminds us of how recent attempts to "open up" the canon encourage us to imagine a text as being representative of an author's experience and that author's experience as somehow illustrative of the concerns of a social group:

> The sense in which a canonical author represents a dominant social group, or a noncanonical author a socially defined minority, is continuous with the sense in which the work is perceived to be immediately expressive of the author's experience as a representative member of some social group. The primacy of the social identity of the author in the pluralist critique of the canon means that the revaluation of works on this basis will inevitably seek its ground in the author's experience, conceived as the experience of a marginalized race, class, or gender identity.... The typical valorization of the noncanonical author's experience as a marginalized social identity necessarily reasserts the transparency of the text to the experience it represents. (Guillory 10)

This sort of essentialism is also harmful in the way that it encourages many professors to focus on better representing the diversity of Canada rather than on covering the diversity of the literatures in this country. The preoccupation with issues of race, gender, or ethnic background serve very well to distract our attention from all the other aspects of the literatures of Canada excluded from the typical course offerings on the literatures of Canada. It is interesting to note in this regard that, while many professors spoke of their efforts to provide better coverage of all of these issues, next to no one described endeavouring to make sure there was a better balance between genres and that marginalized forms like non-fiction, songs, experimental literature, or popular fiction had a place on their courses. In this same way, while many of both my anglophone and francophone interview subjects suggested to me that the strength and reputation of Canada's female writers made gender coverage a non-issue, few people questioned what types of writing by women were being represented or made sure to include some works by feminist writers.

Cultural Nationalism and the Teaching of the Literatures of Canada

The final set of questions I asked in my interviews directly addresses how professors envision the relationship between Canada (or Québec in the case of the French-language universities I visited) and courses that attempt to offer an understanding of its literature(s). I asked my subjects first if they believed that it was "possible to develop in your students a greater sense of Canada (or Québec) through teaching them about its literature" and then, if that was the case, if they designed their syllabi "in such a way so as to facilitate this." My rationale for this posing this question when I departed on my trip was that I believed that the cultural nationalist approach of the 1960s and 1970s was still present, if not in the attitudes of the professors then in the curriculum itself. Interestingly, the constituency from whom I received the most consistent answers on this topic were the francophone professors teaching Québécois literature. Contrary to what I perhaps anticipated, every one of them felt that the nationalistic impulse behind the study of Québécois literature was passé and that any understanding of Québec that students derived from the course, aside from understanding it to have a vibrant literary culture, was purely tangential to the main goals of the course. In English Canada, while there were quite varied responses to this question, roughly 60 per cent of the professors I spoke to responded that this was not one of their main objectives when teaching the course. Ironically, many of these same people also argued strongly for the importance of representing the diversity of Canadian identity through their courses, in part so that their increasingly diverse student body would see themselves reflected in the literature(s) of this country. Course descriptions also frequently support this approach, as did that from the University of British Columbia's 1997–98 course guide, which stated that in English 202 "all sections seek to represent varieties of cultural experiences within Canadian literature."

If, from studying the literatures of Canada, students do inevitably take away some sort of broader vision of their own country, however, the question that needs to be asked is how course structures and curriculum might affect this understanding. While we have already looked at the inherent problems with the notion of using single texts to represent, for instance, multicultural writing or the nineteenth-century novel, we must pay even greater attention to that which is omitted from courses altogether, often in the name of the "literary tradition." In all cases, avoiding these omissions would help students (and faculty) to develop a far more complex picture of the literatures of this country and how they interconnect, interact, and, in many cases, exist independently of the others. In Québec, the traditional lacunae in the curriculum have involved literature not written in French, though, in terms of the inclusion of different genres, the French-language universities in Québec are years ahead of their English counterparts. Even the exclusion of anglophone writing in the notion of the literature(s) of Québec was beginning to change in 1997–98 with the work of professors such as the Université de Montréal's Pierre Nepveu and the Université Laval's François Dumont, who both spoke to me of a growing interest and recognition for "la littérature québécoise anglaise." In the decade following those conversations, this interest has increasingly become a part of mainstream conceptions of Québécois literature.

In the English-language universities, there is far less diversity in the genres considered to merit literary study than there is in Québec. Such a paradigm fosters a vision of the literatures of Canada that only includes fiction, poetry, and sometimes drama. The most crucial gap, however, involves the omission of literature originally written in French from most courses in "Canadian literature." In many cases, apparently, this omission is due primarily to policies in some departments of English that prohibit the teaching of translated works, something many professors told me was both logical and natural. Such policies are tremendously problematic when one considers the fact that Canada is a literary space occupied by two major literatures, each written in a different language, and a significant number of other smaller ones. More troublesome is the degree to which the frequent lack of any translated French-Canadian or Québécois texts on English courses (re)produces the impression that "Canadian literature" consists entirely of literature written in English. Such a limited perspective is remarkably useful to have when trying to articulate a vision of there being a single Canadian or Québécois literary tradition; as Guillory states, though, "one should always bear in mind that the concept of a given tradition is much more revealing about the immediate context in which the tradition is defined than it is about the works retroactively so organized" (Guillory 34).

One of the other primary reasons that Québécois texts in translation rarely make it into courses on "Canadian literature" is that there seems to be so little space for translated works in the small proportion of the overall English curriculum devoted to Canadian literature. Many professors I spoke to justified their exclusion of literature in translation by questioning what they would have to leave out in order to accommodate it. This is precisely what University of Toronto's John O'Connor, who in fact has a master's degree in comparative Canadian literature from the Université de Sherbrooke, describes as being one of his reasons for leaving out translated works:

> I would be a natural in my department to be teaching a lot of French-Canadian lit in translation as part of my course. Of course, there's still the problem of numbers. If I bring in Gabrielle Roy and Yves Beauchemin, who do I kick off? Richler and MacLennan? This is an English Department after all, and with the material being as rich and diverse as it is, I don't have any problem coming up with twelve good English-Canadian books. So, that for me, right away, is the way I decide. (O'Connor)

For most people, however, the question of turf war or room on the course list is a convenient excuse for not envisioning "Canadian literature" as a body of literature containing more than one tradition. As Dennis Duffy, now a professor emeritus of English at the University of Toronto, admitted to me,

There's no doubt about it that I would be challenged if that whole turf war thing were taken away. All I can say in my own defence is that it's a challenge that I hope I would respond to....I'd be up against the limitations of my own training in that I could not teach technique with any great skill. The course would have to be pretty much thematic. That would be a real limitation and I'd be really worried. (Duffy)

The issue of training is an important one, of course, as the vast majority of students graduating with English degrees, whether it is a BA or a PHD, will leave never having been exposed to any literature from Québec that was originally written in French. By excluding it from the curriculum, the English department becomes an effective site of institutional and cultural reproduction, of which the chief aim is to ensure the hegemony of the dominant cultural power. This form of "sanctioned ignorance," as Gayatri Spivak describes it, maintains the status quo in a highly efficient and wholly insidious manner. If the efficacy of this system to reproduce itself was not apparent to me in 1997–98 when discussing these issues with the ninety-four professors I interviewed, it became abundantly clear to me when examining the state of courses on the literatures of Canada taught exactly one decade later.

"The Substance of Forgetting"

A Decade of Changes, Or a Lack Thereof?

5

I was thinking of the other lives. Lives we could have led but did not choose.
Choices we did not make. The alternate paths. That what we choose is
only real because we choose it. Perhaps what we have not chosen is even
more real.

— KRISTJANA GUNNARS, *The Substance of Forgetting*

L'oubli, et je dirai même l'erreur historique, sont un facteur essentiel de la
création d'une nation, et c'est ainsi que le progrès des études historiques est
souvent pour la nationalité un danger....Or l'essence d'une nation est que tous
les individus aient beaucoup de choses en commun, et aussi que tous aient
oublié bien des choses.

— ERNEST RENAN, "Qu'est-ce qu'une nation"[1]

IN THE PREFACE TO HIS ESSAY COLLECTION *Making it Real: The*
Canonization of English-Canadian Literature, Robert Lecker, writing just
before the 1995 Québec referendum, contends "no one can pretend
that it is possible to speak about Canadian literature without interro-
gating the country" (ix). Clearly, through our courses and scholarship

in English Canada, we frequently appear to question and even reshape our ideas of the nation. It seems impossible to do otherwise and, even when we try to avoid having our take on "Canadian literature" confused with our take on Canada, our students do this for us. "[When] it comes to teaching Canadian literature to Canadian students," Lecker submits, "we are inevitably teaching them about their country; for this reason we need a clear sense—or a clearer sense—of the relationship between pedagogy, criticism, and citizenship" (ix). Lecker is absolutely correct; for scholars and teachers perhaps, but especially for students, our courses are always offering a response to Northrop Frye's immortal question, "where is here?" As we will see played out in the shape of the courses offered in 2007–08 at anglophone universities, the answer that we seem to offer to our students is increasingly that Canadian literature (and Canada) is really a post-nineteenth-century phenomenon that occurs only in English. Ironically, for a country that in 1995 saw passionate and well-intentioned citizens fly across the country on the eve of the last referendum to prove that "[their] Canada includes Québec," it seems clear from the courses on our national *literature* and our literary anthologies that our "Canadian Literature" does not.

As with the set of data and interviews collected in 1997–98, the data I gathered for the 2007–08 academic year covers all courses on the literatures of Canada at universities. In part because of the larger argument I am making in this chapter and also because of the difficulties in comparing two entirely different systems at one time, this chapter focuses on the courses taught in English departments at English-language universities on the literatures of Canada. The overall approach offered within French-language institutions in Québec continues to play a vital role in this discussion as an illustration of an entirely viable alternate model that has been incredibly effective in building and disseminating knowledge of the literatures of Québec. The shared lack of awareness (and interest) between the two solitudes conveniently allows every professor and the department to rationalize their own practices and the larger structures of which they are a part as the best, or at least the most logical, way to conceive of the study of the literatures of Canada. A contributing factor to such assumptions, as we have already examined, is our extraordinary lack of (interest in) data that, when collected and studied, can reveal back to us our practices as a field. Like the 1997–98 data, some of the 2007–08 data will surprise people in all levels of the field and will disprove many of the assumptions we make about what books everyone is teaching or the role of, say, First Nations writing in Canada's English departments.

Universities and Departments

As we have seen, from the very beginning of our discipline's history, Canadian literature has been treated, even by many of its strongest advocates, as a supplement to the overall English curriculum. Although the statistics do show, in one or two cases, strong growth of the number of courses and sections taught on English-Canadian literature between 1997–98 and 2007–08, there have been few, if any, meaningful changes to the place of the literatures of Canada in the degree requirements. In fact, of the twenty-two English departments looked at in this study only seven require a student majoring in English to take a Canadian Literature course.[2] The numbers get slightly better for honours degrees, as eleven universities require their students to take courses in Canadian literature. Given the frequent complaints we hear from publishers, writers, and, yes, people who teach courses on the literatures of Canada at Canadian universities regarding how few Canadian works are taught in schools across the country, it is surprising, even shocking, that only one third of the universities require this of the English major, a degree that future school teachers of English pursue more frequently than the honours degree.

As with my data from 1997–98, for the figures from ten years later I looked at both how many courses each department offered and what percentage of these were designated as courses on the literatures of Canada. In this count, courses offered with multiple sections only count as a single course, as students cannot take multiple sections of the same course at the same time. This figure, then, tells us something about the place of courses on the literatures of Canada within the overall course offerings. I did not count courses on more general topics that might have included significant Canadian content, which is, of course, one of the ways in which Canadian literature does enter the classroom and increase the level of Canadian content. It is difficult to quantify such a Canadian presence, however, and so this gets left out of my study. The one exception I made was to include in my count courses with titles such as "North American Aboriginal Literature" or "Aboriginal Literature and Culture," which, rightly, work to trouble our understandings of the border and the boundaries of national literatures; Aboriginal literature, in other words, like Québécois literature, cannot be fairly labelled as "Canadian literature." Yet, Aboriginal literature remains one of the literatures or bodies of literature produced at least partly within the geographic borders of Canada. So, while I included courses on Aboriginal writing, I did not include in my overall count works written by Native authors that were written and published on the other side of the Canada/US border.

Table 5.1 demonstrates the percentage of courses available to students pursuing English degrees,[3] which gives a sense of the opportunity students in those departments have to take courses that focus on the literatures of Canada. For understandable reasons, smaller universities with a more limited staff and no PHD program may have only a few faculty capable of teaching those courses. So, when a member is on sabbatical or administrative leave, smaller departments are forced to offer a smaller number of classes, if they can offer any at all. When I visited the University of New Brunswick in the fall of 1997, for instance, they were only able to mount one such course, taught by a lecturer whose field of expertise was not Canadian literature. Larger departments are much more capable of dealing with these ebbs and flows of available personnel.

Table 5.1 represents the number of distinct courses available to students in a given department, but it does not capture the volume of courses offered. In other words, in the table a survey course on Canadian Literature is counted only once, even if there are five sections of that course available all taught by different professors. Table 5.2, then, looks at what happens to the rankings if we count the place of the sections offered in relation to the overall number of sections offered by the entire department. For some universities, those that teach multiple sections of the same Canadian literature course, this improves their rankings; for others, which might offer one section of Canadian literature and three or four sections of Introduction to Shakespeare, their place in the rankings

TABLE 5.1 *English Universities Ranked by Percentage of Courses Offered on the Literatures of Canada (2007–08)*

University	Department	Cdn. Courses
University of Victoria	Department of English	15.79%
Concordia University	Department of English	15.38%
Carleton University	Department of English Language and Literature	15.25%
University of Saskatchewan	Department of English	14.29%
McMaster University	Department of English and Cultural Studies	13.73%
University of Winnipeg	Department of English	13.04%
Memorial University of Newfoundland	Department of English	12.50%
University of Toronto	Department of English	11.49%
University of Ottawa	Department of English	10.34%
University of Alberta	Department of English and Film Studies	10.13%
York University	Department of English	9.90%
University of New Brunswick—Fredericton	Department of English	9.09%
University of Western Ontario	Department of English	8.00%
Queen's University	Department of English	7.69%
Dalhousie University	Department of English	7.41%
University of British Columbia	Department of English	7.41%
McGill University	Department of English	6.78%
University of Manitoba	Department of English, Film, and Theatre	6.67%
University of Prince Edward Island	Department of English	5.50%
Simon Fraser University	Department of English	5.26%
University of Calgary	Department of English	5.13%
Acadia University	Department of English	4.76%

TABLE 5.2 *English Universities Ranked by Percentage of Course Sections Offered on the Literatures of Canada (2007–08)*

University	Department	Cdn. Sections
Carleton University	Department of English Language and Literature	22.54%
Concordia University	Department of English	12.70%
University of Toronto	Department of English	12.34%
McMaster University	Department of English and Cultural Studies	11.86%
University of Winnipeg	Department of English	10.67%
University of Western Ontario	Department of English	10.11%
York University	Department of English	10.00%
University of British Columbia	Department of English	10.00%
University of Ottawa	Department of English	9.92%
University of Victoria	Department of English	9.21%
Memorial University of Newfoundland	Department of English	8.61%
Queen's University	Department of English	7.69%
McGill University	Department of English	7.63%
University of Saskatchewan	Department of English	6.84%
University of New Brunswick—Fredericton	Department of English	6.70%
University of Alberta	Department of English and Film Studies	6.09%
Simon Fraser University	Department of English	6.06%
University of Prince Edward Island	Department of English	5.56%
Dalhousie University	Department of English	5.06%
University of Manitoba	Department of English, Film, and Theatre	4.76%
Acadia University	Department of English	4.76%
University of Calgary	Department of English	3.25%

drops. For some, the drop can be dramatic, particularly in cases where the department offers multiple sections of first-year English courses that serve both the English major and a faculty-wide English literature requirement. Neither one of these figures, then, can be seen as the sole definitive indicator of the health of the literatures of Canada within a given department. Nevertheless, we cannot underestimate the effect these numbers have on the value judgements made by our students, our colleagues in and outside of our departments, and even ourselves. It is worth considering if the place of dedicated courses on early Canadian writing or on Canadian poetry makes a statement as to the value of studying either of these topics.

Aside from the percentages of sections within a given department, it is also helpful to know the number of sections offered within a given department. Knowing the number of sections of courses offered may seem to tell us something about the place of courses on the literatures of Canada in a given department, but these numbers can also be somewhat misleading. A department with three sections of an intro survey course with each seating 150 students would in fact teach a greater number of students than a university with nine sections with an enrolment of forty students each. On the other hand, students in the department with nine sections would have a much greater opportunity to choose between the approaches of different professors than if they could only choose between two or three professors in the field.

There are, as Table 5.3 demonstrates, some striking figures in the rankings by the number of sections. We can see, for instance, that the very large departments of University of British Columbia and University of Toronto taught twenty-one and nineteen sections, respectively, while the comparatively smaller English departments at Carleton and the University of Victoria were not that far behind those totals with sixteen and fourteen sections, respectively. In many cases, though, these larger departments are those that simply offer many sections of the same courses, meaning that students in fact have a more limited set of options available to them than these figures might appear. As Table 5.4 shows, the University of Victoria comes in first place when one considers that they ran twelve different courses in 2007–08, which may well be connected

TABLE 5.3 *English Universities Ranked by Number of Course Sections Offered on the Literatures of Canada (2007–08)*

University	Department	Cdn. Sections
University of British Columbia	Department of English	21
University of Toronto	Department of English	19
Carleton University	Department of English Language and Literature	16
University of Victoria	Department of English	14
Memorial University of Newfoundland	Department of English	13
University of Ottawa	Department of English	12
University of Alberta	Department of English and Film Studies	12
York University	Department of English	11
University of Western Ontario	Department of English	9
McGill University	Department of English	9
Concordia University	Department of English	8
University of Winnipeg	Department of English	8
University of Saskatchewan	Department of English	8
McMaster University	Department of English and Cultural Studies	7
Simon Fraser University	Department of English	6
Queen's University	Department of English	4
Dalhousie University	Department of English	4
University of Manitoba	Department of English, Film, and Theatre	4
University of Calgary	Department of English	4
University of Prince Edward Island	Department of English	3
Acadia University	Department of English	3
University of New Brunswick—Fredericton	Department of English	2

TABLE 5.4 *English Universities Ranked by Number of Different Courses Offered on the Literatures of Canada (2007–08)*

University	Department	Different Cdn. Courses
University of Victoria	Department of English	12
University of Toronto	Department of English	10
York University	Department of English	10
Carleton University	Department of English Language and Literature	9
Memorial University of Newfoundland	Department of English	9
Concordia University	Department of English	8
McGill University	Department of English	8
University of Alberta	Department of English and Film Studies	8
McMaster University	Department of English and Cultural Studies	7
University of Saskatchewan	Department of English	7
University of Winnipeg	Department of English	6
University of Western Ontario	Department of English	6
University of Ottawa	Department of English	6
University of British Columbia	Department of English	4
Queen's University	Department of English	4
Dalhousie University	Department of English	4
Simon Fraser University	Department of English	3
University of Prince Edward Island	Department of English	3
University of Manitoba	Department of English, Film, and Theatre	3
Acadia University	Department of English	3
University of New Brunswick— Fredericton	Department of English	2
University of Calgary	Department of English	2

to the fact that they are the sole university in Canada in which one can obtain an undergraduate degree specializing in the literatures of Canada.

Courses Offered

One of the recurring themes of my interviews with professors and in my research of course offerings and department structures is that each university organizes their curriculum differently—sometimes very differently—from the others and yet the faculty, and likely the students, take these divisions of knowledge as being natural and logical, assuming that other departments do things in similar ways. Looking at over two hundred courses side by side, one cannot help but be struck by the sheer arbitrariness with which we organize our courses and then quickly forget that these divisions are, in many cases, anything but natural. By looking through all of these courses together it is also possible to make some observations not only about trends that occurred between 1997–98 and 2007–08 but also about some of the common ways in which we do shape our knowledge of our literature through decisions we make about the types of classes we offer.

Chapter Three identified an overreliance on survey courses, which, I argued, can prevent students from gaining a richer knowledge of various periods of our literary history, particularly when a department offers multiple sections of that survey course and thus makes it more difficult for faculty members to teach more specific courses on their particular areas or periods of expertise. Looking at the figures for 2007–08, the number of courses that I tagged as surveys, by which I mean courses that aim to cover all or most of Canada's literary history over a semester or two and usually look at multiple genres of writing, has in fact decreased over the decade. In 1997–98, 30 per cent of the courses I examined were surveys, and a decade later that figure has dropped from sixty-two courses to forty-eight, or 24 per cent of the total course offerings. It seems, therefore, that English departments are gradually moving away from the survey, but what, if anything, is replacing it in the overall course numbers? We can observe significant, even dramatic growth, over ten years in two key areas.

The first area of growth is long overdue and will be of no surprise to anyone. In 1997–98, forty-nine of the classes I catalogued had some content by Aboriginal writers; ten years later, that increased to eighty, a substantial improvement. This increase, although partly connected with the second area of growth I will discuss momentarily, marks a change in the perception of the place of Aboriginal writers in our courses as well as the publication of important works during this era, such as Eden Robinson's *Monkey Beach* and Tomson Highway's *Kiss of the Fur Queen*. More significant, though, is the dramatic increase in courses solely devoted to writing by Aboriginal peoples, which rose from four courses to twenty in 2007–08. Of those twenty courses, six were taught at the University of Alberta thanks to the new curriculum they put in place in 2005–06. These six classes comprised exactly 50 per cent of their Canadian literature offerings in 2007–08.

The second area of extraordinary growth is likely, to some, a troubling one. The primary area that seems to be supplanting the place of the traditional survey course is contemporary literature, and fiction in particular. When recording courses in my database, I tried to tag broadly the historical range of the course. So, for instance, most survey courses get tagged as beginning in the nineteenth century, while others get tagged as beginning with exploration literature or, in rare cases, with the oral traditions of the First Nations. In 1997–98, I found eleven courses that had as their starting point works written in the late 1970s or later, an era I tagged as simply "late twentieth century." The number of courses in 2007–08 tagged as beginning with the late twentieth century in our literary history increased nearly fivefold. Of the 203 courses I recorded for that year, forty-eight focused solely on literature written at the earliest in the late 1970s. Many of these courses, in fact, focused on writing from the very late twentieth to early twenty-first century. Further proof of this huge increase in our attention to recent writing in Canada can be found in the fact that 316 of the 495 titles I recorded as having been taught in courses during 2007–08 were not on the list of books taught just ten years earlier. This means that only 36 per cent (179) of the books taught in 2007–08 were on our syllabi just ten years earlier.

At the same time as our focus on "new" or "contemporary" writing grows, as the course titles describe this work, our attention to "early Canadian literature" seems to be waning. In 1997–98, the number of courses on early Canadian writing was shockingly low. Only eight courses at the time dealt with that period, and in 2007–08 that number dropped to six, which makes up just 3 per cent of the total course offerings that year. While there were twenty-eight other courses in 2007–08 that touched on the nineteenth century, most were survey courses with a heavy focus on the twentieth century. There were only nine of 203 courses in the country that year that paid any attention to work written prior to the nineteenth century and none that focused solely on it. Of those six previously mentioned courses on early Canadian literature, two were taught at the University of Victoria, two were taught at Simon Fraser, and one each was taught at the University of Manitoba and Memorial University. In other words, only four out of the twenty-two (18 per cent) universities surveyed in 2007–08 bothered to teach a course that dealt primarily with early Canadian literature.

One of the focuses of my project all along has been the question of how writing in translation, whether from French or other languages, gets represented in our courses on "Canadian literature." Looking at the figures from 2007–08, we do see a fairly substantial drop in the number of courses in Canada that included works translated from French. In 1997–98, twenty-nine courses on "Canadian literature" included at least one work translated from the French. This drops to twenty courses in 2007–08, with nine of these twenty books being taught at Carleton University primarily in multiple sections of their two core Canadian literature courses, English 2802 and English 3803. Interestingly, there also seems to have been a particular fascination with Jacques Poulin's *Volkswagen Blues* there that year, as it comprised five of the nine occurrences of a French text at Carleton. As we saw with courses in early Canadian literature, the culture and traditional practices of particular departments shape what gets taught and thus the demand for such courses. The twenty French texts in translation were, in fact, taught at only a handful of institutions: Carleton (nine), York (three), Winnipeg (three), Concordia (two), Victoria (two), UBC (two), Manitoba (one), and McGill (one). Although at Carleton these were part of larger survey classes, in most of the other cases the texts taught were chosen because they fit within special topics courses such as courses on life writing, children's literature, or contemporary drama. Rarely in 2007–08 did any works in translation appear on a regular survey course. In total, there were eighteen different French titles in translation that were taught in 2007–08, which from a list of 495 titles taught that year means that roughly 25 per cent of this country's population and literary production was represented by 3.6 per cent of the books taught.[4]

Courses that examine the literatures of Canada via particular genres are also still a relatively strong presence. While theatre or drama programs often do run their own courses on Canadian drama, there were eleven different courses on Canadian drama taught at the twenty-two English universities I targeted with this study. Interestingly, because of its tremendous contribution to this field, drama seems to be one of the few areas in of study in which it is not common practice to neglect Québécois literature. In addition to the Québécois selections in Wassermans's *Modern Canadian Plays Volume 1* (taught three times) and *Modern Canadian Plays Volume 2* (taught five times), the list of texts taught in 2007–08 included two plays by Michel Tremblay, Michel Marc Bouchard's play *Lilies*, and a collection of two plays by Marco Micone. Between the presence of individual courses on drama and the inclusion of plays in larger survey classes, drama texts are relatively prominent in the list of books taught in 2007–08, with playwrights such as Sharon Pollock and Tomson Highway leading the way. Courses on Canadian children's literature and the Canadian short story were also taught across the country, often appearing at universities such as Winnipeg or Ottawa, where there happen to be experts in these fields. As we know, certain courses only get taught if there's someone who wants to teach them and often this desire is connected to the correspondence of a particular topic with that teacher's own area of expertise.

As I recounted earlier, one of the more memorable conversations from 1997–98 was with a professor at the University of Toronto who suggested that they rarely taught courses on Canadian poetry anymore because no one wanted to take them. That issue, if it ever really was one—as we can see in other instances, if courses are offered regularly, they will become options in the minds of students—seems to be on the wane as in English Canada we saw Canadian poetry classes jump from ten to seventeen. Just like with other more "specialized" courses, though, these courses seem to be concentrated at particular universities that, more often than not, have larger English departments and thus the ability to offer a wider variety of courses. The University of Victoria and McGill, for instance, each taught three classes on Canadian poetry that year, which means that those two schools alone accounted for more than one third of the courses on Canadian poetry in English Canada.

Texts and Authors

As with the results from the 1997–98 research, one of the groups of data that most intrigues people and that *seems* to tell us a great deal about the shape of courses on the literatures of Canada at the beginning of the twenty-first century revolves around the question of which books get taught across the country. I use the word *seems* here as a reminder that these lists can only tell us so much. To go back to what Larry McDonald said to me when I spoke with him in 1997–98, the canon is as much, if not more, *how* we teach as it is *what* we teach. As Robert Lecker states in his seminal article "The Canonization of Canadian Literature," "the institution *is* the canon, its members *are* the texts" (7). The texts that appear on the following lists may tell us more, in other words, about the people teaching these courses or the institution itself than it ever will about the books or authors studied. Whether it is the sanctioned ignorance of anything written originally in a language other than English or the exclusion of particular genres from mainstream academia, or the ongoing popularity of individual titles over others long forgotten, the books that are on this list have wound up here for a reason; either a professor assumes a title is so canonical that it must be included in a course (and this can be due to personal canons or regional ones as much as disciplinary ones), it fits within a particular theme or topic being examined in the course, or he or she has chosen it because it serves a particular role in the classroom. As Lecker and others remind us, the classroom does not necessarily equal the curriculum; however, it is clear from these results

TABLE 5.5 *The Twenty-four Most Frequently Taught Texts (2007–08)*

Title	Author	Occurrences
Coursepack of other photocopied readings		41
In the Skin of a Lion	Ondaatje, Michael	27
Green Grass, Running Water	King, Thomas	24
A New Anthology of Canadian Literature in English	Bennett, Donna, and Russell Brown (eds.)	23
As For Me and My House	Ross, Sinclair	20
Monkey Beach	Robinson, Eden	19
Lives of Girls and Women	Munro, Alice	16
The Diviners	Laurence, Margaret	14
The Rez Sisters	Highway, Tomson	13
Fifth Business	Davies, Robertson	12
Running in the Family	Ondaatje, Michael	11
Swamp Angel	Wilson, Ethel	11
Anne of Green Gables	Montgomery, L.M.	11
Canadian Poetry From the Beginnings through the First World War	Gerson, Carole, and Gwendolyn Davies (eds.)	11
Roughing it in the Bush	Moodie, Susanna	10
The Wars	Findley, Timothy	10
Sunshine Sketches of a Little Town	Leacock, Stephen	10
The Imperialist	Duncan, Sara Jeannette	9
15 Canadian Poets x 3	Geddes, Gary (ed.)	9
Wacousta	Richardson, John	8
Obasan	Kogawa, Joy	8
The Collected Works of Billy the Kid	Ondaatje, Michael	8
Fugitive Pieces	Michaels, Anne	8
Disappearing Moon Café	Lee, Sky	8

that a text is much more likely to become canonical if it is regularly included on multiple courses over time.

The list of the most frequently taught texts in Canada in 2007–08 (Table 5.5), like the earlier data from 1997–98, is a great illustration of this process. It offers some surprising results that challenge common assumptions about what the English-Canadian canon might look like in the early part of the twenty-first century.

Because this list comes from a higher number of courses surveyed (161) than in 1997–98 (128), it is not helpful to compare the precise number of occurrences between these two periods. The relative placement of these books on the list, however, tells us a great deal. Most striking is the rise to the top of the list by the ubiquitous "coursepack," which was assembled and used by forty-one different professors in 2007–08 compared to just eight in 1997–98. The exact reasons for this are unclear, but it could be connected to crucial work having fallen out of print or a sense of dissatisfaction with the available anthologies of Canadian literature. *A New Anthology of Canadian Literature in English* edited by Brown and Bennett, however, still holds a strong place on this list and winds up being one of the most frequently used texts across the entire country. That anthology's drop from the first spot on the list in 1997–98 to the fourth isn't significant in terms of the overall sales of the book. What is interesting and significant, though, is to see a popular anthology overtaken by two novels. Looking back at Table 3.5, we see that *In the Skin of a Lion* moves from being taught in fifteen of 128 classes (11.7 per cent) to being taught in twenty-seven of 161 courses (16.7 per cent), an increase in popularity of about 42 per cent. *Green Grass, Running Water* remains close behind it at twenty-four occurrences. Both King's novel and Ondaatje's have clearly overtaken the previous top two works of fiction, *As For Me and My House* and *Sunshine Sketches of a Little Town*. The latter plummets down the rankings, being taught only ten times in 2007–08 compared to twenty in the smaller data set from a decade earlier, while the former remains constant in the number of times it was taught. Because of the larger data set, however, we can see the popularity of Ross's novel waning somewhat, being taught in 15.6 per cent of

TABLE 5.6 *The Twenty Most Frequently Taught Authors (2007–08)*

Author	Occurrences
Ondaatje, Michael	60
Atwood, Margaret	41
King, Thomas	40
Laurence, Margaret	29
Bennett, Donna, and Russell Brown (eds.)	23
Robinson, Eden	22
Ross, Sinclair	22
Findley, Timothy	21
Highway, Tomson	21
Munro, Alice	20
Brand, Dionne	17
Richler, Mordecai	16
Davies, Robertson	12
Montgomery, L.M.	12
Wilson, Ethel	12
Campbell, Maria	10
Duncan, Sara Jeannette	10
Leacock, Stephen	10
Moodie, Susanna	10
Pollock, Sharon	10

all courses in 1997–98 and 12.4 per cent of all classes in 2007–08. Some of the other interesting surprises in the rankings include the speedy rise of Eden Robinson's *Monkey Beach* to being the sixth most frequently taught novel in 161 courses examined. Compared to their popularity ten years earlier, works like *Obasan*, *Wacousta*, and *The Stone Angel* have lost considerable ground in 2007–08, with Margaret Laurence's novel even dropping to thirty-fifth spot with only five occurrences. Also worth noting here is that no text by Margaret Atwood even makes the 2007–08 list. Her most frequently taught novels, *The Handmaid's Tale* (ten occurrences in 1997–98) and *Surfacing* (nine occurrences in 1997–98) were taught only five and six times a decade later. As the 1997–98 data makes clear, however, the importance of a particular author may not be judged best by the list of most frequently taught texts.

Just as in 1997–98, the list of most frequently taught authors (Table 5.6) more closely resembles what many might draw up as a list of English Canada's most important writers. Most striking is the considerable fall in the frequency with which Atwood's and Laurence's books are taught. Atwood was in clear command of the list in 1997–98 with fifty-one occurrences in 128 courses, a figure that means that Atwood was taught in 40 per cent of all Canadian literature classes that year. In 2007–08, though, Atwood's number of occurrences drops despite the larger sample size, meaning that in 2007–08 her books were included in only 25 per cent of courses on the literatures of Canada. Laurence's drop is equally dramatic, moving from forty-four occurrences to twenty-nine over the decade. Strong risers in this list are Thomas King (twenty-one to forty occurrences), Eden Robinson (zero occurrences to twenty-two), and Dionne Brand (six occurrences to seventeen). While the great rise in attention being paid to First Nations writers such as King, Highway, and Robinson, all firmly cemented in the top ten, can explain their increasing presence in this list, the harder things to rationalize are the drops in popularity of Atwood and Laurence. Is it perhaps because of the rise in courses on contemporary literature that we are now cutting back on our more comprehensive (and conservative) survey courses? Is there the assumption that these writers are so popular that students will have already read these books anyhow? Or are we witnessing the beginning of their slow move away from the centre of the canon—or at least our "imagined canon" as Lecker provocatively suggests (Lecker 62)—as we have witnessed happen over time with writers like Davies, Richler, and Findley?

When examining these figures, it is important to remember that we cannot draw a straight line of cause and effect between the curriculum and the canon, if, as Lecker has argued, we even have one at all. "In Canada," Lecker argues, "we have a shifting but identifiable curriculum that is often misread as a canon" (Lecker 55). As I hope some of my earlier observations about how and why certain works wind up on course reading lists have made clear, many works on the list of books taught in 1997–98 and 2007–08 were not taught because they were canonical. Indeed, the excellence of a particular text might not even be a secondary or tertiary reason for its inclusion on a course syllabus. For that matter a text's canonicity may well work *against* its inclusion on the text. The increasing disappearance of Atwood from Canadian literature courses at the same time as her world reputation is reaching even greater heights is likely a function of her high degree of canonicity. In other words, perhaps she has become so canonical that professors chose other writers for their syllabus, not out of any malicious intent, but rather to help *expand* their students' knowledge of Canada's literary landscape. As I hypothesized earlier, it seems that as particular writers gain cultural capital, their body of work and indeed the authors themselves can become more canonical than their individual texts.

The other thing that is crucial to remember is that the absence of a novel or play on a reading list does not automatically indicate that work by that writer is not being taught in that same class. A survey class using an anthology, for instance, might not include a full novel by Atwood or Richler, but might, in fact, discuss in great detail some of their short stories or Atwood's poetry. Anthologies themselves can offer us as much of a view of the canon—or at least a perceived or imagined canon—as the list of books taught across the country in any given year. As much as students sometimes complain about having to buy an enormous and expensive anthology of which they will inevitably be asked to just read a fraction, anthologies can be exceptionally valuable as a reminder to students (and to faculty) of the arbitrariness of the curricular choices made by their professors. Even if they only read the texts assigned to them by their professors, they witness, in the physical form of the anthology, how much there is that they are *not* reading. Simply by flipping through the table of contents, they begin to get an idea of the larger shape of the field, that there is more out there that they can learn. This is comparable to a situation I mentioned earlier about how important it is for our students to have a wide variety of Canadian literature courses from which to choose; even if they only take one or two, the mere presence of those other courses reminds them of the vastness of our field.

Anthologies will always have their critics and perhaps none more vocal than the people who choose to use them in their courses. As we read any anthology, we cannot help but imagine how we would have chosen different texts or written more (or less) extensive footnotes. As we saw in both 1997–98 and 2007–08, the Oxford anthology edited by Donna Bennett, Russell Brown, and, for the 1990 "Revised and Abridged edition," Nathalie Cooke, has long dominated the reading lists from survey courses in English-Canadian literature. In 2007 and 2009, the Oxford anthology, now *A New Anthology of Canadian Literature in English*, faced two new contenders for the throne of the most popular anthology in Canada: *Open Country: Canadian Literature in English*, edited by Robert Lecker, and *Canadian Literature in English: Texts and Contexts*, edited by Cynthia Sugars and Laura Moss. An editor of an anthology must make many key decisions, such as where to begin the timeline, which authors and texts to include, and what types of introductions, footnotes, and other devices they will create to make the anthology a useful text for the classroom, which is always the primary objective of any such text. As with any anthology project, what is of equal interest to critics is what the editors have chosen to leave out.

In Lecker's introduction to *Open Country* and Sugars and Moss's introduction to *Canadian Literature in English*, the editors speak of their aim to represent Canada in some way through their work and their efforts to try to give students as broad a sampling as possible of what "Canadian" literature is all about. They each make many choices different from those made by Brown and Bennett, but in neither anthology do the editors see it at all necessary to include or even discuss literature written originally in French. Moss and Sugars do make note of excluding everything in translation, but they do not describe this as being terribly problematic; rather, they characterize this exclusion as a reflection of how the discipline organizes itself as well as the market for sales of the book (i.e., courses in English-Canadian literature):

> For practical reasons of space restriction, this is an anthology of Canadian literature written in English, so we do not include literary works in translation. Thus, we do not include stories originally told/written in First Nations

languages or Inuktitut, or works originally written in French, or, for example, Icelandic or Ukrainian. Further, courses in French- and English-Canadian literature tend to be separate in most university literature programs, a division that informs our restriction to the literary history of English-Canadian writing. (Moss and Sugars xiii)

What is most interesting about both of these anthology projects is not so much the decisions made by the authors (and more likely the publishers) to exclude translations but the assertion by those parties—and likely the intended audience of professors and students—that this is relatively unproblematic. The sanctioning of this narrow view of Canada's literary landscape is due in great part to how, to go back to Bourdieu and Dubois, locating and embedding the study of "Canadian Literature" in departments of English turns this potentially multilingual, multicultural collection of literatures into a single, English subject that, our curricula across the country suggest, is a natural extension of the British tradition.

The inequities, oversimplifications, and gaps in the studies of the literatures of Canada—whether in the more prominent cases in English courses in "Canadian Literature" or courses in "Littérature Québécoise" at French-language universities in Québec or New Brunswick—are all rooted in the curriculum and how it insidiously shapes our knowledge of our own literatures. The failure in English Canada to achieve a greater proportional representation for the literatures of Canada in English departments has, in many cases, led professors to try to fit an increasingly diverse body of work into the same structures that we had for them in the 1970s and 1980s. Frank Davey's explanation of how this has led to an almost complete omission of literature in translation in such courses offers an interesting perspective on how these limited parameters affect the production of knowledge:

Another thing that has happened is that anglophone Canadian women's writing, Native peoples' writing, lesbian feminist writing, writing by people of colour, writing affected by ethnicity in English—all of these things compete with the francophone. So it used to be that the other in anglophone Canadian literature was Québec. In the 1970s, that's what it was. It was francophone

Québec writing. That was the other. It was something exotic, something you could attend to, something you could construct as an entity which would illuminate by contrast the anglophone work you were studying. Now that role of the other is filled by writing by Rohinton Mistry, by Joseph Škvorecký, by Daphne Marlatt, Gail Scott, and by Maria Campbell. (Davey, Personal interview)

Of course, as we have seen, one can rarely fit more than one of these "others" into a typical survey course. What is most troubling about this is that, while some professors, such as Davey, actually take the time to consider how this has occurred, even fewer try to envision a way out of this dilemma. Most, rather, try to envision ways of doing more with less and, thus, wind up representing the nineteenth century with a single text by Susanna Moodie or Catharine Parr Traill, multicultural writing with *Obasan*, and Native writing in Canada with Thomas King or Tomson Highway. It will not be until we as Canadianists demand a greater place in the English curriculum, the ability for students to specialize in the study of our own literatures, and, as Carlyle King boldly envisioned back in 1944, the creation of at least one department that might focus solely on the literatures of North America that we will ever be able to mind the gaps, let alone mend them.

Afterword

New Ways to "Here"

"History," Stephen said, "is a nightmare from which I am trying to awake."

—JAMES JOYCE, *Ulysses*

THERE ARE AT LEAST SEVERAL BOOKS that could and perhaps will be written solely from the wealth of information I gathered in my interviews with professors of the literatures of Canada. With over one hundred hours worth of tapes from which to work, I was unable to utilize more than a fraction of these conversations in this book. On their own, these tapes represent a valuable oral history of some of the key moments in our field's evolution, not to mention a record of my own journey across the country. It struck me then, and strikes me even more deeply now, that we rarely do enough to share our stories of how we came to study and teach in our field, about pedagogy and the magic of unleashing a text into the classroom, or about our hopes and concerns for the future of the study of our country's rich literary heritage. If the canon is truly as much *how* we teach as it is *what* we teach, then we have failed so far to explore fully this side of our own literary histories. "The truth about stories," Thomas King wisely notes, "is that's all that we are" (1). The thirst I found among our country's professors to tell their stories could not be quenched with an hour-long interview; we all have many stories yet to tell.

It is my hope that some of the data and ideas I have discussed here will lead us to further conversations about the past, present, and future of the study of the literatures of Canada. Though I am not a pessimist at heart by any means, the nature of the university system, departmental structures, and, with a few notable exceptions, the lack of curricular diversity we see across the country make the possibility of any radical changes unlikely. The only change that seems to occur follows the model described by Charles B. Harris in his 1988 article "Canonical Variations and the English Curriculum":

> In cold political terms, the votes necessary for a thorough restructuring of the curriculum are not there yet. It is far more practical and, at least in the short run, probably more effective to wage the curricular battle in guerilla fashion by adding a course in theory here, a course in women's studies there and by unofficially redesigning traditionally described courses by teaching them in theoretically up-to-date ways. (C.B. Harris 12)

There are certainly a number of professors I interviewed who would recognize in Harris's recommendation their own teaching practices and efforts at promoting curricular change. As discussed in Chapter Two, however, this type of seemingly underground resistance to the curriculum is not only accepted by the institution but welcomed by it as it helps to prevent or at least postpone any change that could radically reshape its power structure. For cultural and institutional reproduction to take place, then, such resistance is accommodated in such a way that the institution can see itself as being accepting of change, while in reality it changes very little.

I hope, nevertheless, that in some small way this book works to point out some of the bolder paths we might take to alter in a fundamental way the place of the literatures of Canada in this country's various departments of literature. The contrast between the directions taken by the French-language universities in Québec (and the Université de Moncton) and those taken by English-language universities in Canada should be a revelation to scholars working in either language. Perhaps the most crucial of these differences is the greater proportion of courses on littérature québécoise and littérature acadienne offered at the former compared with those offered in English-Canadian literature at the latter. Of equal importance to the proportion of courses is the variety, and again the French-language universities in this country far outperform their English counterparts. The proportion and variety of such courses are important for two reasons. First, they allow students an opportunity to learn more about these literatures than they would by having a choice of one or two courses that frequently cover the entirety of English Canada's literary history in one year. Second, by offering faculty a chance to teach a wider variety of courses in their field, courses that are far more specialized than a multi-genre, multi-period survey course, such a curriculum invariably results in a larger, more diverse canon and a greater amount of research in these fields that might otherwise be neglected if they did not correspond in some way to the curriculum. The other marked difference between the two sets of universities is that there is a far greater diversity between the literature curricula of the three largest French-language universities, the Université Laval, the Université de Montréal, and the Université du Québec à Montréal, than among any English departments in the country. While there is obviously a huge variation between the number and variety of English courses one might be able to choose from at the University of Prince Edward Island compared to the University of British Columbia, the curriculum at each institution essentially follows the same field coverage model in which an honours or specializing student takes courses covering the major periods of British literary history along with what are not always required courses in American and Canadian literature. The range of courses and differences in the curriculum available at the aforementioned French-language universities mean that an undergraduate student has the option of choosing a department, such as the Université du Québec à Montréal's Département d'études littéraires, whose curriculum is most closely aligned with her or his interests. This, again, contributes to the growth of a wide range of knowledge and approaches to literature.

Creating the infrastructure required for a greater exploration
of Québécois literature through an organization like the Centre de
recherche en littérature québécoise (CRELIQ) at the Université Laval,
and now the Centre de recherche interuniversitaire sur la littérature et
la culture québécoises (CRILCQ),[1] has also resulted in an extraordinary
amount of research done on the literary history of Québec, for instance.
When we look at the type of research that has been done by CRILCQ and
its central role in the community of scholars of Québécois literature,
it is clear that those who study any or all of the literatures of Canada
would benefit endlessly from having access to such an organization
and the research it would generate. One of the longstanding obsta-
cles to the creation of a centre for research in the literatures of Canada,
however, was the distinct lack of a perceived need of such an institute.[2] Thanks to a significant donation from a community member, the
University of Alberta was able to launch a new research centre in 2006.
The Canadian Literature Centre/Centre de littérature canadienne (CLC)
has had considerable success with their wonderful Henry Kreisel Lecture
Series and the resulting published lectures, but, as of 2013, it has yet to
become a major centre of research approaching anything resembling a
centre like CRILCQ. In part, this stems, I presume, from a lack of major
institutional investment in its success. I would argue, however, that the
centre's limited initial reach also stems from the lack of imagination on
the part of the University of Alberta administration. Had it possessed
any sense of the scope of CRILCQ, the University of Alberta might have
set their sights higher. It also speaks volumes that no other institution
in English Canada seems to have ever thought of creating such a centre.
This attitude, I would argue, is a reflection of English-Canadian literature
scholars' lack of awareness of how the literature(s) of Québec are studied
in Québec. This "sanctioned ignorance," in both scholarly communities,
stems primarily from the misperception that the "two literatures" are of
no relation to one another and thus have little reason to be considered
simultaneously. It is clear, however, that there is no neat and seam-
less boundary between the two and that the assumption of some sort
of unity to each literature is erroneous. What makes all the literatures
of Canada worthy of study together in some form or another is the fact

that each responds somehow to a common geography; a shared—if not agreed upon—history and system of government; the experiences and interactions of this country's new immigrants, long-term residents, and original peoples; and concerns that are related to our national identities and our relation(s) to North America and the world.

Ultimately, I am not advocating a wholly integrationist approach to the study of the literatures of Canada at every university in the country or an all-out shift towards the model of comparative Canadian literature. There are valid reasons for studying the literatures of Québec and English Canada entirely independently of one another. What I am calling for, however, is a greater effort to understand Canada as a highly complex literary space in which there are virtually no literatures and elements of the literary institution that do not interact in some way with the others. A movement in this direction is something that could best be achieved by the establishment of at least one Department of the Literatures of Canada at a Canadian university that would comprise faculty members who would otherwise be separated in different departments including those of French, English, or Native studies. As scholars like François Dumont begin to reimagine "littérature québécoise" as including the works of anglophone writers from Québec, so too is there much to be gained from broadening our understanding of prairie literature(s), for instance, to include writers like Gabrielle Roy, Marguérite A. Primeau, or immigrant writers like Stephan G. Stephansson who wrote and published in their native languages. As I have shown, our tendency to do otherwise, to oversimplify this extraordinarily interesting complexity of our literary past, present, and future, serves many purposes, not the least of which is to reinforce and reproduce the arbitrary boundaries placed around literary knowledge through the creation of separate departments of French and departments of English. By ignoring how detrimental these divisions are to our conception of the literatures of our own country, we close ourselves off to the rich and unique nature of Canada as a literary space.

Appendix 1

Universities Visited, Course Offerings in the Literatures of Canada, and Instructors Interviewed, 1997–98

Department	Department of English
Province	Nova Scotia
Year	1997–98
Total courses	33
Canadian literature courses	3
Canadian content	9.1%
Total sections	36
Canadian literature sections	3
Canadian content	8.3%
Different Canadian literature courses	3
Canadian literature required for major	no
Canadian literature required for honours or specialization	no
Professors interviewed	Davies, Gwen
	Davies, Richard
	Smyth, Donna
	Thompson, Hilary
Courses on the literatures of Canada offered in 1997–98	English 2563: Canadian Literature 1
	English 2573: Canadian Literature 2: Modernism to Post-Modernism
	English 3903: Canadian Children's Literature

Department	Department of English
Province	Alberta
Year	1997–98
Total courses	51 Full-course equivalent (FCE)
Canadian literature courses	5.5 FCE
Canadian content	10.8%
Total sections	n/a
Canadian literature sections	7.5 FCE
Canadian content	?
Different Canadian literature courses	9
Canadian literature required for major	no
Canadian literature required for honours or specialization	yes
Professors interviewed	Bracken, Christopher Gittings, Chris Hjartarson, Paul Williamson, Janice
Courses on the literatures of Canada offered in 1997–98	English 271 (1): Canadian Lit.: Major Writers and Movements English 271 (2): Canadian Lit.: Major Writers and Movements English 372: Canadian Literature from 1925 English 373: Canadian Poetry to 1925 English 374: Canadian Literature 1925–1960 English 376 (1): Canadian Literature from 1960 English 376 (2): Canadian Literature from 1960 English 376 (3): Canadian Literature from 1960 English 377: Canadian Drama English 475 (1): St. in Can. Prose: The Theoretical Analysis of Narrative English 475 (2): St. in Can. Prose English 478: Regional Lit. of Canada: West of Where? Contemp. Western Canadian Women's Cultural Work

Department	Comparative Literature Program, Department of Modern Languages and Comparative Studies
Province	Alberta
Year	1997–98
Total courses	21
Canadian literature courses	4
Canadian content	19.0%
Total sections	25
Canadian literature sections	4
Canadian content	16.0%
Different Canadian literature courses	4
Canadian literature required for major	no
Canadian literature required for honours or specialization	no
Professors interviewed	Blodgett, E.D.
Courses on the literatures of Canada offered in 1997–98	Comparative Lit. 171: Intro. to the Comp. Study of the Can. Literatures I Comparative Lit. 172: Intro. to the Comp. Study of the Can. Literatures II Comparative Lit. 372: Intro. to the Comp. Study of Can. Prose Comparative Lit. 472: Advanced Studies in Comparative Canadian Prose

Department	Department of English
Province	British Columbia
Year	1997–98
Total courses	45.5 FCE
Canadian literature courses	4.5 FCE
Canadian content	9.9%
Total sections	137.5 FCE
Canadian literature sections	13 FCE
Canadian content	9.5%
Different Canadian literature courses	8
Canadian literature required for major	no
Canadian literature required for honours or specialization	no
Professors interviewed	Cavell, Richard Fee, Margery Grace, Sherrill Hatch, R. Kroller, Eva-Marie New, W.H. Ricou, Laurie Wasserman, Jerry Weir, Lorraine
Courses on the literatures of Canada offered in 1997–98	English 202/001: Introduction to Canadian Literature English 202/003: Introduction to Canadian Literature English 202/004: Introduction to Canadian Literature English 202/005: Introduction to Canadian Literature English 202/006: Introduction to Canadian Literature English 202/007: Introduction to Canadian Literature English 202/701: Introduction to Canadian Literature English 360: Studies in Can. Lit.: Representations of the Indian English 420/001: Canadian Literature English 420/002: Canadian Literature

English 421: Canadian Poetry
English 423A: Canadian Drama
English 424/001: Canadian Novel
English 424/002: Canadian Novel
English 425/001: Canadian Short Fiction
English 425/002: Canadian Short Fiction
English 426B: Studies in Can. Lit.: Orality and
    Literacy in Canadian Cultural Studies
English 429B: Backgrounds of
    Canadian Literature

UNIVERSITY OF CALGARY

Department	Department of English
Province	Alberta
Year	1997–98
Total courses	49
Canadian literature courses	4
Canadian content	8.2%
Total sections	72
Canadian literature sections	4
Canadian content	5.6%
Different Canadian literature courses	4
Canadian literature required for major	no
Canadian literature required for honours or specialization	no
Professors interviewed	Buss, Helen Davis, R.C.
Courses on the literatures of Canada offered in 1997–98	English 370–01: Canadian Literature English 509.3: Studies in Can. Lit.: 19th-C. Can. Lit. in English English 509.4: Studies in Can. Lit.: M. Laurence and War

Department	Department of English Language and Lit.
Province	Ontario
Year	1997–98
Total courses	38
Canadian literature courses	6
Canadian content	15.8%
Total sections	64
Canadian literature sections	9
Canadian content	14.1%
Different Canadian literature courses	6
Canadian literature required for major	yes
Canadian literature required for honours or specialization	yes
Professors interviewed	Edwards, Mary Jane McDonald, Larry Padolsky, Enoch Ruffo, Armand Steele, James
Courses on the literatures of Canada offered in 1997–98	English 18.282A: Canadian Literature English 18.282B: Canadian Literature English 18.282C: Canadian Literature English 18.282D: Canadian Literature English 18.383A: Canadian Fiction English 18.482: Studies in Can. Ethnic Minority Lit. English 18.486A: Studies in Canadian Literature I English 18.487A: Studies in Canadian Literature II English 18.488: Can. Writing & the Lit. of the First Nations

Department	Department of English
Province	Québec
Year	1997–98
Total courses	37 FCE
Canadian literature courses	3 FCE
Canadian content	8.1%
Total sections	89.5 FCE
Canadian literature sections	6 FCE
Canadian content	6.7%
Different Canadian literature courses	5
Canadian literature required for major	no
Canadian literature required for honours or specialization	yes
Professors interviewed	Groening, Laura
Courses on the literatures of Canada offered in 1997–98	English 290/3 01: Canadian Literature: Survey
	English 290/3 A: Canadian Literature: Survey
	English 290/3 AA: Canadian Literature: Survey
	English 371/2 01: Postwar Canadian Fiction
	English 371/2 AA: Postwar Canadian Fiction
	English 372/4 01: Contemporary Canadian Fiction
	English 372/4 AA: Contemporary Canadian Fiction
	English 375/3 Modern Canadian Poetry and its Roots
	English 470J/4: Nation and Genre (Honours Seminar)

Department	Department of English
Province	Nova Scotia
Year	1997–98
Total courses	26
Canadian literature courses	2
Canadian content	7.7%
Total sections	26
Canadian literature sections	2
Canadian content	7.7%
Different Canadian literature courses	2
Canadian literature required for major	no
Canadian literature required for honours or specialization	no
Professors interviewed	Monk, Patricia Wainwright, A.
Courses on the literatures of Canada offered in 1997–98	English 4357R: Modern Canadian Literature English 2207R: Canadian Literature

Department	Département des littératures
Province	Québec
Year	1997–98
Total courses	35
Canadian literature courses	8
Canadian content	22.9%
Total sections	35
Canadian literature sections	8
Canadian content	22.9%
Different Canadian literature courses	8
Canadian literature required for major	yes
Canadian literature required for honours or specialization	n/a
Professors interviewed	Beaudet, Marie-Andrée Dumont, François Sabor, Peter Saint-Jacques, Denis
Courses on the literatures of Canada offered in 1997–98	FRN-10705: Roman, conte, et nouvelle du Québec (xxe siècle)—Jacques Poulin FRN-10706: Roman, conte, et nouvelle du Québec (xxe siècle)—L'image de l'autochtone dans le roman FRN-10716: Poésie et chanson du Québec (xxe siècle)—La chanson québécoise FRN-10717: Poésie et chanson du Québec (xxe siècle): La génération de l'Hexagone FRN-10729: Essai du Québec (xxe siècle)—L'essai depuis 1960 FRN-18633—Vie Littéraire du Québec (xixe siècle)—La littérature intime au xixe siècle FRN-18639: Littératures du Québec et de la France—La science-fiction en France et au Québec FRN-20492: Littérature québécoise de 1934 à nos jours

Department	Department of English
Province	Manitoba
Year	1997–98
Total courses	19 FCE
Canadian literature courses	3.5
Canadian content	18.4%
Total sections	46.5 FCE
Canadian literature sections	4 FCE
Canadian content	8.6%
Different Canadian literature courses	5
Canadian literature required for major	no
Canadian literature required for honours or specialization	no
Professors interviewed	Arnason, David
	Cooley, Dennis
	Johnson, Chris
	Lenoski, D.S.
	Neijmann, Daisy
Courses on the literatures of Canada offered in 1997–98	English 4.288 (A): Canadian Lit. pre-1967
	English 4.288 (B): Canadian Lit. pre-1967
	English 4.388: Prairie literature
	English 4.289: Canadian Lit. post-1967: "The Postmodern Novel in Canada"
	English 4.479: 20th-Century Short fiction: Cdn. stories in World Contexts
	English 4.290: Genre—Canadian Drama

Department	Department of English
Province	Québec
Year	1997–98
Total courses	36
Canadian literature courses	8
Canadian content	22.2%
Total sections	40
Canadian literature sections	8
Canadian content	20.0%
Different Canadian literature courses	8
Canadian literature required for major	yes
Canadian literature required for honours or specialization	yes
Professors interviewed	Lecker, Robert Rimstead, Roxanne Trehearne, Brian
Courses on the literatures of Canada offered in 1997–98	English 110–228A: Canadian Literature I English 110–229B: Canadian Literature II English 110–328D: The Development of Can. Poetry English 110–391B: Special Topics in Cultural St. (Autobiographies, Oral Histories, and Cultural Memory in Canada) English 110–410B: Studies in a Theme or Movement in Can. Lit. (Klein, Layton, Cohen) English 110–411B: Studies in Can. Fiction (Multicultural Fictions) English 110–414A: Studies in 20th C. Lit. I (Can. novel) English 110–460A: Studies in Lit. Theory (Native Voices and Images of Natives in Canada)

Department	Department of English
Province	Ontario
Year	1997–98
Total courses	54
Canadian literature courses	5
Canadian content	9.3%
Total sections	63
Canadian literature sections	7
Canadian content	11.1%
Different Canadian literature courses	5
Canadian literature required for major	no
Canadian literature required for honours or specialization	no
Professors interviewed	Coleman, Daniel King, James York, Lorraine
Courses on the literatures of Canada offered in 1997–98	English 4TF3: Timothy Findley and the Construction of Masculinities English 2K6/WS 2K6: Women and Literature: Contemporary African-Canadian Women Writers English 2G06A: Canadian Literature English 2G06B: Canadian Literature English 4GM3: Canadian Fictions of Gender and Migration English 4ML3: Margaret Laurence English 2G06C: Canadian Literature

Department	Department of English Language and Literature
Province	Newfoundland
Year	1997–98
Total courses	34
Canadian literature courses	5
Canadian content	14.7%
Total sections	42
Canadian literature sections	5
Canadian content	11.9%
Different Canadian literature courses	5
Canadian literature required for major	no
Canadian literature required for honours or specialization	yes
Professors interviewed	Balisch, L. Faith
	Golfman, Noreen
	Legge, Valerie
	Lynde, Denyse
	Mathews, Lawrence
	Wallace, Ronald
Courses on the literatures of Canada offered in 1997–98	English 2150: Modern Canadian Fiction
	English 2160: North American Native Literature
	English 3155: Newfoundland Literature
	English 3156: Modern Canadian Drama
	English 4821: Canadian Literature in Context I
	English 4822: Can. Lit. in Context II: The Politics of Culture/Identity and Canadian Literature: Ideologies, "Isms" and "Others"

Department	Département d'études françaises
Province	New Brunswick
Year	1997–98
Total courses	9 FCE
Canadian literature courses	3.5 FCE
Canadian content	38.9%
Total sections	9 FCE
Canadian literature sections	3.5 FCE
Canadian content	38.9%
Different Canadian literature courses	7
Canadian literature required for major	yes
Canadian literature required for honours or specialization	n/a
Professors interviewed	Boudreau, Raoul Morency, Jean
Courses on the literatures of Canada offered in 1997–98	FR 2291: Panorama de la littérature canadienne-française FR 2671: Folklore acadien I FR 3206: Essai québécois FR 3285: Théâtre et roman acadiens FR 3672: Folklore acadien II FR 4254: Roman québécois jusqu'en '39 FR 4263: Poésie québécoise de 1939 à nos jours

Department	Département d'études françaises
Province	Québec
Year	1997–98
Total courses	48
Canadian literature courses	12
Canadian content	25.0%
Total sections	48
Canadian literature sections	12
Canadian content	25.0%
Different Canadian literature courses	12
Canadian literature required for major	yes
Canadian literature required for honours or specialization	yes
Professors interviewed	Godin, Jean Cléo Nepveu, Pierre
Courses on the literatures of Canada offered in 1997–98	FRA 1602: Classiques de la poésie québécoise FRA 1603: Classiques du roman québécois FRA 1700D: La littérature québécoise depuis 1960 (télévisé) FRA 2604: Nouvelle et conte québécois FRA 2605: Écrits de la Nouvelle France FRA 2608: Poésie québécoise 1 (autour de Jacques Brault) FRA 2611: Roman québécois 1 (Réjean Ducharme) FRA 2614: Théâtre québécois FRA 2615: Questions de la littérature québécoise (Lectures de Saint-Denys Garneau) FRA 3024: Questions d'histoire littéraire (posées à la littérature québécoise) FRA 3823: Auteurs québécois 2 (Jacques Ferron) FRA 3861: Littérature du Québec: groupes culturels (L'écriture juive et l'espace montréalais)

Department	Department of English
Province	New Brunswick
Year	1997–98
Total courses	35
Canadian literature courses	1
Canadian content	2.9%
Total sections	n/a
Canadian literature sections	1
Canadian content	?
Different Canadian literature courses	1
Canadian literature required for major	no
Canadian literature required for honours or specialization	no
Professors interviewed	Steele, Tony
Courses on the literatures of Canada offered in 1997–98	English 3610: Canadian Prose and Poetry

Department	Department of English
Province	Ontario
Year	1997–98
Total courses	48
Canadian literature courses	5
Canadian content	10.4%
Total sections	65
Canadian literature sections	10
Canadian content	15.4%
Different Canadian literature courses	5
Canadian literature required for major	no
Canadian literature required for honours or specialization	yes
Professors interviewed	Hallett, David Lynch, Gerald Mayne, Seymour Staines, David
Courses on the literatures of Canada offered in 1997–98	English 2400A: Introduction to Canadian Literature English 2400B: Introduction to Canadian Literature English 2400C: Introduction to Canadian Literature English 2400D: Introduction to Canadian Literature English 3321A: The Canadian Short Story English 3386A: Canadian Fiction of the 20th Century to Mid-Century English 3387A: Canadian Fiction of the 20th Century Since Mid-Century English 4182: Seminar: "Jargoning City": A.M. Klein's Montreal and Its Poetic Solitudes English 3321B: Canadian Short Story English 3387B: Canadian Fiction of the 20th Century Since Mid-Century

Department	Department of English
Province	Prince Edward Island
Year	1997–98
Total courses	41
Canadian literature courses	2
Canadian content	4.9%
Total sections	n/a
Canadian literature sections	2
Canadian content	?
Different Canadian literature courses	2
Canadian literature required for major	no
Canadian literature required for honours or specialization	yes
Professors interviewed	Gammel, Irene Lemm, Richard MacLaine, Brent
Courses on the literatures of Canada offered in 1997–98	English 322: English-Canadian Poetry English 492: L.M. Montgomery

Department	Département d'études littéraires
Province	Québec
Year	1997–98
Total courses	76
Canadian literature courses	14
Canadian content	18.4%
Total sections	76
Canadian literature sections	14
Canadian content	18.4%
Different Canadian literature courses	14
Canadian literature required for major	yes
Canadian literature required for honours or specialization	n/a
Professors interviewed	Andrès, Bernard Robert, Lucie Roy, Max
Courses on the literatures of Canada offered in 1997–98	LIT 1035: Canadian Literature LIT 1060: Québec literature in English LIT 1605: Panorama de la littérature québécoise LIT 200A: Auteurs québécois en littérature de jeunesse LIT 252R: Corpus d'auteur: Jacques Brault LIT 3310: Essai québécois LIT 3412: Dramaturgie québécoise LIT 3430: Textes littéraires québécois et didactique LIT 351S: Séminaire: Naissance de l'écrivain québécois LIT 351V: Séminaire: Hubert Aquin ou l'écriture de l'inavouable LIT 3710: Écoles et mouvements littéraires au Québec LIT 4195: Chanson québécoise LIT 4230: Poésie québécoise LIT 4235: Poésie québécoise contemporaine

Department	Department of English Language and Literature
Province	Ontario
Year	1997–98
Total courses	39
Canadian literature courses	2
Canadian content	5.1%
Total sections	56
Canadian literature sections	3
Canadian content	5.4%
Different Canadian literature courses	2
Canadian literature required for major	no
Canadian literature required for honours or specialization	no
Professors interviewed	Soderlind, Sylvia Willmott, Glen
Courses on the literatures of Canada offered in 1997–98	English 283: Contemporary Canadian Literature English 380 (A): Literature and Culture in Canada English 380 (B): Literature and Culture in Canada

Department	Department of English
Province	Saskatchewan
Year	1997–98
Total courses	40
Canadian literature courses	5
Canadian content	12.5%
Total sections	43
Canadian literature sections	6
Canadian content	14.0%
Different Canadian literature courses	5
Canadian literature required for major	no
Canadian literature required for honours or specialization	no
Professors interviewed	Beddoes, Julie Denham, P. Zichy, F.
Courses on the literatures of Canada offered in 1997–98	English 251.6: Canadian Poetry in English English 253.6 (01): Canadian Literature in English English 253.6 (02): Canadian Literature in English English 259.3: Western Canadian Literature English 466.3: Topics in 20th Century Can. Lit.: The Canadian Short Story in English English 488.3: Topics in Genre and Contexts of Literature: Canadian Literature of Exploration

UNIVERSITÉ DE SHERBROOKE

Department	Département des lettres et communications
Province	Québec
Year	1997–98
Total courses	Data unavailable
Canadian literature courses	Data unavailable
Canadian content	Data unavailable
Total sections	Data unavailable
Canadian literature sections	Data unavailable
Canadian content	Data unavailable
Different Canadian literature courses	Data unavailable
Canadian literature required for major	yes
Canadian literature required for honours or specialization	yes
Professors interviewed	Giguere, Richard Reid, Greg Siemerling, Winfried Sutherland, Ronald
Courses on the literatures of Canada offered in 1997–98	None

Department	Department of English
Province	British Columbia
Year	1997–98
Total courses	56
Canadian literature courses	5
Canadian content	8.9%
Total sections	97
Canadian literature sections	8
Canadian content	8.2%
Different Canadian literature courses	5
Canadian literature required for major	yes
Canadian literature required for honours or specialization	yes
Professors interviewed	Bowering, George Gerson, Carole Miki, Roy St. Pierre, Paul Stouck, David
Courses on the literatures of Canada offered in 1997–98	English 354: Canadian Literature to 1920 English 357 (1): Canadian Literature Since 1920 English 357 (2): Canadian Literature Since 1920 English 359 (1): Literature of British Columbia English 359 (2): Literature of British Columbia English 360: Studies in Can. Lit.: Representations of the Indian English 360 (2): Studies in Canadian Literature English 394: World Lit. in English II: Contemporary Asian Canadian Cultural/ Textual Production

Department	Department of English
Province	Ontario
Year	1997–98
Total courses	67
Canadian literature courses	7
Canadian content	10.4%
Total sections	128 FCE
Canadian literature sections	9 FCE
Canadian content	7.0%
Different Canadian literature courses	8
Canadian literature required for major	yes
Canadian literature required for honours or specialization	yes
Professors interviewed	Brandeis, R. Brown, Russell Cullen, A. Duffy, Dennis Murray, Heather O'Connor, John Podnieks, Elizabeth Solecki, Sam
Courses on the literatures of Canada offered in 1997–98	English 215S: The Canadian Short Story English 216Y: 20th C Canadian Fiction L0101 English 216Y: 20th C Canadian Fiction L0201 English 216Y: 20th C Canadian Fiction L0301 English 216Y: 20th C Canadian Fiction L5101 English 252Y: Canadian Literature L0101 English 252Y: Canadian Literature L5101 English 350F: Early Canadian Literature English 350F: Topics in Canadian Literature English 430F: Studies in a Canadian Writer L0101 English 431S: Studies in a Canadian Writer L5101 English 431S: Studies in a Canadian Writer L5101 (Michael Ondaatje)

Department	Department of English
Province	British Columbia
Year	1997–98
Total courses	36.5 FCE
Canadian literature courses	5.5 FCE
Canadian content	15.1%
Total sections	54 FCE
Canadian literature sections	5.5 FCE
Canadian content	10.2%
Different Canadian literature courses	9
Canadian literature required for major	yes
Canadian literature required for honours or specialization	yes
Professors interviewed	Scobie, Stephen Smith, Nelson Vautier, Marie
Courses on the literatures of Canada offered in 1997–98	English 202 (UVIC): An Introduction to Canadian Literature English 448: Special Studies in Can. Lit.: Contemp. Can. Drama English 450: Modern Canadian Fiction: I English 451: Modern Canadian Fiction: II English 452: Modern Canadian Poetry: I English 453: Modern Canadian Poetry: II English 457: Traditions in Canadian Literature English 458/French 487: Comparative Studies in French and Engl. Can. Lit. English 459: Early Canadian Prose Literature

Department	Department of English
Province	Ontario
Year	1997–98
Total courses	64
Canadian literature courses	8
Canadian content	12.5%
Total sections	n/a
Canadian literature sections	11
Canadian content	?
Different Canadian literature courses	8
Canadian literature required for major	no
Canadian literature required for honours or specialization	no
Professors interviewed	Bentley, D.M.R.
	Davey, Frank
	Dragland, Stan
	Hair, D.S.
	Tausky, Tom
	Zezulka, J.
Courses on the literatures of Canada offered in 1997–98	English 274E (1): Canadian Literature
	English 160E: Contemporary Canadian Literature
	English 274E (2): Canadian Literature
	English 474F: Canadian Gothic
	English 274E (3): Canadian Literature
	English 296G: First Nations Theatre
	English 287G: Canadian Drama
	English 475F: Jung & the Fiction of Robertson Davies
	English 475G: Cultural Memory in Canada, 1759–1997
	English 476G: Archetypal Patterns in the Fiction of Margaret Atwood
	English 274E (4): Canadian Literature

Department	Department of English
Province	Manitoba
Year	1997–98
Total courses	30
Canadian literature courses	4
Canadian content	13.3%
Total sections	47
Canadian literature sections	6
Canadian content	12.8%
Different Canadian literature courses	4
Canadian literature required for major	no
Canadian literature required for honours or specialization	yes
Professors interviewed	Besner, Neil Jewison, Don
Courses on the literatures of Canada offered in 1997–98	English 17.3713: Contexts in Canadian Literature English 17.4712: Topics in Canadian Literature English 17.2116/001: Canadian Children's Literature English 17.2116/002: Canadian Children's Literature English 17.2116/003: Canadian Children's Literature English 17.4341: Individual Author I: Jane Rule

Department	Department of English
Province	Ontario
Year	1997–98
Total courses	74
Canadian literature courses	9
Canadian content	12.2%
Total sections	84
Canadian literature sections	9
Canadian content	10.7%
Different Canadian literature courses	9
Canadian literature required for major	no
Canadian literature required for honours or specialization	no
Professors interviewed	Early, Len
	Goldie, Terry
	Hopkins, Elizabeth
	Lennox, John
	Thomas, Clara
	Zeifman, Hersh
Courses on the literatures of Canada offered in 1997–98	English 2450: Canadian Literature
	English 3160A: Canadian Drama
	English 3340: Modern Canadian Fiction
	English 3350: Modern Canadian Poetry
	English 4270A: The Canadian Short Story
	English 4270B: Beginnings of Canadian Literature
	English 3430A: Studies in Women Writers: Cdn. Women Writers
	English 3440: Post-Colonial Writing in Canada
	English 4270C: Studies in Can. Lit.: Poetry

Appendix 2

Texts Taught in English and Comparative Literature Courses on the
Literatures of Canada in 1997–98 (Ranked by Frequency)

Title	Author	Occurrences
As For Me and My House	Ross, Sinclair	20
Sunshine Sketches of a Little Town	Leacock, Stephen	20
Anthology of Canadian Literature in English (1 vol.)	Bennett, Donna, and Russell Brown (eds.)	20
Wacousta	Richardson, John	16
Green Grass, Running Water	King, Thomas	16
Roughing it in the Bush	Moodie, Susanna	15
Obasan	Kogawa, Joy	15
In the Skin of a Lion	Ondaatje, Michael	15
The Diviners	Laurence, Margaret	14
The Imperialist	Duncan, Sara Jeannette	14
15 Canadian Poets x 2	Geddes, Gary (ed.)	14
The English Patient	Ondaatje, Michael	13
Coursepack of other photocopied readings		13
The Double Hook	Watson, Sheila	12
Fifth Business	Davies, Robertson	11
The Mountain and the Valley	Buckler, Ernest	10
The Handmaid's Tale	Atwood, Margaret	10
Dry Lips Oughta Move to Kapuskasing	Highway, Tomson	10
The Stone Angel	Laurence, Margaret	9
Surfacing	Atwood, Margaret	9

Title	Author	Occurrences
Lives of Girls and Women	Munro, Alice	9
Tay John	O'Hagan, Howard	9
The Rez Sisters	Tomson Highway	8
Settlers of the Marsh	Grove, Frederick Philip	8
The Journals of Susanna Moodie	Atwood, Margaret	8
Disappearing Moon Café	Lee, Sky	8
Canadian Poetry From the Beginnings through the First World War	Gerson, Carole, and Gwendolyn Davies (eds.)	8
A Strange Manuscript Found in a Copper Cylinder	De Mille, James	7
Who Do You Think You Are?	Munro, Alice	7
The Wars	Findley, Timothy	7
Famous Last Words	Findley, Timothy	7
Not Wanted on the Voyage	Findley, Timothy	7
Lady Oracle	Atwood, Margaret	7
The Clockmaker	Haliburton, T.C.	6
La Guerre, Yes Sir!	Carrier, Roch	6
Ana Historic	Marlatt, Daphne	6
Arcadian Adventures with the Idle Rich	Leacock, Stephen	6
Swamp Angel	Wilson, Ethel	6
Wild Geese	Ostenso, Martha	6
A Jest of God	Laurence, Margaret	6
The Fire-Dwellers	Laurence, Margaret	6
The Studhorse Man	Kroetsch, Robert	6
The Stone Diaries	Shields, Carol	6
The Collected Works of Billy the Kid	Ondaatje, Michael	5
The Sacrifice	Wiseman, Adele	5
The Watch that Ends the Night	MacLennan, Hugh	5
The Tin Flute	Roy, Gabrielle	5
Medicine River	King, Thomas	5
Coming Through Slaughter	Ondaatje, Michael	5
Solomon Gursky Was Here	Richler, Mordecai	5
Wilderness Tips	Atwood, Margaret	5
Who Has Seen the Wind	Mitchell, W.O.	4
The History of Emily Montague	Brooke, Frances	4
Pélagie	Maillet, Antonine	4

Title	Author	Occurrences
Canadian Short Fiction	New, W.H. (ed.)	4
Anne of Green Gables	Montgomery, L.M.	4
A Bird in the House	Laurence, Margaret	4
The Englishman's Boy	Vanderhaeghe, Guy	4
Malcolm's Katie	Crawford, Isabella Valancy	4
A Mixture of Frailties	Davies, Robertson	4
Such is My Beloved	Callaghan, Morley	4
Halfbreed	Campbell, Maria	4
Barometer Rising	MacLennan, Hugh	4
Canadian Poetry (2 vols.)	Lecker, Robert, and Jack David (eds.)	4
Beautiful Losers	Cohen, Leonard	4
The Second Scroll	Klein, A.M.	4
Making a Difference: Canadian Multicultural Literature	Kamboureli, Smaro	4
Improved by Cultivation: English Canadian Prose to 1914	Moyles, R.G.	4
The Jade Peony	Choy, Wayson	4
The Book of Jessica	Griffiths, L., and M. Campbell	4
Running in the Family	Ondaatje, Michael	3
Les Belles Soeurs	Tremblay, Michel	3
Blood Relations	Pollock, Sharon	3
Goodnight Desdemona (Good Morning Juliet)	MacDonald, Ann-Marie	3
Antoinette de Mirecourt	Leprohon, Rosanna	3
Alias Grace	Atwood, Margaret	3
Two Solitudes	MacLennan, Hugh	3
Away	Urquhart, Jane	3
The Loved and the Lost	Callaghan, Morley	3
Mauve Desert	Brossard, Nicole	3
A Discovery of Strangers	Wiebe, Rudy	3
Funny Boy	Selvadurai, Shyam	3
The Lamp at Noon and Other Stories	Ross, Sinclair	3
Bear	Engel, Marian	3
What's Bred in the Bone	Davies, Robertson	3
The Apprenticeship of Duddy Kravitz	Richler, Mordecai	3

Title	Author	Occurrences
Looking for Livingstone: An Odyssey of Silence	Philip, Marlene Nourbese	3
In Another Place, Not Here	Brand, Dionne	3
The Luck of Ginger Coffey	Moore, Brian	3
The Man From Glengarry	Connor, Ralph	3
The Afterlife of George Carwright	Steffler, John	3
The Invention of the World	Hodgins, Jack	3
St. Urbain's Horseman	Richler, Mordecai	3
No New Land	Vassanji, M.G.	3
Badlands	Kroetsch, Robert	3
Chorus of Mushrooms	Goto, Hiromi	3
Write It On Your Heart	Robinson, Harry	3
In Search of April Raintree	Culleton, Beatrice	3
Bear Bones and Feathers	Halfe, Louise Bernice	3
Generals Die in Bed	Harrison, Charles Yale	3
Leaven of Malice	Davies, Robertson	3
An Anthology of Canadian Native Literature in English	Moses, Daniel David, and Terry Goldie (eds.)	3
Under the Volcano	Lowry, Malcolm	3
The Ecstasy of Rita Joe	Ryga, George	2
The Edible Woman	Atwood, Margaret	2
Riot	Moodie, Andrew	2
Poor Super Man	Fraser, Brad	2
The Backwoods of Canada	Traill, Catharine Parr	2
Canadian Crusoes	Traill, Catharine Parr	2
They Shall Inherit the Earth	Callaghan, Morley	2
Thirty Acres	Ringuet	2
Kamouraska	Hébert, Anne	2
Swann	Shields, Carol	2
In the Village of Viger and Other Stories	Scott, Duncan Campbell	2
Home Truths: Selected Canadian Stories	Gallant, Mavis	2
Open Secrets	Munro, Alice	2
Anthology of Canadian Literature in English (2 vols.)	Bennett, Donna, and Russell Brown (eds.)	2
The Temptations of Big Bear	Wiebe, Rudy	2
Fugitive Pieces	Michaels, Anne	2

Title	Author	Occurrences
She Tries Her Tongue, Her Silence Softly Breaks	Philip, Marlene Nourbese	2
Van de Graaff Days	Begamudré, Ven	2
Fortune, My Foe	Davies, Robertson	2
Emily of New Moon	Montgomery, L.M.	2
Friend of My Youth	Munro, Alice	2
This Side Jordan	Laurence, Margaret	2
The Tomorrow-Tamer	Laurence, Margaret	2
Arctic Dreams and Nightmares	Ipellie, Alootook	2
Stranger Music: Selected Poems and Songs	Cohen, Leonard	2
Execution	McDougall, Colin	2
The Lost Salt Gift of Blood	MacLeod, Alistair	2
Cat's Eye	Atwood, Margaret	2
The Colonial Century: English-Canadian Writing Before Confederation	Smith, A.J.M. (ed.)	2
Cabbagetown	Garner, Hugh	2
Bodily Harm	Atwood, Margaret	2
Confessions of an Immigrant's Daughter	Salverson, Laura Goodman	2
Sojourner's Truth	Maracle, Lee	2
Food and Spirits	Brant, Beth	2
Princess Pocahontas and the Blue Spots	Mojica, Monique	2
Whylah Falls	Clarke, George Elliott	2
Ravensong	Maracle, Lee	2
The Scorched-Wood People	Wiebe, Rudy	2
The Engineer of Human Souls	Škvorecký, Josef	2
The Manticore	Davies, Robertson	2
World of Wonders	Davies, Robertson	2
Rebel Angels	Davies, Robertson	2
Poets Between the Wars	Wilson, Milton (ed.)	2
Man Descending	Vanderhaeghe, Guy	2
We So Seldom Look on Love	Gowdy, Barbara	2
Modern Canadian Plays (vol. 1)	Wasserman, Jerry (ed.)	2
The Fat Woman Next Door is Pregnant	Tremblay, Michel	2
Klee Wyck	Carr, Emily	2
Mrs. Golightly and Other Stories	Wilson, Ethel	2
Ghost in the Wheels	Birney, Earle	2

Title	Author	Occurrences
Canadian Poetry: Volume One	David, Jack, and Robert Lecker (eds.)	2
The Medium is the Massage	McLuhan, Marshall, and Quentin Fiore	2
Technology and the Canadian Mind	Kroker, Arthur	2
Hamlet's Twin	Aquin, Hubert	2
Ink and Strawberries: An Anthology of Quebec Women's Fiction	Daurio, Beverley, and Louise von Flotow (eds.)	2
Generation X: Tales for an Accelerated Culture	Coupland, Douglas	2
Burning Water	Bowering, George	2
The Cure for Death by Lightning	Anderson-Dargatz, Gail	2
Balconville	Fennario, David	2
Quiet in the Land	Chislett, Anne	1
Fronteras Americanas	Verdecchia, Guillermo	1
1837: The Farmers' Revolt	Salutin, Rick, and Theatre Passe Muraille	1
Under the Skin	Lambert, Betty	1
Little Sister	MacLeod, Joan	1
The Soldier Dreams	MacIvor, Daniel	1
Creeps	Freeman, David	1
Lion in the Streets	Thompson, Judith	1
Love and Anger	Walker, George F.	1
Life in the Clearings	Moodie, Susanna	1
Voyages: Short Narratives of Susanna Moodie	Moodie, Susanna	1
Forest and Other Gleanings: The Fugitive Writings of Catharine Parr Traill	Traill, Catharine Parr	1
The Golden Dog	Kirby, William	1
Fruits of the Earth	Grove, Frederick Philip	1
A Dream Like Mine	Kelly, M.T.	1
Where Nests the Water Hen	Roy, Gabrielle	1
The Moons of Jupiter	Munro, Alice	1
The New Long Poem Anthology	Thesen, Sharon (ed.)	1
Other Selves	Minni, C.D.	1
Sans Souci and Other Stories	Brand, Dionne	1
Morley Callaghan's Stories	Callaghan, Morley	1

Title	Author	Occurrences
Joshua Then and Now	Richler, Mordecai	1
Book of Secrets	Vassanji, M.G.	1
Fables From the Women's Quarters	Harris, Claire	1
Drawing Down a Daughter	Harris, Claire	1
Dipped in Shadow	Harris, Claire	1
Borrowed Beauty	Tynes, Maxine	1
Woman Talking Woman	Tynes, Maxine	1
The Door of My Heart	Tynes, Maxine	1
Women Do This Every Day: Selected Poems of Lillian Allen	Allen, Lillian	1
Black Girl Talk	The Black Girl Talk Collective	1
Harriet's Daughter	Philip, Marlene Nourbese	1
Martha and Elvira: A One-Act Play	Braithwaite, Diana	1
No Language is Neutral	Brand, Dionne	1
Earth Day Magic	Brand, Dionne	1
The Last of the Crazy People	Findley, Timothy	1
The Butterfly Plague	Findley, Timothy	1
Stones	Findley, Timothy	1
Headhunter	Findley, Timothy	1
You Went Away	Findley, Timothy	1
The Origin of Waves	Clarke, Austin	1
The Prowler	Gunnars, Kristjana	1
Caprice	Bowering, George	1
Slash	Armstrong, Jeannette	1
Casino and Other Stories	Burnard, Bonnie	1
Poems Twice Told: The Boatman and Welcoming Disaster	Macpherson, Jay	1
The Donnellys	Reaney, James	1
Winter Studies and Summer Rambles	Jameson, Anna	1
My Present Age	Vanderhaeghe, Guy	1
Time as History	Grant, George	1
Legends of Vancouver	Johnson, Pauline	1
Tecumseh	Mair, Charles	1
Technology and Empire	Grant, George	1
Essential McLuhan	McLuhan, Eric, and Frank Zingrone (eds.)	1

Title	Author	Occurrences
Cambodia	Fawcett, Brian	1
Kyotopolis	Moses, Daniel David	1
An H in the Heart	Nichol, bp	1
Canadian Anthology	Klinck, C.F., and R.E. Watters	1
Return of the Sphinx	MacLennan, Hugh	1
Oxford Book of Canadian Short Stories in English	Atwood, Margaret, and Robert Weaver (eds.)	1
Selected Poems	Klein, A.M.	1
A Search for America	Grove, Frederick Philip	1
Equations of Love	Wilson, Ethel	1
A Wild and Peculiar Joy: Selected Poems 1945–89	Layton, Irving	1
Walsh	Pollock, Sharon	1
The Book of Small	Carr, Emily	1
The Whirlpool	Urquhart, Jane	1
Canadian Brothers	Richardson, John	1
Jalna	De La Roche, Mazo	1
The Black Madonna	Paci, F.G.	1
Other Solitudes: Canadian Multicultural Fiction	Hutcheon, Linda, and Marion Richmond (eds.)	1
All My Relations	King, Thomas	1
Riverrun	Such, Peter	1
Stories by Canadian Women	Sullivan, Rosemary	1
Intertidal Life	Thomas, Audrey	1
The Canadian Postmodern	Hutcheon, Linda	1
Fire on the Water: An Anthology of Black Nova Scotian Writing	Clarke, George Elliott	1
In This City	Clarke, Austin	1
Some Great Thing	Hill, Lawrence	1
The Betrayal	Kreisel, Henry	1
Yellow Boots	Lysenko, Vera	1
Geography of Voice: Canadian Literature of the South Asian Diaspora	McGifford, Diane (ed.)	1
In a Glass House	Ricci, Nino	1
The Salvation of Yasch Siemens	Wiebe, Armin	1
House of Hate	Janes, Percy	1
Story of Bobby O'Malley	Johnston, Wayne	1

Title	Author	Occurrences
For Those Who Hunt the Wounded Down	Richards, David Adams	1
Fall on Your Knees	MacDonald, Ann-Marie	1
The Book of Eve	Beresford-Howe, Constance	1
The Marriage Bed	Beresford-Howe, Constance	1
Night Studies	Beresford-Howe, Constance	1
Prospero's Daughter	Beresford-Howe, Constance	1
A Serious Widow	Beresford-Howe, Constance	1
The Constance Beresford-Howe Papers	Steele, Appolonia (ed.)	1
Sacred Legends	Ray, Carl, and James Stevens (eds.)	1
Someday	Taylor, Drew Hayden	1
Keeper'n Me	Wagamese, Richard	1
Breath Tracks	Armstrong, Jeannette	1
Native Canadiana	Scofield, Gregory	1
A Season in the Life of Emmanuel	Blais, Marie-Claire	1
Rockbound	Day, Frank Parker	1
Great Canadian Animal Stories	Whitaker, Muriel	1
Magic for Marigold	Montgomery, L.M.	1
Waiting for the Whales	McFarlane, Sheryl	1
Eating Between the Lines	Major, Kevin	1
Oliver's Wars	Wilson, Budge	1
Stranger at Bay	Aker, Don	1
Jonathan Cleaned Up and Then He Heard a Sound	Munsch, Robert	1
Anne's House of Dreams	Montgomery, L.M.	1
Rilla of Ingleside	Montgomery, L.M.	1
Anne of Ingleside	Montgomery, L.M.	1
The Blue Castle	Montgomery, L.M.	1
Jane of Lantern Hill	Montgomery, L.M.	1
The Fragrance of Sweet-Grass: L.M. Montgomery's Heroines and the Pursuit of Romance	Epperly, Elizabeth	1
Harvesting Thistles: The Textual Garden of L.M. Montgomery, Essays on Her Novels and Journals	Rubio, Mary	1
Such a Long Journey	Mistry, Rohinton	1
Pale as Real Ladies: Poems for Pauline Johnson	Crate, Joan	1

Title	Author	Occurrences
The New Oxford Book of Canadian Verse in English	Atwood, Margaret (ed.)	1
Blood Ties	Richards, David Adams	1
Mister Sandman	Gowdy, Barbara	1
Sticks and Stones	Reaney, James	1
Wild Animals I Have Known	Seton, E.T.	1
Rooms for Rent in the Outer Planets	Purdy, Al	1
Brébeuf and His Brethren	Pratt, E.J.	1
Towards the Last Spike	Pratt, E.J.	1
Dance on the Earth	Laurence, Margaret	1
Fortune, My Foe and Eros at Breakfast	Davies, Robertson	1
Tempest-Tost	Davies, Robertson	1
The Cinnamon Peeler: Selected Poems	Ondaatje, Michael	1
Canadian Culture: An Introductory Reader	Cameron, Elspeth	1
New Contexts of Canadian Criticism	Heble, Ajay, Donna Palmateer Penee, and J.R. (Tim) Struthers (eds.)	1
Inspecting the Vaults	McCormack, Eric	1
From the Fifteenth District	Gallant, Mavis	1
Inscriptions	Cooley, Dennis (ed.)	1
A/long Prairie Lines	Lenoski, Daniel (ed.)	1
Fox	Sweatman, Margaret	1
The Trouble with Heroes	Vanderhaeghe, Guy	1
Nineteenth Century Canadian Stories	Arnason, David (ed.)	1
Under the Ribs of Death	Marlyn, John	1
By Grand Central Station I Sat Down and Wept	Smart, Elizabeth	1
Crackpot	Wiseman, Adele	1
The Quebec Anthology (1830–1990)	Cohen, Matt, and Wayne Grady (eds.)	1
Tamarind Mem	Rau Badami, Anita	1
In the Shadow of the Wind	Hébert, Anne	1
The Gutenberg Galaxy	McLuhan, Marshall	1
Maps and Dreams	Brody, Hugh	1
The Yellow Pages	Markotic, Nicole	1
Playing Dead: A Contemplation Concerning the Arctic	Wiebe, Rudy	1

Title	Author	Occurrences
Zoom Away	Wynne-Jones, Tim	1
The Only Snow in Havana	Hay, Elizabeth	1
Harpoon of the Hunter	Markoosie	1
The Occupation of Wendy Rose	Lill, Wendy	1
Modern Canadian Plays (Vol. 2)	Wasserman, Jerry (ed.)	1
7 Stories	Panych, Morris	1
2000	MacLeod, Joan	1
The Stepsure Letters	McCulloch, T.	1
E.J. Pratt: Selected Poems	Pratt, E.J.	1
The Glass Air: Selected Poems	Page, P.K.	1
Word of Mouth	Farrant, M.A.C.	1
Daughters of Copper Woman	Cameron, Ann	1
Dance Me Outside	Kinsella, W.P.	1
Many-Mouthed Birds: Contemporary Writing by Chinese Canadians	Lee, Bennet, and Jim Wong-Chu (eds.)	1
No More Watno Dur	Binning, Sadhu	1
Diamond Grill	Wah, Fred	1
Vancouver Short Stories	Gerson, Carole (ed.)	1
The Rain Barrel	Bowering, George	1
Completed Field Notes	Kroetsch, Robert	1
Salvage	Marlatt, Daphne	1
This is For You, Anna	The Anna Project	1
Rumours of Our Death	Walker, George F.	1
The Saga of the Wet Hens	Marchessault, Jovette	1
Polygraph	Lepage, Robert, and M. Brassard	1
Ever Loving	Hollingsworth, Margaret	1
Diving	Hollingsworth, Margaret	1
Canadian Short Stories: Fifth Series	Weaver, Robert (ed.)	1
Nights Below Station Street	Richards, David Adams	1
The Vision Tree: Selected Poems	Webb, Phyllis	1
Aurora	Thesen, Sharon	1
Aqueduct	Shikatanti, Gerry	1
The Martyrology: Books 1 and 2	Nichol, bp	1
Frog Moon	Tostevin, Lola Lemire	1
The Russian Album	Ignatieff, Michael	1

Title	Author	Occurrences
The Mechanical Bride: Folklore of Industrial Man	McLuhan, Marshall	1
Iroquois Fires	Dawendine [Bernice Loft Winslow]	1
Anatomy of Criticism	Frye, Northrop	1
To Master, A Long Goodnight	Gysin, Brion	1
Plague of the Gorgeous and Other Tales	Armstrong, Gordon, et al.	1
The Indian Medicine Shows	Moses, Daniel David	1
Blade, Job's Wife, and Video: 3 Plays	Nolan, Yvette	1
Doc	Pollock, Sharon	1
Mother Tongue	Quan, Betty	1
Afrika Solo	Sears, Djanet	1
The Bootlegger Blues	Taylor, Drew Hayden	1
The Other Side of the Dark	Thompson, Judith	1
Don't: A Woman's Word	Danica, Elly	1
A Really Good Brown Girl	Dumont, Marilyn	1
Zero Hour	Gunnars, Kristjana	1
The First Garden	Hébert, Anne	1
Amnesia	Cooper, Douglas	1
Ricordi: Things Remembered. An Anthology of Short Stories	Minni, C.D.	1
The Substance of Forgetting	Gunnars, Kristjana	1
Over Prairie Trails	Grove, Frederick Philip	1
Peckertracks	Dragland, Stan	1
Murder in the Dark	Atwood, Margaret	1
Uhuru Street	Vassanji, M.G.	1
Aspiring Women: Short Stories by Canadian Women, 1880–1990	McMullen, Lorraine, and Sandra Campbell (eds.)	1
As Birds Bring Forth the Sun	MacLeod, Alistair	1
Things as They Are?	Vanderhaeghe, Guy	1
The Moslem Wife and Other Stories	Gallant, Mavis	1
Six Canadian Plays	Hamill, Tony (ed.)	1
Places Far From Ellesmere	Van Herk, Aritha	1
The Green Library	Kulyk-Keefer, Janice	1
Krekshuns	Bolen, Dennis	1
Antiphonary	Aquin, Hubert	1
No Man in the House	Foster, Cecil	1

232   **Appendix 2**

Title	Author	Occurrences
Son of a Smaller Hero	Richler, Mordecai	1
The Innocent Traveller	Wilson, Ethel	1
The Robber Bride	Atwood, Margaret	1
Canadian Exploration Literature	Warkentin, Germaine (ed.)	1
Sketches of Upper Canada	Howison, John	1
Troutstream	Lynch, Gerald	1
Civil Elegies	Lee, Dennis	1
Selected Stories of E.W. Thompson	Thompson, E.W.	1
Keep That Candle Burning Bright	Wallace, Bronwen	1
readings on library reserve		1
Lives of the Saints	Ricci, Nino	1
The Lyre of Orpheus	Davies, Robertson	1
The Cunning Man	Davies, Robertson	1
The Nymph and the Lamp	Raddall, Thomas H.	1
The Incomparable Atuk	Richler, Mordecai	1
The Work of Margaret Laurence	Sorfleet, J. (ed.)	1
The Blue Mountains of China	Wiebe, Rudy	1
Quebec Fiction: The English Fact	Sorfleet, J. (ed.)	1
The Poems of Bliss Carman	Sorfleet, J. (ed.)	1
Selected Poetry of Duncan Campbell Scott	Scott, Duncan Campbell	1
Selected Poems by Margaret Avison	Avison, Margaret	1
An Exchange of Gifts: Poems New and Selected	Nowlan, Alden	1
The Circle Game	Atwood, Margaret	1
Desert of the Heart	Rule, Jane	1
After the Fire	Rule, Jane	1
Against the Season	Rule, Jane	1
Memory Board	Rule, Jane	1
This is Not For You	Rule, Jane	1
The Young in One Another's Arms	Rule, Jane	1
Inland Passage	Rule, Jane	1

Appendix 3

Texts Taught in English and Comparative Literature Courses on the
Literatures of Canada in 1997–98 (Sorted by Author)

Author	Title	Occurrences
Aker, Don	Stranger at Bay	1
Allen, Lillian	Women Do This Every Day: Selected Poems of Lillian Allen	1
Anderson-Dargatz, Gail	The Cure for Death by Lightning	2
The Anna Project	This is For You, Anna	1
Aquin, Hubert	Antiphonary	1
Aquin, Hubert	Hamlet's Twin	2
Armstrong, Gordon, et al.	Plague of the Gorgeous and Other Tales	1
Armstrong, Jeannette	Slash	1
Armstrong, Jeannette	Breath Tracks	1
Arnason, David (ed.)	Nineteenth Century Canadian Stories	1
Atwood, Margaret	Alias Grace	3
Atwood, Margaret	Bodily Harm	2
Atwood, Margaret	Cat's Eye	2
Atwood, Margaret	The Circle Game	1
Atwood, Margaret	The Edible Woman	2
Atwood, Margaret	The Handmaid's Tale	10
Atwood, Margaret	The Journals of Susanna Moodie	8
Atwood, Margaret	Lady Oracle	7
Atwood, Margaret	Murder in the Dark	1
Atwood, Margaret	The Robber Bride	1
Atwood, Margaret	Surfacing	9

Author	Title	Occurrences
Atwood, Margaret	*Wilderness Tips*	5
Atwood, Margaret (ed.)	*The New Oxford Book of Canadian Verse in English*	1
Atwood, Margaret, and Robert Weaver (eds.)	*Oxford Book of Canadian Short Stories in English*	1
Avison, Margaret	*Selected Poems by Margaret Avison*	1
Begamudré, Ven	*Van de Graaff Days*	2
Beresford-Howe, Constance	*The Book of Eve*	1
Beresford-Howe, Constance	*The Marriage Bed*	1
Beresford-Howe, Constance	*Night Studies*	1
Beresford-Howe, Constance	*Prospero's Daughter*	1
Beresford-Howe, Constance	*A Serious Widow*	1
Binning, Sadhu	*No More Watno Dur*	1
Birney, Earle	*Ghost in the Wheels*	2
The Black Girl Talk Collective	*Black Girl Talk*	1
Blais, Marie-Claire	*A Season in the Life of Emmanuel*	1
Bolen, Dennis	*Krekshuns*	1
Bowering, George	*Burning Water*	2
Bowering, George	*Caprice*	1
Bowering, George	*The Rain Barrel*	1
Braithwaite, Diana	*Martha and Elvira: A One-Act Play*	1
Brand, Dionne	*Earth Day Magic*	1
Brand, Dionne	*In Another Place, Not Here*	3
Brand, Dionne	*No Language is Neutral*	1
Brand, Dionne	*Sans Souci and Other Stories*	1
Brant, Beth	*Food and Spirits*	2
Brody, Hugh	*Maps and Dreams*	1
Brooke, Frances	*The History of Emily Montague*	4
Brossard, Nicole	*Mauve Desert*	3
Brown, Russell, Donna Bennett, and Nathalie Cooke (eds.)	*Anthology of Canadian Literature in English* (1 vol.)	20
Brown, Russell, Donna Bennett, and Nathalie Cooke (eds.)	*Anthology of Canadian Literature in English* (2 vols.)	2
Buckler, Ernest	*The Mountain and the Valley*	10
Burnard, Bonnie	*Casino and Other Stories*	1

Author	Title	Occurrences
Callaghan, Morley	*The Loved and the Lost*	3
Callaghan, Morley	*Morley Callaghan's Stories*	1
Callaghan, Morley	*Such is My Beloved*	4
Callaghan, Morley	*They Shall Inherit the Earth*	2
Cameron, Ann	*Daughters of Copper Woman*	1
Cameron, Elspeth	*Canadian Culture: An Introductory Reader*	1
Campbell, Maria	*Halfbreed*	4
Carr, Emily	*The Book of Small*	1
Carr, Emily	*Klee Wyck*	2
Carrier, Roch	*La Guerre, Yes Sir!*	6
Chislett, Anne	*Quiet in the Land*	1
Choy, Wayson	*The Jade Peony*	4
Clarke, Austin	*In This City*	1
Clarke, Austin	*The Origin of Waves*	1
Clarke, George Elliott	*Fire on the Water: An Anthology of Black Nova Scotian Writing*	1
Clarke, George Elliott	*Whylah Falls*	2
Cohen, Leonard	*Beautiful Losers*	4
Cohen, Leonard	*Stranger Music: Selected Poems and Songs*	2
Cohen, Matt, and Wayne Grady (eds.)	*The Quebec Anthology (1830–1990)*	1
Connor, Ralph	*The Man From Glengarry*	3
Cooley, Dennis (ed.)	*Inscriptions*	1
Cooper, Douglas	*Amnesia*	1
Coupland, Douglas	*Generation X: Tales for an Accelerated Culture*	2
Crate, Joan	*Pale as Real Ladies: Poems for Pauline Johnson*	1
Crawford, Isabella Valancy	*Malcolm's Katie*	4
Culleton, Beatrice	*In Search of April Raintree*	3
Danica, Elly	*Don't: A Woman's Word*	1
Daurio, Beverley, and Louise von Flotow (eds.)	*Ink and Strawberries: An Anthology of Quebec Women's Fiction*	2
David, Jack, and Robert Lecker (eds.)	*Canadian Poetry: Volume One*	2
Davies, Robertson	*The Cunning Man*	1

Author	Title	Occurrences
Davies, Robertson	Fifth Business	11
Davies, Robertson	Fortune, My Foe and Eros at Breakfast	1
Davies, Robertson	Fortune, My Foe	2
Davies, Robertson	Leaven of Malice	3
Davies, Robertson	The Lyre of Orpheus	1
Davies, Robertson	The Manticore	2
Davies, Robertson	A Mixture of Frailties	4
Davies, Robertson	Rebel Angels	2
Davies, Robertson	Tempest-Tost	1
Davies, Robertson	What's Bred in the Bone	3
Davies, Robertson	World of Wonders	2
Dawendine [Bernice Loft Winslow]	Iroquois Fires	1
Day, Frank Parker	Rockbound	1
De La Roche, Mazo	Jalna	1
De Mille, James	A Strange Manuscript Found in a Copper Cylinder	7
Dragland, Stan	Peckertracks	1
Dumont, Marilyn	A Really Good Brown Girl	1
Duncan, Sara Jeannette	The Imperialist	14
Engel, Marian	Bear	3
Epperly, Elizabeth	The Fragrance of Sweet-Grass: L.M. Montgomery's Heroines and the Pursuit of Romance	1
Farrant, M.A.C.	Word of Mouth	1
Fawcett, Brian	Cambodia	1
Fennario, David	Balconville	2
Findley, Timothy	The Butterfly Plague	1
Findley, Timothy	Famous Last Words	7
Findley, Timothy	Headhunter	1
Findley, Timothy	The Last of the Crazy People	1
Findley, Timothy	Not Wanted on the Voyage	7
Findley, Timothy	Stones	1
Findley, Timothy	The Wars	7
Findley, Timothy	You Went Away	1
Foster, Cecil	No Man in the House	1
Fraser, Brad	Poor Super Man	2

Author	Title	Occurrences
Freeman, David	Creeps	1
Frye, Northrop	Anatomy of Criticism	1
Gallant, Mavis	From the Fifteenth District	1
Gallant, Mavis	Home Truths: Selected Canadian Stories	2
Gallant, Mavis	The Moslem Wife and Other Stories	1
Garner, Hugh	Cabbagetown	2
Geddes, Gary (ed.)	15 Canadian Poets x 2	14
Gerson, Carole (ed.)	Vancouver Short Stories	1
Gerson, Carole, and Gwendolyn Davies (eds.)	Canadian Poetry From the Beginnings through the First World War	8
Goto, Hiromi	Chorus of Mushrooms	3
Gowdy, Barbara	Mister Sandman	1
Gowdy, Barbara	We So Seldom Look on Love	2
Grant, George	Technology and Empire	1
Grant, George	Time as History	1
Griffiths, Linda, and Maria Campbell	The Book of Jessica	4
Grove, Frederick Philip	Fruits of the Earth	1
Grove, Frederick Philip	Over Prairie Trails	1
Grove, Frederick Philip	A Search for America	1
Grove, Frederick Philip	Settlers of the Marsh	8
Gunnars, Kristjana	The Prowler	1
Gunnars, Kristjana	The Substance of Forgetting	1
Gunnars, Kristjana	Zero Hour	1
Gysin, Brion	To Master, A Long Goodnight	1
Halfe, Louise Bernice	Bear Bones and Feathers	3
Haliburton, T.C.	The Clockmaker	6
Hamill, Tony (ed.)	Six Canadian Plays	1
Harris, Claire	Dipped in Shadow	1
Harris, Claire	Drawing Down a Daughter	1
Harris, Claire	Fables From the Women's Quarters	1
Harrison, Charles Yale	Generals Die in Bed	3
Hay, Elizabeth	The Only Snow in Havana	1
Hébert, Anne	The First Garden	1
Hébert, Anne	In the Shadow of the Wind	1
Hébert, Anne	Kamouraska	2

Author	Title	Occurrences
Heble, Ajay, Donna Palmateer Penee, and J.R. (Tim) Struthers (eds.)	New Contexts of Canadian Criticism	1
Highway, Tomson	Dry Lips Oughta Move to Kapuskasing	10
Hill, Lawrence	Some Great Thing	1
Hodgins, Jack	The Invention of the World	3
Hollingsworth, Margaret	Diving	1
Hollingsworth, Margaret	Ever Loving	1
Howison, John	Sketches of Upper Canada	1
Hutcheon, Linda	The Canadian Postmodern	1
Hutcheon, Linda, and Marion Richmond (eds.)	Other Solitudes: Canadian Multicultural Fiction	1
Ignatieff, Michael	The Russian Album	1
Ipellie, Alootook	Arctic Dreams and Nightmares	2
Jameson, Anna	Winter Studies and Summer Rambles	1
Janes, Percy	House of Hate	1
Johnson, Pauline	Legends of Vancouver	1
Johnston, Wayne	Story of Bobby O'Malley	1
Kamboureli, Smaro	Making a Difference: Canadian Multicultural Literature	4
Kelly, M.T.	A Dream Like Mine	1
King, Thomas	All My Relations	1
King, Thomas	Green Grass, Running Water	16
King, Thomas	Medicine River	5
Kinsella, W.P.	Dance Me Outside	1
Kirby, William	The Golden Dog	1
Klein, A.M.	The Second Scroll	4
Klein, A.M.	Selected Poems	1
Klinck, C.F., and R.E. Watters	Canadian Anthology	1
Kogawa, Joy	Obasan	15
Kreisel, Henry	The Betrayal	1
Kroetsch, Robert	Badlands	3
Kroetsch, Robert	Completed Field Notes	1
Kroetsch, Robert	The Studhorse Man	6
Kroker, Arthur	Technology and the Canadian Mind	2
Kulyk-Keefer, Janice	The Green Library	1
Lambert, Betty	Under the Skin	1

Author	Title	Occurrences
Laurence, Margaret	A Bird in the House	4
Laurence, Margaret	Dance on the Earth	1
Laurence, Margaret	The Diviners	14
Laurence, Margaret	The Fire-Dwellers	6
Laurence, Margaret	A Jest of God	6
Laurence, Margaret	The Stone Angel	9
Laurence, Margaret	This Side Jordan	2
Laurence, Margaret	The Tomorrow-Tamer	2
Layton, Irving	A Wild and Peculiar Joy: Selected Poems 1945–89	1
Leacock, Stephen	Arcadian Adventures with the Idle Rich	6
Leacock, Stephen	Sunshine Sketches of a Little Town	20
Lecker, Robert, and Jack David (eds.)	Canadian Poetry (2 vols.)	4
Lee, Bennet, and Jim Wong-Chu (eds.)	Many-Mouthed Birds: Contemporary Writing by Chinese Canadians	1
Lee, Dennis	Civil Elegies	1
Lee, Sky	Disappearing Moon Café	8
Lenoski, Daniel (ed.)	A/long Prairie Lines	1
Lepage, Robert, and M. Brassard	Polygraph	1
Leprohon, Rosanna	Antoinette de Mirecourt	3
Lill, Wendy	The Occupation of Wendy Rose	1
Lowry, Malcolm	Under the Volcano	3
Lynch, Gerald	Troutstream	1
Lysenko, Vera	Yellow Boots	1
MacDonald, Ann-Marie	Fall on Your Knees	1
MacDonald, Ann-Marie	Goodnight Desdemona (Good Morning Juliet)	3
MacIvor, Daniel	The Soldier Dreams	1
MacLennan, Hugh	Barometer Rising	4
MacLennan, Hugh	Return of the Sphinx	1
MacLennan, Hugh	Two Solitudes	3
MacLennan, Hugh	The Watch that Ends the Night	5
MacLeod, Alistair	As Birds Bring Forth the Sun	1
MacLeod, Alistair	The Lost Salt Gift of Blood	2
MacLeod, Joan	2000	1

Author	Title	Occurrences
MacLeod, Joan	*Little Sister*	1
Macpherson, Jay	*Poems Twice Told: The Boatman and Welcoming Disaster*	1
Maillet, Antonine	*Pélagie*	4
Mair, Charles	*Tecumseh*	1
Major, Kevin	*Eating Between the Lines*	1
Maracle, Lee	*Ravensong*	2
Maracle, Lee	*Sojourner's Truth*	2
Marchessault, Jovette	*The Saga of the Wet Hens*	1
Markoosie	*Harpoon of the Hunter*	1
Markotic, Nicole	*The Yellow Pages*	1
Marlatt, Daphne	*Ana Historic*	6
Marlatt, Daphne	*Salvage*	1
Marlyn, John	*Under the Ribs of Death*	1
McCormack, Eric	*Inspecting the Vaults*	1
McCulloch, T.	*The Stepsure Letters*	1
McDougall, Colin	*Execution*	2
McFarlane, Sheryl	*Waiting for the Whales*	1
McGifford, Diane (ed.)	*Geography of Voice: Canadian Literature of the South Asian Diaspora*	1
McLuhan, Eric, and Frank Zingrone (eds.)	*Essential McLuhan*	1
McLuhan, Marshall	*The Gutenberg Galaxy*	1
McLuhan, Marshall	*The Mechanical Bride: Folklore of Industrial Man*	1
McLuhan, Marshall, and Quentin Fiore	*The Medium is the Massage*	2
McMullen, Lorraine, and Sandra Campbell (eds.)	*Aspiring Women: Short Stories by Canadian Women, 1880–1990*	1
Michaels, Anne	*Fugitive Pieces*	2
Minni, C.D.	*Other Selves*	1
Minni, C.D.	*Ricordi: Things Remembered. An Anthology of Short Stories*	1
Mistry, Rohinton	*Such a Long Journey*	1
Mitchell, W.O.	*Who Has Seen the Wind*	4
Mojica, Monique	*Princess Pocahontas and the Blue Spots*	2
Montgomery, L.M.	*Anne of Green Gables*	4

Author	Title	Occurrences
Montgomery, L.M.	Anne of Ingleside	1
Montgomery, L.M.	Anne's House of Dreams	1
Montgomery, L.M.	The Blue Castle	1
Montgomery, L.M.	Emily of New Moon	2
Montgomery, L.M.	Jane of Lantern Hill	1
Montgomery, L.M.	Magic for Marigold	1
Montgomery, L.M.	Rilla of Ingleside	1
Moodie, Andrew	Riot	2
Moodie, Susanna	Life in the Clearings	1
Moodie, Susanna	Roughing it in the Bush	15
Moodie, Susanna	Voyages: Short Narratives of Susanna Moodie	1
Moore, Brian	The Luck of Ginger Coffey	3
Moses, Daniel David	The Indian Medicine Shows	1
Moses, Daniel David	Kyotopolis	1
Moses, Daniel David, and Terry Goldie (eds.)	An Anthology of Canadian Native Literature in English	3
Moyles, R.G.	Improved by Cultivation: English Canadian Prose to 1914	4
Munro, Alice	Friend of My Youth	2
Munro, Alice	Lives of Girls and Women	9
Munro, Alice	The Moons of Jupiter	1
Munro, Alice	Open Secrets	2
Munro, Alice	Who Do You Think You Are?	7
Munsch, Robert	Jonathan Cleaned Up and Then He Heard a Sound	1
New, W.H. (ed.)	Canadian Short Fiction	4
Nichol, bp	An H in the Heart	1
Nichol, bp	The Martyrology: Books 1 and 2	1
Nolan, Yvette	Blade, Job's Wife, and Video: 3 Plays	1
Nowlan, Alden	An Exchange of Gifts: Poems New and Selected	1
O'Hagan, Howard	Tay John	9
Ondaatje, Michael	The Cinnamon Peeler: Selected Poems	1
Ondaatje, Michael	The Collected Works of Billy the Kid	5
Ondaatje, Michael	Coming Through Slaughter	5
Ondaatje, Michael	The English Patient	13

Author	Title	Occurrences
Ondaatje, Michael	*In the Skin of a Lion*	15
Ondaatje, Michael	*Running in the Family*	3
Ostenso, Martha	*Wild Geese*	6
Paci, F.G.	*The Black Madonna*	1
Page, P.K.	*The Glass Air: Selected Poems*	1
Panych, Morris	*7 Stories*	1
Philip, Marlene Nourbese	*Harriet's Daughter*	1
Philip, Marlene Nourbese	*Looking for Livingstone: An Odyssey of Silence*	3
Philip, Marlene Nourbese	*She Tries Her Tongue, Her Silence Softly Breaks*	2
Pollock, Sharon	*Blood Relations*	3
Pollock, Sharon	*Doc*	1
Pollock, Sharon	*Walsh*	1
Pratt, E.J.	*Brébeuf and His Brethren*	1
Pratt, E.J.	*E.J. Pratt: Selected Poems*	1
Pratt, E.J.	*Towards the Last Spike*	1
Purdy, Al	*Rooms for Rent in the Outer Planets*	1
Quan, Betty	*Mother Tongue*	1
Raddall, Thomas H.	*The Nymph and the Lamp*	1
Rau Badami, Anita	*Tamarind Mem*	1
Ray, Carl, and James Stevens (eds.)	*Sacred Legends*	1
Reaney, James	*The Donnellys*	1
Reaney, James	*Sticks and Stones*	1
Ricci, Nino	*In a Glass House*	1
Ricci, Nino	*Lives of the Saints*	1
Richards, David Adams	*Blood Ties*	1
Richards, David Adams	*For Those Who Hunt the Wounded Down*	1
Richards, David Adams	*Nights Below Station Street*	1
Richardson, John	*Canadian Brothers*	1
Richardson, John	*Wacousta*	16
Richler, Mordecai	*The Apprenticeship of Duddy Kravitz*	3
Richler, Mordecai	*The Incomparable Atuk*	1
Richler, Mordecai	*Joshua Then and Now*	1
Richler, Mordecai	*Solomon Gursky Was Here*	5
Richler, Mordecai	*Son of a Smaller Hero*	1

Author	Title	Occurrences
Richler, Mordecai	St. Urbain's Horseman	3
Ringuet	Thirty Acres	2
Robinson, Harry	Write It On Your Heart	3
Ross, Sinclair	As For Me and My House	20
Ross, Sinclair	The Lamp at Noon and Other Stories	3
Roy, Gabrielle	The Tin Flute	5
Roy, Gabrielle	Where Nests the Water Hen	1
Rubio, Mary	Harvesting Thistles: The Textual Garden of L.M. Montgomery, Essays on Her Novels and Journals	1
Rule, Jane	After the Fire	1
Rule, Jane	Against the Season	1
Rule, Jane	Desert of the Heart	1
Rule, Jane	Inland Passage	1
Rule, Jane	Memory Board	1
Rule, Jane	This is Not For You	1
Rule, Jane	The Young in One Another's Arms	1
Ryga, George	The Ecstasy of Rita Joe	2
Salutin, Rick, and Theatre Passe Muraille	1837: The Farmers' Revolt	1
Salverson, Laura Goodman	Confessions of an Immigrant's Daughter	2
Scofield, Gregory	Native Canadiana	1
Scott, Duncan Campbell	In the Village of Viger and Other Stories	2
Scott, Duncan Campbell	Selected Poetry of Duncan Campbell Scott	1
Sears, Djanet	Afrika Solo	1
Selvadurai, Shyam	Funny Boy	3
Seton, E.T.	Wild Animals I Have Known	1
Shields, Carol	The Stone Diaries	6
Shields, Carol	Swann	2
Shikatanti, Gerry	Aqueduct	1
Škvorecký, Josef	The Engineer of Human Souls	2
Smart, Elizabeth	By Grand Central Station I Sat Down and Wept	1
Smith, A.J.M. (ed.)	The Colonial Century: English-Canadian Writing Before Confederation	2
Sorfleet, J. (ed.)	The Poems of Bliss Carman	1
Sorfleet, J. (ed.)	Quebec Fiction: The English Fact	1

Author	Title	Occurrences
Sorfleet, J. (ed.)	The Work of Margaret Laurence	1
Steele, Appolonia (ed.)	The Constance Beresford-Howe Papers	1
Steffler, John	The Afterlife of George Cartwright	3
Such, Peter	Riverrun	1
Sullivan, Rosemary	Stories by Canadian Women	1
Sweatman, Margaret	Fox	1
Taylor, Drew Hayden	The Bootlegger Blues	1
Taylor, Drew Hayden	Someday	1
Thesen, Sharon	Aurora	1
Thesen, Sharon (ed.)	The New Long Poem Anthology	1
Thomas, Audrey	Intertidal Life	1
Thompson, E.W.	Selected Stories of E.W. Thompson	1
Thompson, Judith	Lion in the Streets	1
Thompson, Judith	The Other Side of the Dark	1
Tomson Highway	The Rez Sisters	8
Tostevin, Lola Lemire	Frog Moon	1
Traill, Catharine Parr	The Backwoods of Canada	2
Traill, Catharine Parr	Canadian Crusoes	2
Traill, Catharine Parr	Forest and Other Gleanings: The Fugitive Writings of Catharine Parr Traill	1
Tremblay, Michel	Les Belles Soeurs	3
Tremblay, Michel	The Fat Woman Next Door is Pregnant	2
Tynes, Maxine	Borrowed Beauty	1
Tynes, Maxine	The Door of My Heart	1
Tynes, Maxine	Woman Talking Woman	1
Urquhart, Jane	Away	3
Urquhart, Jane	The Whirlpool	1
Van Herk, Aritha	Places Far From Ellesmere	1
Vanderhaeghe, Guy	The Englishman's Boy	4
Vanderhaeghe, Guy	Man Descending	2
Vanderhaeghe, Guy	My Present Age	1
Vanderhaeghe, Guy	Things as They Are?	1
Vanderhaeghe, Guy	The Trouble with Heroes	1
Vassanji, M.G.	Book of Secrets	1
Vassanji, M.G.	No New Land	3

Author	Title	Occurrences
Vassanji, M.G.	Uhuru Street	1
Verdecchia, Guillermo	Fronteras Americanas	1
Wagamese, Richard	Keeper'n Me	1
Wah, Fred	Diamond Grill	1
Walker, George F.	Love and Anger	1
Walker, George F.	Rumours of Our Death	1
Wallace, Bronwen	Keep That Candle Burning Bright	1
Warkentin, Germaine (ed.)	Canadian Exploration Literature	1
Wasserman, Jerry (ed.)	Modern Canadian Plays (vol. 1)	2
Wasserman, Jerry (ed.)	Modern Canadian Plays (vol. 2)	1
Watson, Sheila	The Double Hook	12
Weaver, Robert (ed.)	Canadian Short Stories: Fifth Series	1
Webb, Phyllis	The Vision Tree: Selected Poems	1
Whitaker, Muriel	Great Canadian Animal Stories	1
Wiebe, Armin	The Salvation of Yasch Siemens	1
Wiebe, Rudy	The Blue Mountains of China	1
Wiebe, Rudy	A Discovery of Strangers	3
Wiebe, Rudy	Playing Dead: A Contemplation Concerning the Arctic	1
Wiebe, Rudy	The Scorched-Wood People	2
Wiebe, Rudy	The Temptations of Big Bear	2
Wilson, Budge	Oliver's Wars	1
Wilson, Ethel	Equations of Love	1
Wilson, Ethel	The Innocent Traveller	1
Wilson, Ethel	Mrs. Golightly and Other Stories	2
Wilson, Ethel	Swamp Angel	6
Wilson, Milton (ed.)	Poets Between the Wars	2
Wiseman, Adele	Crackpot	1
Wiseman, Adele	The Sacrifice	5
Wynne-Jones, Tim	Zoom Away	1
coursepack of other photocopied readings		13
readings on library reserve		1

Appendix 4

Texts Taught in English and Comparative Literature Courses on the
Literatures of Canada in 2007–08 (Ranked by Frequency)

Title	Author	Occurrences
Coursepack of other photocopied readings		41
In the Skin of a Lion	Ondaatje, Michael	27
Green Grass, Running Water	King, Thomas	24
A New Anthology of Canadian Literature in English	Bennett, Donna, and Russell Brown (eds.)	23
As For Me and My House	Ross, Sinclair	20
Monkey Beach	Robinson, Eden	19
Lives of Girls and Women	Munro, Alice	16
The Diviners	Laurence, Margaret	14
The Rez Sisters	Highway, Tomson	13
Fifth Business	Davies, Robertson	12
Running in the Family	Ondaatje, Michael	11
Swamp Angel	Wilson, Ethel	11
Anne of Green Gables	Montgomery, L.M.	11
Canadian Poetry From the Beginnings through the First World War	Gerson, Carole, and Gwendolyn Davies (eds.)	11
Roughing it in the Bush	Moodie, Susanna	10
The Wars	Findley, Timothy	10
Sunshine Sketches of a Little Town	Leacock, Stephen	10
The Imperialist	Duncan, Sara Jeannette	9
15 Canadian Poets x 3	Geddes, Gary (ed.)	9
Wacousta	Richardson, John	8

Title	Author	Occurrences
Obasan	Kogawa, Joy	8
The Collected Works of Billy the Kid	Ondaatje, Michael	8
Fugitive Pieces	Michaels, Anne	8
Disappearing Moon Café	Lee, Sky	8
The Mountain and the Valley	Buckler, Ernest	7
The Apprenticeship of Duddy Kravitz	Richler, Mordecai	7
The Double Hook	Watson, Sheila	7
Halfbreed	Campbell, Maria	7
Diamond Grill	Wah, Fred	7
Doc	Pollock, Sharon	7
Surfacing	Atwood, Margaret	6
The Studhorse Man	Kroetsch, Robert	6
What We All Long For	Brand, Dionne	6
The Stone Angel	Laurence, Margaret	5
The Handmaid's Tale	Atwood, Margaret	5
Not Wanted on the Voyage	Findley, Timothy	5
A Bird in the House	Laurence, Margaret	5
Barometer Rising	MacLennan, Hugh	5
An Anthology of Canadian Native Literature in English	Moses, Daniel David, and Terry Goldie (eds.)	5
Modern Canadian Plays (vol. 2)	Wasserman, Jerry (ed.)	5
A Complicated Kindness	Toews, Miriam	5
Stanley Park	Taylor, Timothy	5
Volkswagen Blues	Poulin, Jacques	5
Kiss of the Fur Queen	Highway, Tomson	5
Childhood	Alexis, André	5
A Strange Manuscript Found in a Copper Cylinder	De Mille, James	4
Away	Urquhart, Jane	4
The Journals of Susanna Moodie	Atwood, Margaret	4
Cat's Eye	Atwood, Margaret	4
Whylah Falls	Clarke, George Elliott	4
Bloodletting and Miraculous Cures	Lam, Vincent	4
Alligator	Moore, Lisa	4
FareWel	Ross, Ian	4
Three Day Road	Boyden, Joseph	4

Title	Author	Occurrences
Canadian Short Stories	Brown, Russell, and Donna Bennett (eds.)	4
A Short History of Indians in Canada	King, Thomas	4
Truth and Bright Water	King, Thomas	4
All that Matters	Choy, Wayson	4
The Ecstasy of Rita Joe	Ryga, George	3
Goodnight Desdemona (Good Morning Juliet)	MacDonald, Ann-Marie	3
Alias Grace	Atwood, Margaret	3
Bear	Engel, Marian	3
No Language is Neutral	Brand, Dionne	3
Lady Oracle	Atwood, Margaret	3
Tay John	O'Hagan, Howard	3
Canadian Anthology	Klinck, C.F., and R.E. Watters	3
The Stone Diaries	Shields, Carol	3
Coming Through Slaughter	Ondaatje, Michael	3
Improved by Cultivation: English Canadian Prose to 1914	Moyles, R.G.	3
Generals Die in Bed	Harrison, Charles Yale	3
Modern Canadian Plays (vol. 1)	Wasserman, Jerry (ed.)	3
The Book of Jessica	Griffiths, Linda, and Maria Campbell	3
Klee Wyck	Carr, Emily	3
Divisadero	Ondaatje, Michael	3
A Map to the Door of No Return: Notes to Belonging	Brand, Dionne	3
The Colony of Unrequited Dreams	Johnston, Wayne	3
The Truth About Stories	King, Thomas	3
Strike/Slip	McKay, Don	3
Oryx and Crake	Atwood, Margaret	3
George and Rue	Clarke, George Elliott	3
Barney's Version	Richler, Mordecai	3
Life of Pi	Martel, Yann	3
Steveston	Marlatt, Daphne, and Robert Minden	3
The Lesser Blessed	Van Camp, Richard	3
City Treaty	Francis, Marvin	3

Title	Author	Occurrences
Indian School Days	Johnston, Basil	3
The Electrical Field	Sakamoto, Kerri	3
Selected Poems 1966–1984	Atwood, Margaret	3
Early Writing in Canada: English 274E Anthology (Coursepack)	Bentley, D.M.R. (ed.)	3
Moderns and Contemporaries: Canadian Poetry from 1900 to the Present (English 274E Anthology) (Coursepack)	Zezulka, Joseph (ed.)	3
Two Months in the Camp of Big Bear: The Life and Adventures of Theresa Gowanlock and Theresa Delaney	Gowanlock, Theresa, and Theresa Delaney	3
The Second Life of Samuel Tyne	Edugyan, Esi	3
Unhomely States: Theorizing Canadian Postcolonialism	Sugars, Cynthia (ed.)	3
Lion in the Streets	Thompson, Judith	2
The Backwoods of Canada	Traill, Catharine Parr	2
Antoinette de Mirecourt	Leprohon, Rosanna	2
Fruits of the Earth	Grove, Frederick Philip	2
The English Patient	Ondaatje, Michael	2
A Discovery of Strangers	Wiebe, Rudy	2
Home Truths	Gallant, Mavis	2
The Lamp at Noon and Other Stories	Ross, Sinclair	2
In Another Place, Not Here	Brand, Dionne	2
Stones	Findley, Timothy	2
Wild Geese	Ostenso, Martha	2
The Fire-Dwellers	Laurence, Margaret	2
The Englishman's Boy	Vanderhaeghe, Guy	2
St. Urbain's Horseman	Richler, Mordecai	2
Selected Poems by A.M. Klein	Klein, A.M.	2
Such is My Beloved	Callaghan, Morley	2
The Lost Salt Gift of Blood	MacLeod, Alistair	2
All My Relations	King, Thomas	2
Dry Lips Oughta Move to Kapuskasing	Highway, Tomson	2
Some Great Thing	Hill, Lawrence	2
Solomon Gursky Was Here	Richler, Mordecai	2
In Search of April Raintree	Culleton, Beatrice	2
Someday	Taylor, Drew Hayden	2

Title	Author	Occurrences
Keeper'n Me	Wagamese, Richard	2
Making a Difference: Canadian Multicultural Literature	Kamboureli, Smaro	2
Wilderness Tips	Atwood, Margaret	2
Ravensong	Maracle, Lee	2
The Cinnamon Peeler: Selected Poems	Ondaatje, Michael	2
Crackpot	Wiseman, Adele	2
The Jade Peony	Choy, Wayson	2
Tamarind Mem	Rau Badami, Anita	2
In Search of April Raintree	Culleton, Beatrice	2
The Vision Tree: Selected Poems	Webb, Phyllis	2
A Really Good Brown Girl	Dumont, Marilyn	2
Hold Fast	Major, Kevin	2
Johnny Kellock Died Today	Dyer, Hadley	2
Grey Owl: The Mystery of Archie Belaney	Ruffo, Armand Garnet	2
Mercy Among the Children	Richards, David Adams	2
Canadian Exploration Literature	Warkentin, Germanine (ed.)	2
The Navigator of New York	Johnston, Wayne	2
Path with No Moccasins	Cheechoo, Shirley	2
Hosanna	Tremblay, Michel	2
Simple Recipes	Thien, Madeleine	2
Elizabeth Rex	Findley, Timothy	2
Maria Chapdelaine	Hémon, Louis	2
Orphan Love	Bozak, Nadia	2
The Road Past Altamont	Roy, Gabrielle	2
No Fixed Address: An Amourous Journey	Van Herk, Aritha	2
E. Pauline Johnson, Tekahionwake: Collected Poems and Selected Stories	Johnson, E. Pauline	2
I Knew Two Métis Women: The Lives of Dorothy Scofield and Georgina Houle Young	Scofield, Gregory	2
Billy Bishop Goes to War	Gray, John, and Eric Peterson	2
The White Bone	Gowdy, Barbara	2
Traplines	Robinson, Eden	2
The Favourite Game	Cohen, Leonard	2
Autobiography of Red: A Novel in Verse	Carson, Anne	2
Anil's Ghost	Ondaatje, Michael	2
Johnny Kellock Died Today	Dyer, Hadley	2

Title	Author	Occurrences
Growing Pains: The Autobiography of Emily Carr	Carr, Emily	2
Lives of the Saints	Ricci, Nino	2
American Standard/Canada Dry	Cain, Stephen	2
Hamburger Valley, California	McGimpsey, David	2
That Summer in Paris	Callaghan, Morley	2
Memoirs of Montparnasse	Glassco, John	2
In an Iron Glove	Martin, Claire	2
In the Company of Strangers	Meigs, Mary	2
Of This Earth: A Mennonite Boyhood in the Boreal Forest	Wiebe, Rudy	2
The Prophet's Camel Bell	Laurence, Margaret	2
Someday	Taylor, Drew Hayden	2
The Adventures of Ali & Ali and the Axes of Evil: A Divertimento for Warlords	Youssef, Marcus	2
April Raintree	Culleton, Beatrice	2
My Name is Seepeetza	Sterling, Shirley	2
The Kappa Child	Goto, Hiromi	2
Moon Honey	Mayr, Suzette	2
Hopeful Monsters	Goto, Hiromi	2
He Drown She in the Sea	Mootoo, Shani	2
Sojourners and Sundogs	Maracle, Lee	2
Delible	Stone, Anne	2
A Story As Sharp As a Knife	Bringhurst, Robert	2
Short Haul Engine	Solie, Karen	2
Crow Lake	Lawson, Mary	2
City of Glass: Douglas Coupland's Vancouver	Coupland, Douglas	2
Dead Girls	Nancy Lee	2
Salt Fish Girl	Lai, Larissa	2
Soucoyant	Chariandy, David	2
Woodsmen of the West	Grainger, Martin	2
Who Has Seen the Wind	Mitchell, W.O.	1
Les Belles Soeurs	Tremblay, Michel	1
Riot	Moodie, Andrew	1
Blood Relations	Pollock, Sharon	1
Under the Skin	Lambert, Betty	1
Poor Super Man	Fraser, Brad	1

Title	Author	Occurrences
The History of Emily Montague	Brooke, Frances	1
The Golden Dog	Kirby, William	1
Settlers of the Marsh	Grove, Frederick Philip	1
The Moons of Jupiter	Munro, Alice	1
Ana Historic	Marlatt, Daphne	1
Funny Boy	Selvadurai, Shyam	1
15 Canadian Poets x 2	Geddes, Gary (ed.)	1
The New Long Poem Anthology	Thesen, Sharon (ed.)	1
Open Secrets	Munro, Alice	1
Joshua Then and Now	Richler, Mordecai	1
The Temptations of Big Bear	Wiebe, Rudy	1
The Sacrifice	Wiseman, Adele	1
She Tries Her Tongue, Her Silence Softly Breaks	Philip, Marlene Nourbese	1
Harriet's Daughter	Philip, Marlene Nourbese	1
The Luck of Ginger Coffey	Moore, Brian	1
The Origin of Waves	Clarke, Austin	1
The Prowler	Gunnars, Kristjana	1
Blood Relations	Pollock, Sharon	1
The Tin Flute	Roy, Gabrielle	1
The Donnellys	Reaney, James	1
The Invention of the World	Hodgins, Jack	1
Winter Studies and Summer Rambles	Jameson, Anna	1
A Jest of God	Laurence, Margaret	1
Arctic Dreams and Nightmares	Ipellie, Alootook	1
Stranger Music: Selected Poems and Songs	Cohen, Leonard	1
Execution	McDougall, Colin	1
In the Village of Viger	Scott, D.C.	1
New Oxford Book of Canadian Short Stories in English	Atwood, Margaret, and Robert Weaver (eds.)	1
Walsh	Pollock, Sharon	1
The Book of Small	Carr, Emily	1
The Whirlpool	Urquhart, Jane	1
Jalna	De La Roche, Mazo	1
The Black Madonna	Paci, F.G.	1
Bodily Harm	Atwood, Margaret	1

Title	Author	Occurrences
Badlands	Kroetsch, Robert	1
House of Hate	Janes, Percy	1
Fall on Your Knees	MacDonald, Ann-Marie	1
Sacred Legends	Ray, Carl, and James Stevens (eds.)	1
Write It On Your Heart	Robinson, Harry	1
Sojourner's Truth	Maracle, Lee	1
Arctic Dreams and Nightmares	Ipellie, Alootook	1
Princess Pocahontas and the Blue Spots	Mojica, Monique	1
Beautiful Losers	Cohen, Leonard	1
The Second Scroll	Klein, A.M.	1
Rockbound	Day, Frank Parker	1
The Blue Castle	Montgomery, L.M.	1
Such a Long Journey	Mistry, Rohinton	1
The New Oxford Book of Canadian Verse in English	Atwood, Margaret (ed.)	1
The Scorched-Wood People	Wiebe, Rudy	1
Wild Animals I Have Known	Seton, E.T.	1
Rooms for Rent in the Outer Planets	Purdy, Al	1
The New Athens	Hood, Hugh	1
New Contexts of Canadian Criticism	Heble, Ajay, Donna Palmateer Penee, and J.R. (Tim) Struthers (eds.)	1
From the Fifteenth District	Gallant, Mavis	1
Fox	Sweatman, Margaret	1
Nineteenth Century Canadian Stories	Arnason, David (ed.)	1
By Grand Central Station I Sat Down and Wept	Smart, Elizabeth	1
Man Descending	Vanderhaeghe, Guy	1
E.J. Pratt: Selected Poems	Pratt, E.J.	1
Dance Me Outside	Kinsella, W.P.	1
The Indian Medicine Shows	Moses, Daniel David	1
The Medium is the Massage	McLuhan, Marshall, and Quentin Fiore	1
Generation X: Tales for an Accelerated Culture	Coupland, Douglas	1
Over Prairie Trails	Grove, Frederick Philip	1

Title	Author	Occurrences
Burning Water	Bowering, George	1
Tales from the Firozha Baag	Mistry, Rohinton	1
Marine Life	Svendsen, Linda	1
Moral Disorder	Atwood, Margaret	1
Invitation to the Game	Hughes, Monica	1
Windows and Words: A Look at Canadian Children's Literature	Hudson, Aida	1
Stormy Night	Lemieux, Michèle	1
This Land is My Land	Littlechild, George	1
The Maestro	Wynne-Jones, Tim	1
Awake and Dreaming	Pearson, Kit	1
Four Pictures of Emily Carr	Debon, Nicolas	1
Hockey Dreams: Memoirs of a Man Who Couldn't Play	Richards, David Adams	1
Going Top Shelf: An Anthology of Canadian Hockey Poetry	Kennedy, Michael P.J. (ed.)	1
Words on Ice: A Collection of Hockey Prose	Kennedy, Michael P.J. (ed.)	1
The Divine Ryans	Johnston, Wayne	1
Ladies and Gentlemen... Mr. Leonard Cohen	Brittain, Donald, and Don Owen (dirs.)	1
Thirty-Two Short Films about Glenn Gould	Girard, François (dir.)	1
From Ink Lake	Ondaatje, Michael (ed.)	1
Icefields	Wharton, Thomas	1
To The New World	McGrath, Carmelita	1
The Hour of Bad Decisions	Wangersky, Russell	1
Going Around with Bachelors	Walsh, Agnes	1
An Island in the Sky: Selected Poetry of Al Pittman	Pittman, Al	1
Inside	Harvey, Kenneth J.	1
Scarecrow	Callanan, Mark	1
Shadow Side of Grace	Hallett, Michelle Butler	1
Hard Light	Crummey, Michael	1
Wreckhouse	Barry, Frank	1
Gaff Topsails	Kavanagh, Patrick	1
There, There	Warner, Patrick	1
Morning in the Burned House	Atwood, Margaret	1
Processional	Compton, Anne	1

Title	Author	Occurrences
Camber: Selected Poems 1983–2000	McKay, Don	1
Wreckage	Crummey, Michael	1
Muinji'j Becomes a Man	Mi'sel Joe, Saqamaw	1
Love Medicine and One Song	Scofield, Gregory	1
Two Plays: Butler's Marsh, Tempting Providence	Chafe, Robert	1
The Door	Atwood, Margaret	1
Short Talks	Carson, Anne	1
Days Into Flatspin	Babstock, Ken	1
Loop	Simpson, Anne	1
With English Subtitles	Starnino, Carmine	1
The Drawer Boy	Healey, Michael	1
The Farm Show: A Collective Creation	Theatre Passe Muraille	1
Burridge Unbound	Cumyn, Alan	1
Open Country	Lecker, Robert	1
Miriam Waddington: Collected Poems	Waddington, Miriam	1
The Self-Completing Tree	Livesay, Dorothy	1
Planet Earth: Poems Selected and New	Page, P.K.	1
Ernestine Shuswap Gets Her Trout: A "String Quartet" for Four Female Actors	Highway, Tomson	1
The Shape of a Girl and Jewel	MacLeod, Joan	1
Half Life	Mighton, John	1
Hetty Dorval	Wilson, Ethel	1
Winona, or The Foster Sisters	Crawford, Isabella Valancy	1
Brébeuf's Ghost	Moses, Daniel David	1
The Fiddlehead (subscription)		1
Glengarry School Days	Connor, Ralph	1
The Widows	Mayr, Suzette	1
Each Man's Son	MacLennan, Hugh	1
The Last Crossing	Vanderhaeghe, Guy	1
Early Canadian Short Stories: Short Stories in English Before World War I: A Critical Edition	Dean, Misao (ed.)	1
And Other Stories	Bowering, George (ed.)	1
All My Friends Are Superheroes	Kaufman, Andrew	1
The Martyrology: Books 3 and 4	Nichol, bp	1

Title	Author	Occurrences
I Dream Myself Into Being: Collected Poems	Thompson, John	1
The Kerrisdale Elegies	Bowering, George	1
Waiting for Saskatchewan	Wah, Fred	1
Seed Catalogue	Kroetsch, Robert	1
Little Buffalo River	Beaulieu, Frances	1
The Epic of Qayaq: The Longest Story Ever Told By My People	Oman, Lela Kiana	1
Sacred Legends	Ray, Carl, and James R. Stevens	1
Out of the Depths: The Experiences of Mi'kmaw Children at the Indian Residential School at Shubenacadie, Nova Scotia	Knockwood, Isabelle	1
It's Like the Legend: Innu Women's Voices	Fouillard, Camille	1
The Pale Indian	Alexie, Robert Arthur	1
The Heart of the Ancient Wood	Roberts, Charles G.D.	1
Pilgrims of the Wild	Grey Owl	1
Last of the Curlews	Bodsworth, Fred	1
Never Cry Wolf	Mowat, Farley	1
Coyote City: A Play in Two Acts	Moses, Daniel David	1
The Baby Blues	Taylor, Drew Hayden	1
Apartment Seven: Essays Selected and New	Waddington, Miriam	1
The Street	Richler, Mordecai	1
The Rent Collector	Rotchin, Glen	1
The Age of Longing	Wright, Richard B.	1
Neuromancer	Gibson, William	1
Two Murders in My Double Life	Škvorecký, Josef	1
The In-between World of Vikram Lall	Vassanji, M.G.	1
Still Life with June	Greer, Darren	1
This Will All End in Tears	Ollmann, Joe	1
Wimbledon Green: The Greatest Comic Book Collector in the World	Seth	1
Secular Love	Ondaatje, Michael	1
Rex Zero and the End of the World	Wynne-Jones, Tim	1
Odd Man Out	Ellis, Sarah	1
Digging Up the Mountains	Bissoondath, Neil	1
Random Passage	Morgan, Bernice	1

Title	Author	Occurrences
The Adventures of a Black Girl in Search of God	Sears, Djanet	1
Problem Child	Walker, George F.	1
Sister Woman	Sime, J.G.	1
Paper Shadows	Choy, Wayson	1
When She Was Queen	Vassanji, M.G.	1
Only Drunks and Children Tell the Truth	Taylor, Drew Hayden	1
The Swinging Bridge	Espinet, Ramabai	1
Behind the Face of Winter	Thomas, H. Nigel	1
Italian Canadian Voices: A Literary Anthology, 1946–2004	Di Giovanni, Caroline (ed.)	1
Roman Candles: An Anthology of Poems by Seventeen Italo-Canadian Poets	Di Cicco, Pier Giorgio	1
Stranger in You: Selected Poems and New	Di Michele, Mary	1
Homeground: A Play	Edwards, Caterina	1
Two Plays: Voiceless People and Addorata	Micone, Marco	1
Marshall McLuhan: The Book of Probes	McLuhan, Marshall	1
Laws of Media	McLuhan, Marshall	1
The Medium is the Massage	McLuhan, Marshall	1
The Educated Imagination	Frye, Northrop	1
The Great Code: The Bible and Literature	Frye, Northrop	1
The Double Vision: Language and Meaning in Religion	Frye, Northrop	1
Eunoia	Bök, Christian	1
Liar	Crosbie, Lynn	1
The Bare Plum of Winter Rain	Lane, Patrick	1
Yesno	Lee, Dennis	1
Hologram: A Book of Glosas	Page, P.K.	1
Ontological Necessities	Uppal, Priscila	1
The Concubine's Children: Portrait of a Family Divided	Chong, Denise	1
Walking Since Daybreak: A Story of Eastern Europe, World War II, and the Heart of Our Century	Eksteins, Modris	1
Travels By Night: A Memoir of the Sixties	Fetherling, Douglas	1
A Safe House: Holland 1940–45	Jacobs, Maria	1
The Danger Tree	Macfarlane, David	1

Title	Author	Occurrences
Clearing in the West: My Own Story	McClung, Nellie	1
Enchantment and Sorrow: The Autobiography of Gabrielle Roy	Roy, Gabrielle	1
Pause: A Sketch Book	Carr, Emily	1
Love and Sweet Food: A Culinary Memoir	Clarke, Austin	1
Incorrigible	Demerson, Velma	1
The Tightrope Walker: Autobiographical Writings of Anne Wilkinson	Wilkinson, Anne	1
Inside Memory	Findley, Timothy	1
The Piano Man's Daughter	Findley, Timothy	1
Survival	Atwood, Margaret	1
Some Other Garden	Urquhart, Jane	1
Storm Glass	Urquhart, Jane	1
The Stone Carvers	Urquhart, Jane	1
Changing Heaven	Urquhart, Jane	1
Runaway	Munro, Alice	1
Almighty Voice and His Wife	Moses, Daniel David	1
Unnatural and Accidental Women	Clements, Marie	1
Angélique	Gale, Lorena	1
Reading Hebron	Sherman, Jason	1
Blood Sports	Robinson, Eden	1
The Cure for Death by Lightning	Anderson-Dargatz, Gail	1
Just Some Stuff I Wrote	Bell, William	1
Secrets: Stories Selected by Marthe Jocelyn	Jocelyn, Marthe (ed.)	1
Juliana and the Medicine Fish	MacDonald, Jake	1
Beckoners	Mac, Carrie	1
The Freak	Matas, Carol	1
A Thief in the House of Memory	Wynne-Jones, Tim	1
Frost	Luiken, Nicole	1
Road to Chlifa	Marineau, Michèle	1
Yellow Line	Olsen, Sylvia	1
Harriet's Daughter	Philip, Marlene Nourbese	1
Dust	Slade, Arthur	1
No Man's Land	Major, Kevin	1
A Coyote Columbus Story	King, Thomas	1

Title	Author	Occurrences
As Long as the Rivers Flow: A Last Summer Before Residential School	Loyie, Larry with Constance Brissenden	1
Nanabosho and the Woodpecker	McLellan, Joseph	1
Little Voice	Slipperjack, Ruby	1
Chuck in the City	Wheeler, Jordan	1
Awful Disclosures of Maria Monk, or, The Hidden Secrets of a Nun's Life in a Convent Exposed	Monk, Maria	1
On the Eve of Uncertain Tomorrows	Bissoondath, Neil	1
Fiery Spirits and Voices: Canadian Writers of African Descent	Black, Ayanna (ed.)	1
The Meeting Point	Clarke, Austin	1
The Nutmeg Princess	Keens-Douglas, Richardo	1
Forbidden Voice: Reflections of a Mohawk Indian	Greene, Alma (Gah-wonh-nos-doh)	1
Will's Garden	Maracle, Lee	1
A Quality of Light	Wagamese, Richard	1
A Fine Balance	Mistry, Rohinton	1
The Minor Keys: A Romantic Comedy	Belke, David	1
A Teatro Trilogy: Selected Plays	Lemoine, Stewart	1
Tornado Magnet: A Salute to Trailer Court Women	Hagen, Darrin	1
Our Story: Aboriginal Voices on Canada's Past	King, Thomas (ed.)	1
Angel Wing Splash Pattern	Van Camp, Richard	1
Elle	Glover, Douglas	1
Sweetness in the Belly	Gibb, Camilla	1
Trudeau: Long March Shining Path	Clarke, George Elliott	1
Inventory	Brand, Dionne	1
Letters and Journals of Simon Fraser, 1806–1808	Fraser, Simon	1
Roland Graeme: Knight. A Novel of Our Time	Machar, Agnes Maule	1
Cousin Cinderella	Duncan, Sara Jeannette	1
Mirabel	Nepveu, Pierre	1
Thirsty	Brand, Dionne	1

Title	Author	Occurrences
The Life, History, and Travels of Kah-GE-Ga-Gah-Bowh	Copway, George	1
The Diary of Abraham Ulrikab: Text and Context	Lutz, Hartmut, and Alootook Ipellie	1
Thunder Through My Veins: Memories of a Métis Childhood	Scofield, Gregory	1
For Joshua: An Ojibway Father Teaches His Son	Wagamese, Richard	1
Louis Riel: A Comic Strip Biography	Brown, Chester	1
No Love Lost	Munro, Alice	1
Field Marks: The Poetry of Don McKay	McKay, Don	1
No Great Mischief	MacLeod, Alistair	1
When Fox is a Thousand	Lai, Larissa	1
A Sunday at the Pool in Kigali	Courtemanche, Gil	1
Borderlands: How We Talk About Canada	New, W.H.	1
Innocent Cities	Hodgins, Jack	1
Lake of the Prairies	Cariou, Warren	1
Vancouver Walking	Quartermain, Meredith	1
Kingsway	Turner, Michael	1
The Letter Opener	Maclear, Kyo	1
Forage	Wong, Rita	1
Certainty	Thien, Madeleine	1
Sexing the Maple: A Canadian Sourcebook	Cavell, Richard, and Peter Dickinson (eds.)	1
The Hero's Walk	Badami, Anita Rau	1
Charles the Bold	Beauchemin, Yves	1
Seminal: The Anthology of Canada's Gay Male Poets	Barton, John, and Billeh Nickerson (eds.)	1
Love and Human Remains	Fraser, Brad	1
Lilies	Bouchard, Michel Marc	1
Glass, Irony, and God	Carson, Anne	1
Keep That Candle Burning Bright and Other Poems	Wallace, Bronwen	1
He Who Hunted Birds in His Father's Village: The Dimensions of Haida Myth	Snyder, Gary	1
Pieces of Map, Pieces of Music	Bringhurst, Robert	1
The Resurrection of Joseph Bourne	Hodgins, Jack	1

Title	Author	Occurrences
ReCalling Early Canada: Reading the Political in Literary and Cultural Production	Blair, Jennifer, et al. (eds.)	1
The Young in One Another's Arms	Rule, Jane	1
Plainsong	Huston, Nancy	1
Strange Fugitive	Callaghan, Morley	1
The Circle Game	Atwood, Margaret	1
The Age of Cities	Grubisic, Brett Josef	1
Carole Frechette: Two Plays	Frechette, Carole	1
The Pornographer's Poem	Turner, Michael	1
Pornography	Nathan, Debbie	1
Jitters	French, David	1
Small Arguments	Thammavongsa, Souvankham	1
Shift and Switch: New Canadian Poetry	Beaulieu, Derek, Jason Christie, and Angela Rawlings (eds.)	1
Whiskey Bullets: Cowboy and Indian Heritage Poems	Gottfriedson, Garry	1
Mrs. Blood	Thomas, Audrey	1
What Lies Before Us	Panych, Morris	1
Chimera	Lill, Wendy	1
Stretching Hide	Lakevold, Dale, and Darrell Racine	1
Whispering in Shadows	Armstrong, Jeannette	1
Is Canada Postcolonial?: Unsettling Canadian Literature	Moss, Laura (ed.)	1
Story House	Taylor, Timothy	1
The Birth House	McKay, Ami	1
Kindred of the Wild	Roberts, Charles G.D.	1
Land to Light On	Brand, Dionne	1
Selected Animal Stories: A Critical Edition	Roberts, Charles G.D.	1
One Good Story, That One	King, Thomas	1
Furious Observations of a Blue-eyed Ojibway	Taylor, Drew Hayden	1
Fearless Warriors	Taylor, Drew Hayden	1
Flint and Feather	Johnson, E. Pauline	1
The Weight of Oranges	Michaels, Anne	1
The Blue Hour of the Day: Selected Poems	Crozier, Lorna	1

Title	Author	Occurrences
Re:Zoom	Wilson, Sheri-D	1
Jaguar Rain: The Margaret Mee Poems	Conn, Jan	1
Coastlines: The Poetry of Atlantic Canada	Compton, Anne (ed.)	1
Jacob's Wake	Cook, Michael	1
The Glace Bay Miner's Museum	Currie, Sheldon	1
Sylvanus Now	Morrissey, Donna	1
Quilt	Smyth, Donna	1

Appendix 5

Texts Taught in English and Comparative Literature Courses on the
Literatures of Canada in 2007–08 (Sorted by Author)

Title	Author	Occurrences
Coursepack of other photocopied readings		41
The Fiddlehead (subscription)		1
The Pale India	Alexie, Robert Arthur	1
Childhood	Alexis, André	5
The Cure for Death by Lightning	Anderson-Dargatz, Gail	1
Whispering in Shadows	Armstrong, Jeannette	1
Nineteenth Century Canadian Stories	Arnason, David (ed.)	1
Surfacing	Atwood, Margaret	6
Alias Grace	Atwood, Margaret	3
The Journals of Susanna Moodie	Atwood, Margaret	4
The Handmaid's Tale	Atwood, Margaret	5
Lady Oracle	Atwood, Margaret	3
Cat's Eye	Atwood, Margaret	4
Bodily Harm	Atwood, Margaret	1
Wilderness Tips	Atwood, Margaret	2
Moral Disorder	Atwood, Margaret	1
Morning in the Burned House	Atwood, Margaret	1
The Door	Atwood, Margaret	1
Oryx and Crake	Atwood, Margaret	3
Selected Poems 1966–1984	Atwood, Margaret	3
Survival	Atwood, Margaret	1
The Circle Game	Atwood, Margaret	1

Title	Author	Occurrences
The New Oxford Book of Canadian Verse in English	Atwood, Margaret (ed.)	1
New Oxford Book of Canadian Short Stories in English	Atwood, Margaret, and Robert Weaver (eds.)	1
Days Into Flatspin	Babstock, Ken	1
The Hero's Walk	Badami, Anita Rau	1
Wreckhouse	Barry, Frank	1
Seminal: The Anthology of Canada's Gay Male Poets	Barton, John, and Billeh Nickerson (eds.)	1
Charles the Bold	Beauchemin, Yves	1
Shift and Switch: New Canadian Poetry	Beaulieu, Derek, Jason Christie, and Angela Rawlings (eds.)	1
Little Buffalo River	Beaulieu, Frances	1
The Minor Keys: A Romantic Comedy	Belke, David	1
Just Some Stuff I Wrote	Bell, William	1
Early Writing in Canada: English 274E Anthology (Coursepack)	Bentley, D.M.R. (ed.)	3
Digging Up the Mountains	Bissoondath, Neil	1
On the Eve of Uncertain Tomorrows	Bissoondath, Neil	1
Fiery Spirits and Voices: Canadian Writers of African Descent	Black, Ayanna (ed.)	1
ReCalling Early Canada: Reading the Political in Literary and Cultural Production	Blair, Jennifer, et al. (eds.)	1
Last of the Curlews	Bodsworth, Fred	1
Eunoia	Bök, Christian	1
Lilies	Bouchard, Michel Marc	1
Burning Water	Bowering, George	1
The Kerrisdale Elegies	Bowering, George	1
And Other Stories	Bowering, George (ed.)	1
Three Day Road	Boyden, Joseph	4
Orphan Love	Bozak, Nadia	2
No Language is Neutral	Brand, Dionne	3
In Another Place, Not Here	Brand, Dionne	2
A Map to the Door of No Return: Notes to Belonging	Brand, Dionne	3
What We All Long For	Brand, Dionne	6

Title	Author	Occurrences
Inventory	Brand, Dionne	1
Thirsty	Brand, Dionne	1
Land to Light On	Brand, Dionne	1
A Story As Sharp As a Knife	Bringhurst, Robert	2
Pieces of Map, Pieces of Music	Bringhurst, Robert	1
Ladies and Gentlemen... *Mr. Leonard Cohen*	Brittain, Donald, and Don Owen (dirs.)	1
The History of Emily Montague	Brooke, Frances	1
Louis Riel: A Comic Strip Biography	Brown, Chester	1
Canadian Short Stories	Brown, Russell, and Donna Bennett (eds.)	4
The Mountain and the Valley	Buckler, Ernest	7
American Standard/Canada Dry	Cain, Stephen	2
Such is My Beloved	Callaghan, Morley	2
That Summer in Paris	Callaghan, Morley	2
Strange Fugitive	Callaghan, Morley	1
Scarecrow	Callanan, Mark	1
Halfbreed	Campbell, Maria	7
Lake of the Prairies	Cariou, Warren	1
The Book of Small	Carr, Emily	1
Klee Wyck	Carr, Emily	3
Growing Pains: The Autobiography of Emily Carr	Carr, Emily	2
Pause: A Sketch Book	Carr, Emily	1
Short Talks	Carson, Anne	1
Autobiography of Red: A Novel in Verse	Carson, Anne	2
Glass, Irony, and God	Carson, Anne	1
Sexing the Maple: A Canadian Sourcebook	Cavell, Richard, and Peter Dickinson (eds.)	1
Two Plays: Butler's Marsh, Tempting Providence	Chafe, Robert	1
Soucoyant	Chariandy, David	2
Path with No Moccasins	Cheechoo, Shirley	2
The Concubine's Children: Portrait of a Family Divided	Chong, Denise	1
The Jade Peony	Choy, Wayson	2
Paper Shadows	Choy, Wayson	1

Title	Author	Occurrences
All that Matters	Choy, Wayson	4
The Origin of Waves	Clarke, Austin	1
Love and Sweet Food: A Culinary Memoir	Clarke, Austin	1
The Meeting Point	Clarke, Austin	1
Whylah Falls	Clarke, George Elliott	4
George and Rue	Clarke, George Elliott	3
Trudeau: Long March Shining Path	Clarke, George Elliott	1
Unnatural and Accidental Women	Clements, Marie	1
Stranger Music: Selected Poems and Songs	Cohen, Leonard	1
Beautiful Losers	Cohen, Leonard	1
The Favourite Game	Cohen, Leonard	2
Processional	Compton, Anne	1
Coastlines: The Poetry of Atlantic Canada	Compton, Anne (ed.)	1
Jaguar Rain: The Margaret Mee Poems	Conn, Jan	1
Glengarry School Days	Connor, Ralph	1
Jacob's Wake	Cook, Michael	1
The Life, History, and Travels of Kah-GE-Ga-Gah-Bowh	Copway, George	1
Generation X: Tales for an Accelerated Culture	Coupland, Douglas	1
City of Glass: Douglas Coupland's Vancouver	Coupland, Douglas	2
A Sunday at the Pool in Kigali	Courtemanche, Gil	1
Winona, or The Foster Sisters	Crawford, Isabella Valancy	1
Liar	Crosbie, Lynn	1
The Blue Hour of the Day: Selected Poems	Crozier, Lorna	1
Hard Light	Crummey, Michael	1
Wreckage	Crummey, Michael	1
In Search of April Raintree	Culleton, Beatrice	2
Burridge Unbound	Cumyn, Alan	1
The Glace Bay Miner's Museum	Currie, Sheldon	1
Fifth Business	Davies, Robertson	12
Rockbound	Day, Frank Parker	1
Jalna	De La Roche, Mazo	1
A Strange Manuscript Found in a Copper Cylinder	De Mille, James	4

Title	Author	Occurrences
Early Canadian Short Stories: Short Stories in English before World War I: A Critical Edition	Dean, Misao (ed.)	1
Four Pictures of Emily Carr	Debon, Nicolas	1
Incorrigible	Demerson, Velma	1
Roman Candles: An Anthology of Poems by Seventeen Italo-Canadian Poets	Di Cicco, Pier Giorgio (ed.)	1
Stranger in You: Selected Poems and New	Di Michele, Mary	1
Italian Canadian Voices: A Literary Anthology, 1946–2004	Di Giovanni, Caroline (ed.)	1
A Really Good Brown Girl	Dumont, Marilyn	2
The Imperialist	Duncan, Sara Jeannette	9
Cousin Cinderella	Duncan, Sara Jeannette	1
Johnny Kellock Died Today	Dyer, Hadley	2
A New Anthology of Canadian Literature in English	Bennett, Donna, and Russell Brown (eds.)	23
The Second Life of Samuel Tyne	Edugyan, Esi	3
Homeground: A Play	Edwards, Caterina	1
Walking Since Daybreak: A Story of Eastern Europe, World War II, and the Heart of Our Century	Eksteins, Modris	1
Odd Man Out	Ellis, Sarah	1
Bear	Engel, Marian	3
The Swinging Bridge	Espinet, Ramabai	1
Travels By Night: A Memoir of the Sixties	Fetherling, Douglas	1
The Wars	Findley, Timothy	10
Not Wanted on the Voyage	Findley, Timothy	5
Stones	Findley, Timothy	2
Elizabeth Rex	Findley, Timothy	2
Inside Memory	Findley, Timothy	1
The Piano Man's Daughter	Findley, Timothy	1
It's Like the Legend: Innu Women's Voices	Fouillard, Camille	1
City Treaty	Francis, Marvin	3
Poor Super Man	Fraser, Brad	1
Love and Human Remains	Fraser, Brad	1
Letters and Journals of Simon Fraser, 1806–1808	Fraser, Simon	1

Title	Author	Occurrences
Carole Frechette: Two Plays	Frechette, Carole	1
Jitters	French, David	1
The Educated Imagination	Frye, Northrop	1
The Great Code: The Bible and Literature	Frye, Northrop	1
The Double Vision: Language and Meaning in Religion	Frye, Northrop	1
Angélique	Gale, Lorena	1
Home Truths	Gallant, Mavis	2
From the Fifteenth District	Gallant, Mavis	1
15 Canadian Poets x 2	Geddes, Gary (ed.)	1
15 Canadian Poets x 3	Geddes, Gary (ed.)	9
Canadian Poetry From the Beginnings through the First World War	Gerson, Carole, and Gwendolyn Davies (eds.)	11
Sweetness in the Belly	Gibb, Camilla	1
Neuromancer	Gibson, William	1
Thirty-Two Short Films about Glenn Gould	Girard, François (dir.)	1
Memoirs of Montparnasse	Glassco, John	2
Elle	Glover, Douglas	1
The Kappa Child	Goto, Hiromi	2
Hopeful Monsters	Goto, Hiromi	2
Whiskey Bullets: Cowboy and Indian Heritage Poems	Gottfriedson, Garry	1
Two Months in the Camp of Big Bear: The Life and Adventures of Theresa Gowanlock and Theresa Delaney	Gowanlock, Theresa, and Theresa Delaney	3
The White Bone	Gowdy, Barbara	2
Woodsmen of the West	Grainger, Martin	2
Billy Bishop Goes to War	Gray, John, and Eric Peterson	2
Forbidden Voice: Reflections of a Mohawk Indian	Greene, Alma (Gah-wonh-nos-doh)	1
Still Life with June	Greer, Darren	1
Pilgrims of the Wild	Grey Owl	1
The Book of Jessica	Griffiths, Linda, and Maria Campbell	3
Fruits of the Earth	Grove, Frederick Philip	2
Settlers of the Marsh	Grove, Frederick Philip	1
Over Prairie Trails	Grove, Frederick Philip	1
The Age of Cities	Grubisic, Brett Josef	1

Title	Author	Occurrences
The Prowler	Gunnars, Kristjana	1
Tornado Magnet: A Salute to Trailer Court Women	Hagen, Darrin	1
Shadow Side of Grace	Hallett, Michelle Butler	1
Generals Die in Bed	Harrison, Charles Yale	3
Inside	Harvey, Kenneth J.	1
The Drawer Boy	Healey, Michael	1
New Contexts of Canadian Criticism	Heble, Ajay, Donna Palmateer Penee, and J.R. (Tim) Struthers (eds.)	1
Maria Chapdelaine	Hémon, Louis	2
The Rez Sisters	Highway, Tomson	13
Dry Lips Oughta Move to Kapuskasing	Highway, Tomson	2
Ernestine Shuswap Gets Her Trout: A "String Quartet" for Four Female Actors	Highway, Tomson	1
Kiss of the Fur Queen	Highway, Tomson	5
Some Great Thing	Hill, Lawrence	2
The Invention of the World	Hodgins, Jack	1
Innocent Cities	Hodgins, Jack	1
The Resurrection of Joseph Bourne	Hodgins, Jack	1
The New Athens	Hood, Hugh	1
Windows and Words: A Look at Canadian Children's Literature	Hudson, Aida	1
Invitation to the Game	Hughes, Monica	1
Plainsong	Huston, Nancy	1
Arctic Dreams and Nightmares	Ipellie, Alootook	1
A Safe House: Holland 1940–45	Jacobs, Maria	1
Winter Studies and Summer Rambles	Jameson, Anna	1
House of Hate	Janes, Percy	1
Secrets: Stories Selected by Marthe Jocelyn	Jocelyn, Marthe (ed.)	1
E. Pauline Johnson, Tekahionwake: Collected Poems and Selected Stories	Johnson, E. Pauline	2
Flint and Feather	Johnson, E. Pauline	1
Indian School Days	Johnston, Basil	3
The Divine Ryans	Johnston, Wayne	1
The Colony of Unrequited Dreams	Johnston, Wayne	3
The Navigator of New York	Johnston, Wayne	2

Title	Author	Occurrences
Making a Difference: Canadian Multicultural Literature	Kamboureli, Smaro	2
All My Friends Are Superheroes	Kaufman, Andrew	1
Gaff Topsails	Kavanagh, Patrick	1
The Nutmeg Princess	Keens-Douglas, Richardo	1
Going Top Shelf: An Anthology of Canadian Hockey Poetry	Kennedy, Michael P.J. (ed.)	1
Words on Ice: A Collection of Hockey Prose	Kennedy, Michael P.J. (ed.)	1
Green Grass, Running Water	King, Thomas	24
All My Relations	King, Thomas	2
The Truth About Stories	King, Thomas	3
A Short History of Indians in Canada	King, Thomas	4
Truth and Bright Water	King, Thomas	4
A Coyote Columbus Story	King, Thomas	1
One Good Story, That One	King, Thomas	1
Our Story: Aboriginal Voices on Canada's Past	King, Thomas (ed.)	1
Dance Me Outside	Kinsella, W.P.	1
The Golden Dog	Kirby, William	1
Selected Poems by A.M. Klein	Klein, A.M.	2
The Second Scroll	Klein, A.M.	1
Canadian Anthology	Klinck, C.F., and R.E. Watters	3
Out of the Depths: The Experiences of Mi'kmaw Children at the Indian Residential School at Shubenacadie, Nova Scotia	Knockwood, Isabelle	1
Obasan	Kogawa, Joy	8
The Studhorse Man	Kroetsch, Robert	6
Badlands	Kroetsch, Robert	1
Seed Catalogue	Kroetsch, Robert	1
When Fox is a Thousand	Lai, Larissa	1
Salt Fish Girl	Lai, Larissa	2
Stretching Hide	Lakevold, Dale, and Darrell Racine	1
Bloodletting and Miraculous Cures	Lam, Vincent	4
Under the Skin	Lambert, Betty	1
The Bare Plum of Winter Rain	Lane, Patrick	1
The Stone Angel	Laurence, Margaret	5

Title	Author	Occurrences
The Diviners	Laurence, Margaret	14
A Jest of God	Laurence, Margaret	1
The Fire-Dwellers	Laurence, Margaret	2
A Bird in the House	Laurence, Margaret	5
The Prophet's Camel Bell	Laurence, Margaret	2
Crow Lake	Lawson, Mary	2
Sunshine Sketches of a Little Town	Leacock, Stephen	10
Open Country	Lecker, Robert	1
Yesno	Lee, Dennis	1
Disappearing Moon Café	Lee, Sky	8
Stormy Night	Lemieux, Michèle	1
A Teatro Trilogy: Selected Plays	Lemoine, Stewart	1
Antoinette de Mirecourt	Leprohon, Rosanna	2
Chimera	Lill, Wendy	1
This Land is My Land	Littlechild, George	1
The Self-Completing Tree	Livesay, Dorothy	1
As Long as the Rivers Flow: A Last Summer before Residential School	Loyie, Larry with Constance Brissenden	1
Frost	Luiken, Nicole	1
The Diary of Abraham Ulrikab: Text and Context	Lutz, Hartmut, and Alootook Ipellie	1
Beckoners	Mac, Carrie	1
Goodnight Desdemona (Good Morning Juliet)	MacDonald, Ann-Marie	3
Fall on Your Knees	MacDonald, Ann-Marie	1
Juliana and the Medicine Fish	MacDonald, Jake	1
The Danger Tree	Macfarlane, David	1
Roland Graeme: Knight. A Novel of Our Time	Machar, Agnes Maule	1
The Letter Opener	Maclear, Kyo	1
Barometer Rising	MacLennan, Hugh	5
Each Man's Son	MacLennan, Hugh	1
The Lost Salt Gift of Blood	MacLeod, Alistair	2
No Great Mischief	MacLeod, Alistair	1
The Shape of a Girl and Jewel	MacLeod, Joan	1
Hold Fast	Major, Kevin	2
No Man's Land	Major, Kevin	1

Title	Author	Occurrences
Sojourner's Truth	Maracle, Lee	1
Ravensong	Maracle, Lee	2
Will's Garden	Maracle, Lee	1
Sojourners and Sundogs	Maracle, Lee	2
Road to Chlifa	Marineau, Michèle	1
Ana Historic	Marlatt, Daphne	1
Steveston	Marlatt, Daphne, and Robert Minden	3
Life of Pi	Martel, Yann	3
In an Iron Glove	Martin, Claire	2
The Freak	Matas, Carol	1
The Widows	Mayr, Suzette	1
Moon Honey	Mayr, Suzette	2
Clearing in the West: My Own Story	McClung, Nellie	1
Execution	McDougall, Colin	1
Hamburger Valley, California	McGimpsey, David	2
To The New World	McGrath, Carmelita	1
The Birth House	McKay, Ami	1
Camber: Selected Poems 1983–2000	McKay, Don	1
Strike/Slip	McKay, Don	3
Field Marks: The Poetry of Don McKay	McKay, Don	1
Nanabosho and the Woodpecker	McLellan, Joseph	1
Marshall McLuhan: The Book of Probes	McLuhan, Marshall	1
Laws of Media	McLuhan, Marshall	1
The Medium is the Massage	McLuhan, Marshall, and Quentin Fiore	1
In the Company of Strangers	Meigs, Mary	2
Muinji'j Becomes a Man	Mi'sel Joe, Saqamaw	1
Fugitive Pieces	Michaels, Anne	8
The Weight of Oranges	Michaels, Anne	1
Two Plays: Voiceless People and Addorata	Micone, Marco	1
Half Life	Mighton, John	1
Such a Long Journey	Mistry, Rohinton	1
A Fine Balance	Mistry, Rohinton	1
Tales from the Firozha Baag	Mistry, Rohinton	1
Who Has Seen the Wind	Mitchell, W.O.	1

Title	Author	Occurrences
Princess Pocahontas and the Blue Spots	Mojica, Monique	1
Awful Disclosures of Maria Monk, or, The Hidden Secrets of a Nun's Life in a Convent Exposed	Monk, Maria	1
Anne of Green Gables	Montgomery, L.M.	11
The Blue Castle	Montgomery, L.M.	1
Riot	Moodie, Andrew	1
Roughing it in the Bush	Moodie, Susanna	10
The Luck of Ginger Coffey	Moore, Brian	1
Alligator	Moore, Lisa	4
He Drown She in the Sea	Mootoo, Shani	2
Random Passage	Morgan, Bernice	1
Sylvanus Now	Morrissey, Donna	1
The Indian Medicine Shows	Moses, Daniel David	1
Brébeuf's Ghost	Moses, Daniel David	1
Coyote City: A Play in Two Acts	Moses, Daniel David	1
Almighty Voice and His Wife	Moses, Daniel David	1
An Anthology of Canadian Native Literature in English	Moses, Daniel David, and Terry Goldie (eds.)	5
Is Canada Postcolonial?: Unsettling Canadian Literature	Moss, Laura (ed.)	1
Never Cry Wolf	Mowat, Farley	1
Improved by Cultivation: English Canadian Prose to 1914	Moyles, R.G.	3
The Moons of Jupiter	Munro, Alice	1
Open Secrets	Munro, Alice	1
Lives of Girls and Women	Munro, Alice	16
Runaway	Munro, Alice	1
No Love Lost	Munro, Alice	1
Dead Girls	Nancy Lee	2
Pornography	Nathan, Debbie	1
Mirabel	Nepveu, Pierre	1
Borderlands: How We Talk About Canada	New, W.H.	1
The Martyrology: Books 3 and 4	Nichol, bp	1
Tay John	O'Hagan, Howard	3
This Will All End in Tears	Ollmann, Joe	1

Title	Author	Occurrences
Yellow Line	Olsen, Sylvia	1
The Epic of Qayaq: The Longest Story Ever Told by My People	Oman, Lela Kiana	1
Running in the Family	Ondaatje, Michael	11
In the Skin of a Lion	Ondaatje, Michael	27
The English Patient	Ondaatje, Michael	2
The Collected Works of Billy the Kid	Ondaatje, Michael	8
Coming Through Slaughter	Ondaatje, Michael	3
The Cinnamon Peeler: Selected Poems	Ondaatje, Michael	2
Divisadero	Ondaatje, Michael	3
Secular Love	Ondaatje, Michael	1
Anil's Ghost	Ondaatje, Michael	2
From Ink Lake	Ondaatje, Michael (ed.)	1
Wild Geese	Ostenso, Martha	2
The Black Madonna	Paci, F.G.	1
Planet Earth: Poems Selected and New	Page, P.K.	1
Hologram: A Book of Glosas	Page, P.K.	1
What Lies Before Us	Panych, Morris	1
Awake and Dreaming	Pearson, Kit	1
She Tries Her Tongue, Her Silence Softly Breaks	Philip, Marlene Nourbese	1
Harriet's Daughter	Philip, Marlene Nourbese	1
An Island in the Sky: Selected Poetry of Al Pittman	Pittman, Al	1
Blood Relations	Pollock, Sharon	1
Walsh	Pollock, Sharon	1
Doc	Pollock, Sharon	7
Volkswagen Blues	Poulin, Jacques	5
E.J. Pratt: Selected Poems	Pratt, E.J.	1
Rooms for Rent in the Outer Planets	Purdy, Al	1
Vancouver Walking	Quartermain, Meredith	1
Tamarind Mem	Rau Badami, Anita	2
Sacred Legends	Ray, Carl, and James R. Stevens (eds.)	1
The Donnellys	Reaney, James	1
Lives of the Saints	Ricci, Nino	2

Title	Author	Occurrences
Hockey Dreams: Memoirs of a Man Who Couldn't Play	Richards, David Adams	1
Mercy Among the Children	Richards, David Adams	2
Wacousta	Richardson, John	8
Joshua Then and Now	Richler, Mordecai	1
The Apprenticeship of Duddy Kravitz	Richler, Mordecai	7
St. Urbain's Horseman	Richler, Mordecai	2
Solomon Gursky Was Here	Richler, Mordecai	2
Barney's Version	Richler, Mordecai	3
The Street	Richler, Mordecai	1
The Heart of the Ancient Wood	Roberts, Charles G.D.	1
Kindred of the Wild	Roberts, Charles G.D.	1
Selected Animal Stories: A Critical Edition	Roberts, Charles G.D.	1
Monkey Beach	Robinson, Eden	19
Traplines	Robinson, Eden	2
Blood Sports	Robinson, Eden	1
Write It On Your Heart	Robinson, Harry	1
FareWel	Ross, Ian	4
As For Me and My House	Ross, Sinclair	20
The Lamp at Noon and Other Stories	Ross, Sinclair	2
The Rent Collector	Rotchin, Glen	1
The Tin Flute	Roy, Gabrielle	1
The Road Past Altamont	Roy, Gabrielle	2
Enchantment and Sorrow: The Autobiography of Gabrielle Roy	Roy, Gabrielle	1
Grey Owl: The Mystery of Archie Belaney	Ruffo, Armand Garnet	2
The Young in One Another's Arms	Rule, Jane	1
The Ecstasy of Rita Joe	Ryga, George	3
The Electrical Field	Sakamoto, Kerri	3
Love Medicine and One Song	Scofield, Gregory	1
I Knew Two Métis Women: The Lives of Dorothy Scofield and Georgina Houle Young	Scofield, Gregory	2
Thunder Through My Veins: Memories of a Métis Childhood	Scofield, Gregory	1
In the Village of Viger	Scott, D.C.	1
The Adventures of a Black Girl in Search of God	Sears, Djanet	1

Title	Author	Occurrences
Funny Boy	Selvadurai, Shyam	1
Wimbledon Green: The Greatest Comic Book Collector in the World	Seth	1
Wild Animals I Have Known	Seton, E.T.	1
Reading Hebron	Sherman, Jason	1
The Stone Diaries	Shields, Carol	3
Sister Woman	Sime, J.G.	1
Loop	Simpson, Anne	1
Two Murders in My Double Life	Škvorecký, Josef	1
Dust	Slade, Arthur	1
Little Voice	Slipperjack, Ruby	1
By Grand Central Station I Sat Down and Wept	Smart, Elizabeth	1
Quilt	Smyth, Donna	1
He Who Hunted Birds in His Father's Village: The Dimensions of Haida Myth	Snyder, Gary	1
Short Haul Engine	Solie, Karen	2
With English Subtitles	Starnino, Carmine	1
My Name is Seepeetza	Sterling, Shirley	2
Delible	Stone, Anne	2
Unhomely States: Theorizing Canadian Postcolonialism	Sugars, Cynthia (ed.)	3
Marine Life	Svendsen, Linda	1
Fox	Sweatman, Margaret	1
The Baby Blues	Taylor, Drew Hayden	1
Only Drunks and Children Tell the Truth	Taylor, Drew Hayden	1
Someday	Taylor, Drew Hayden	2
Furious Observations of a Blue-eyed Ojibway	Taylor, Drew Hayden	1
Fearless Warriors	Taylor, Drew Hayden	1
Stanley Park	Taylor, Timothy	5
Story House	Taylor, Timothy	1
Small Arguments	Thammavongsa, Souvankham	1
The Farm Show: A Collective Creation	Theatre Passe Muraille	1
The New Long Poem Anthology	Thesen, Sharon (ed.)	1
Simple Recipes	Thien, Madeleine	2
Certainty	Thien, Madeleine	1
Mrs. Blood	Thomas, Audrey	1

Title	Author	Occurrences
Behind the Face of Winter	Thomas, H. Nigel	1
I Dream Myself Into Being: Collected Poems	Thompson, John	1
Lion in the Streets	Thompson, Judith	2
A Complicated Kindness	Toews, Miriam	5
The Backwoods of Canada	Traill, Catharine Parr	2
Les Belles Soeurs	Tremblay, Michel	1
Hosanna	Tremblay, Michel	2
Kingsway	Turner, Michael	1
The Pornographer's Poem	Turner, Michael	1
Ontological Necessities	Uppal, Priscila	1
Away	Urquhart, Jane	4
The Whirlpool	Urquhart, Jane	1
Some Other Garden	Urquhart, Jane	1
Storm Glass	Urquhart, Jane	1
The Stone Carvers	Urquhart, Jane	1
Changing Heaven	Urquhart, Jane	1
The Lesser Blessed	Van Camp, Richard	3
Angel Wing Splash Pattern	Van Camp, Richard	1
No Fixed Address: An Amourous Journey	Van Herk, Aritha	2
The Englishman's Boy	Vanderhaeghe, Guy	2
Man Descending	Vanderhaeghe, Guy	1
The Last Crossing	Vanderhaeghe, Guy	1
The In-between World of Vikram Lall	Vassanji, M.G.	1
When She Was Queen	Vassanji, M.G.	1
Miriam Waddington: Collected Poems	Waddington, Miriam	1
Apartment Seven: Essays Selected and New	Waddington, Miriam	1
Keeper'n Me	Wagamese, Richard	2
A Quality of Light	Wagamese, Richard	1
For Joshua: An Ojibway Father Teaches His Son	Wagamese, Richard	1
Diamond Grill	Wah, Fred	7
Waiting for Saskatchewan	Wah, Fred	1
Problem Child	Walker, George F.	1
Keep That Candle Burning Bright and Other Poems	Wallace, Bronwen	1
Going Around with Bachelors	Walsh, Agnes	1

Title	Author	Occurrences
The Hour of Bad Decisions	Wangersky, Russell	1
Canadian Exploration Literature	Warkentin, Germaine (ed.)	2
There, There	Warner, Patrick	1
Modern Canadian Plays (vol. 1)	Wasserman, Jerry (ed.)	3
Modern Canadian Plays (vol. 2)	Wasserman, Jerry (ed.)	5
The Double Hook	Watson, Sheila	7
The Vision Tree: Selected Poems	Webb, Phyllis	2
Icefields	Wharton, Thomas	1
Chuck in the City	Wheeler, Jordan	1
A Discovery of Strangers	Wiebe, Rudy	2
The Temptations of Big Bear	Wiebe, Rudy	1
The Scorched-Wood People	Wiebe, Rudy	1
Of This Earth: A Mennonite Boyhood in the Boreal Forest	Wiebe, Rudy	2
The Tightrope Walker: Autobiographical Writings of Anne Wilkinson	Wilkinson, Anne	1
Swamp Angel	Wilson, Ethel	11
Hetty Dorval	Wilson, Ethel	1
Re:Zoom	Wilson, Sheri-D	1
The Sacrifice	Wiseman, Adele	1
Crackpot	Wiseman, Adele	2
Forage	Wong, Rita	1
The Age of Longing	Wright, Richard B.	1
The Maestro	Wynne-Jones, Tim	1
Rex Zero and the End of the World	Wynne-Jones, Tim	1
A Thief in the House of Memory	Wynne-Jones, Tim	1
The Adventures of Ali & Ali and the Axes of Evil: A Divertimento for Warlords	Youssef, Marcus	2
Moderns and Contemporaries: Canadian Poetry from 1900 to the Present (English 274E Anthology) (Coursepack)	Zezulka, Joseph (ed.)	3

Notes

Introduction

1. Because my initial study included both the University of Alberta's Department of English and what was in 1997–98 the Department of Modern Languages and Comparative Studies at the University of Alberta, my research then included twenty-eight departments but only twenty-seven universities.

2. The Association of Canadian University Teachers of English, later changed its name to the Association of Canadian College and University Teachers of English. Mathews's essay was first published in *English Quarterly* in 1972. A revised version was later published in *Canadian Literature: Surrender or Revolution* (1978).

3. I am alluding here to the slogan used by federalists during the 1995 Québec referendum campaign.

4. Once the tagline in McClelland & Stewart's brand, their claim to be "The Canadian Publisher" is questionable at best. In 2000, owner Avie Bennett sold 25 per cent of the company to Random House of Canada and donated the remaining 75 per cent to the University of Toronto. Even though Random House became full owners in 2011, the company still refers to themselves on their website as "the Canadian Publishers" ("McClelland & Stewart"). Needless to say, regardless of how many Canadian titles McClelland & Stewart publishes, there is a considerable difference between being one of many imprints of a massive multinational publisher and an independent Canadian-owned publisher.

5. The exclusion of Native literatures from this conception of Canadian literature(s), of course, also makes it far simpler to consider the term "Literature" as signifying only written texts.

6. On a larger scale, speaking of the literatures of Canada can also allow us to take into account marginalized genres such as science fiction, comics and graphic novels, and romance fiction. One of the most successful Canadian publishing ventures ever remains that of Harlequin Romance, founded in Winnipeg in 1949. Why such genres are rarely examined in the context of the literatures of Canada has far more to do with the definitions of "Literature" espoused by university literature departments than it does the significance of these bodies of work.

1 The "People's Literature"

1. "The other languages of the hexagon can produce popular poetry, French, itself, produces literature: this nuance is important and characteristic of the century."

2. In fact, the system of colleges in Québec "adopted the same programs, used the same textbooks, and followed the same evolution."

3. "The value of the classical education comes in large part from how it represents a homogenous cultural home for the entire duration of the education of the adolescent."

4. Laval's origins date back to the founding of the Séminaire du Québec in 1663, making it Canada's oldest university and the fourth oldest in North America.

5. "Rationally and historically, the Latin and French genius, in Québec, could be nothing but national and religious, an effective rampart against the Saxon genius and the Protestant heresy at the same time."

6. "Representatives of the Latin race, in the face of the Anglo-Saxon element whose excessive expansion and abnormal influence must be balanced, as it is in Europe, for the progress of civilization, our mission and that of the societies who share our same origin, scattered over this continent, is to place a counterweight against it by gathering our forces, to place in opposition to the Anglo-American positivism, to its materialist instincts, to its crude egoism, the most elevated tendencies, which are the privilege of the Latin races, an uncontested superiority in the moral order and in the domain of thought."

7. "Let us put an end to this abnormal sight of a Canadian literature that develops itself, which is to say that recruits its active workers, largely alongside and outside our educational institutions."

8. Pacey says much the same thing in his seminal 1973 article "The Study of Canadian Literature." Disputing notions held by some of his colleagues that Canadian literature is a "'soft' option," Pacey writes, "I should never myself counsel a student to take a course wholly devoted to Canadian literature unless he already had a good grounding in Chaucer, Spenser, Milton, Pope, and Wordsworth" (70).

9. "The teaching of this literature could orient itself in part towards a study of the sociological aspects that make up literary works and could attach itself in this way to a sort of cultural anthropology or national psychology."

10. "The adoption of a socio-historic perspective on the one hand, and the will to create a sense of identification on the other. This identification seems to have been created by the means of nationalism."

11. Sarah M. Corse's reference to this article in *Nationalism and Literature: The Politics of Culture in Canada and the United States* (1997) is the only one I have found. Lucas's article provides both valuable data and a fascinating glimpse at the movement to challenge what some described as the increasing "Americanization" of Canadian institutions.

12. As Robin Mathews and James Steele pointed out in their highly public campaign for the Canadianization of Canadian universities, the mid-to-late 1960s saw a great number of Americans hired to fill tenure-track positions. In their 1969 book *The Struggle for Canadian Universities*, they estimate that "between 1963 and 1965 roughly 58% of new appointments went to non-Canadians; between 1965 and 1967, this figure appears to have risen to 72%; in 1968, it may have been as high as 86%." (1).

13. Commissioned in 1972 by the Association of Universities and Colleges of Canada, the Symons Report examined the place of teaching and research on Canadian topics at Canada's universities. In this report, published in 1976 under the title *To Know Ourselves*, Thomas H.B. Symons called not only for greater attention to be paid to the study of Canada at the post-secondary level, but for the Government of Canada to provide greater support to Canadian studies both nationally and internationally.

14. A redefinition "would undoubtedly signify the change of status of the literary: freed from its traditional genres that, since the 1950s, have served as the basis for the structuring of courses, literature allows for new forms more and more....This modification implies simultaneously the redefinition of the literary and the redefinition of the objectives and the structures of its teaching."

15. "You will see that it is very diversified, it is very different from one university to another, and the difference often masks the regularities. One must not let oneself be deceived by these differences."

2   "A Prisoner of Its Own Amnesia"

1.   There are, of course, other models that are very applicable to a study of the literary institution in Canada, most notably Itamar Even-Zohar's polysystem theory or some of the work that has been done on the literary institutions of other countries such as Germany and South Africa. As this book is not solely a study of the Canadian literary institution, I have opted not to discuss them here.

2.   "The mechanism of the institution can remain barely visible insofar as it only exerts its constraints in implicit ways on symbolic practices."

3.   There are, of course, exceptions to this general observation. Critics such as Frank Davey, Robert Lecker, Margery Fee, Carole Gerson, and E.D. Blodgett are some of the most prominent critics to have published work in this area. One of the most valuable

contributions to this field was the series of conferences and their proceedings sponsored during the 1980s and 1990s by the University of Alberta's Research Institute for Comparative Literature under the title "Towards a History of the Literary Institution in Canada."

4.   "Literature had just disengaged itself from religious ideology and refused to serve bourgeois ideology. It thus positioned itself as independent of any type of ideology."

5.   "Classical writing thus exploded, and all of Literature, from Flaubert to our time, became a problem of language." "Literature (the word was only born recently before this) was definitively consecrated as an object."

6.   "There is no autonomous position in the autonomized field; every position is always and in advance a function of the others. Consequently, the writer is always, from the moment he writes, someone who seeks his place in this game of positions, and the status of his writings, he knows, will pass without fail through the mediation of the processes that exert symbolic authority."

7.   "In this respect, [the school] does a bit more than conserve and celebrate the works of the past, for it introduces them into the logic of a system that necessarily projects its principles and categories on the productions of the present—productions into which the system is, moreover, always ready to integrate after their selection."

8.   "Pedagogical work (whether it is exerted by School, by a Church, or by a party) has the effect of producing individuals durably and systematically modified by a prolonged action of transformation aiming to endow them with the same durable formation (habitus), which is to say common frameworks of thinking, perception, appreciation, and action."

9.   "(1) social structures generate the habitus; (2) the habitus determines practices (notably esthetic); (3) practices reproduce the structures."

10. "Practice is the product of a relation between a situation and a habitus."

11. "The serial production of identically programmed individuals requires and gives rise to the production of programming agents who are themselves identically programmed and standardized instruments of conservation and transmission."

12. "The ideology of the dominant class operates insidiously, constituting itself in general discourse, in the discourse of everyone, even if the dominated groups reorient and reinterpret that discourse according to their own positions. It is, as one says, what cements the social formation."

13. "The geopolitical border of Québec is not in itself very clear-cut: whatever one says and whatever are our collective or individual aspirations, Québec has borders that are permeable, permeable to Canada and to francophone communities outside of Québec, in France, in the United States. I cannot construct a history that would be founded on the fiction of political, economic, and cultural autonomy: that of the Québécois literary institution."

14. The Bertelsmann website speaks to its overwhelming economic power when it notes that Random House "presents a broad spectrum of editorial voices comprised of 200 editorially independent imprints in 15 countries" (Bertelsmann).

15. While there are no real French-language branch-plant publishers operating in Canada—no Gallimard Québec, for instance—some of Québec's most important authors have been published by prestigious French publishers. The late Anne Hébert had an exclusive publishing contract with Seuil while Réjean Ducharme publishes with Gallimard.

16. For a more detailed explanation of these changes and their impact on the place of Québécois literature in the CÉGEP curriculum, see Max Roy's insightful study *La litté-rature québécoise au collège (1990–1996)* (Montréal: XYZ éditeur, 1998).

17. "The teaching of a culture different from the surrounding culture and presented as the foundational culture inevitably implies a value judgement."

18. "Leads to a splitting up of knowledges, of disciplines, and competencies. These divisions, however inoffensive since their only objective is to facilitate the administration of the university enterprise, become mental divisions."

19. "The principle of 'division' is equally a principle of 'vision.'"

20. This edition replaced Brown, Bennett, and Cooke's "revised and abridged edition" of *An Anthology of Canadian Literature in English* (1990), which replaced Brown and Bennett's earlier two-volume edition of *An Anthology of Canadian Literature in English* (1983). It is worth noting that Brown and Bennett swap the order of their names on the later editions of the anthology. My references to these texts use the order in which the editors list their names.

21. New Canadian Library editions of *The Double Hook*, *The Stone Angel*, and *The Apprenticeship of Duddy Kravitz* were published in 1966, 1968, and 1969, respectively (Friskney). Janet Friskney also notes that "mass market editions of Laurence's work in Seal [Books] in the mid-1970s had an impact on her NCL sales—the [mass market] editions were cheaper and Seal books were marketed to academics for student use, something that upset Laurence" (Friskney).

22. "Its influence eventually measures itself in reading habits and theatre attendance which signifies multiple repercussions. From this perspective, the situation of the teaching of literature and theatre at the college level merits the attention of those interested in the arts and letters, whether it be authors, distributors, booksellers, producers, or the instructors themselves."

23. "Their reason for being, always, is the transmission of knowledge. Not by an empirical transmission, according to circumstances and individuals, but by an authorized trans-mission, officially recognized, that leads to a sanction in the form of a diploma."

24. "Paradoxically...disinterest is rewarded with 'distinction' in the scientific economy. More specifically, the impersonal nature of one's exposition becomes the sovereign argument for its credibility."

25. According to Québec's Société de développement des entreprises culturelles, a government organization that looks after the state of the cultural industries in Québec, in 1999–2000 Québécois publishers received $2,775,000 from the Québec government, with an additional $5,700,000 going to the book industry. In comparison, Alberta publishers received $335,000 from their provincial government and Ontario publishers $572,000 from theirs.

26. While some programs such as that in Canadian literature at the University of Victoria or the graduate program in comparative Canadian literature at the Université de Sherbrooke work against this model, the only department in English Canada to which this statement does not apply is the University of Alberta's Comparative Literature Program. With its over forty-year history of teaching courses in comparative Canadian literature, it posits the literatures of Canada as part of the larger body of world literature and does not tie the study of the subject in any way to the study of the literatures of England or France.

27. It is important to note here that for a number of years Laval had a separate department devoted to "littérature canadienne-française." This department eventually rejoined the Département d'études françaises, but the strength and depth of course offerings in Québécois literature continues to this day.

3 Field Notes

1. Notably, most universities in Canada have more than one department that regularly offers courses that include the literatures of Canada. The most frequent examples of these other course are found in departments or programs that offer courses based around the study of languages other than their university's primary language of instruction. While this mostly applies to English language and literature programs at French-language universities and programs in French language and literature at English-language universities, it can also be expected that, for instance, programs in German, Russian, or Chinese, might in fact feature Canadian literature written originally in those languages—if not in dedicated courses on immigrant literature in Canada, then as part of more general literature or language courses. In any case, I have chosen in this study to focus only on departments whose main function is the teaching of literature. While I chose to do so partly to impose limits on the number of interviews I would conduct and departments I would visit, I based my decision primarily on the fact that there is always at least an implicit sense that the study of literature in another language in conjunction with the study of that language serves in part to educate the student about the culture of that nation or language group. While, obviously, I will be making the case that literature departments play precisely this same role, part of their "distinction," to employ Bourdieu's use of the term, derives from their apparent disinterest and denial of filling this function.

2. In 2002, CRELIQ joined with the Université de Montréal's Centre d'études québécoises (CÉTUQ) and researchers from the Université du Québec à Montréal to form the Centre de recherche interuniversitaire sur la littérature et la culture québécoises (CRILCQ).

3. I was helped tremendously in this process by Lu Ziola who created the first three FileMakerPro databases, which I then proceeded to expand and adjust as necessary.

4. The University of Sherbrooke is omitted from this list, as I looked primarily at its graduate programs in comparative Canadian literature and did not collect statistics on its undergraduate programs in French literature.

5. The departments of English at the University of Alberta, the University of New Brunswick in Fredericton, the University of Prince Edward Island, and the University of Western Ontario are excluded from these rankings as these institutions were unable to provide me with an accurate number of the total course sections for the 1997–98 academic year. The figures for Memorial University only include those courses offered in the fall term.

6. In French "littérature intime" is a categorization that includes texts such as diaries, correspondence, memoirs, and autobiographies. The fact that an undergraduate course could be offered on nineteenth-century Québec texts of this sort speaks to the depth of specialization that exists in the curriculum at the Université Laval.

7. "The principle of 'division' is equally a principle of 'vision.'"

8. In this section, I am using the word "texts" to refer to books. A number of the books taught, in fact, contain multiple texts (e.g., Brown, Bennett, and Cooke's *Anthology of Canadian Literature in English* or Geddes's *15 Canadian Poets x 2*), but it is frequently unclear which selections from such works were taught in the classroom. Therefore, this list actually privileges books over texts and does not endeavour to try to break its assessment of *what* is taught to this more specific level. On the other hand, although it is difficult to know which selections from anthologies or short story collections are included in the curriculum, the knowledge of which anthologies were used can frequently help us to predict what was *not* taught. The fact that the aforementioned *Anthology of Canadian Literature in English* (1990) includes no selections from the Native oral tradition, no selections translated from other languages such as French, no selections from any genres other than poetry and fiction, and in 1997–98 was nearly eight years out of date, reveals a lot about the content of a course when examined in conjunction with the other texts on the syllabus.

9. Works on the ranked list of titles most frequently taught are ordered by number of occurrences. Works with the same number of occurrences are then listed alphabetically. Thus, though a work like *Roughing it in the Bush* is listed here in eighth place, a better way to describe its position would be as one of three works that are the third most frequently taught texts.

10. Aside from writers like Ondaatje and Atwood who publish both poetry and prose, poets fare poorly on the list of most frequently taught writers. Were my statistics able to account for the choices made by instructors as to which works they teach from a given anthology, we would have a much better idea about which poets and poems are taught most frequently in English and comparative literature courses.

4   Mind the Gaps

1. Some of the people to whom I spoke were not in fact teaching courses in the literatures of Canada during that particular term or academic year. In such cases, I oriented my questions more towards the subjects' past experiences teaching such courses and the general issues raised by my questions.

2. "The objective of this course is to identify the currents and dominant literary practices and to gain knowledge of the outstanding works in the corpus of Québécois literature. The approach will be more historical and we will cover the whole of the corpus, from the writings of New France to contemporary writing."

3. The Bibliothèque Québécoise series, it is worth noting, is in fact a joint endeavour between three Québec publishers: les Éditions Fides, les Éditions Hurtubise HMH, and Leméac Éditeur.

4. "There is practically no Native literature written in French. Of the few who are francophone, there is almost no one who writes."

5   "The Substance of Forgetting"

1. "Forgetting, and I will say even historical error, is an essential factor in the creation of a nation, and it is in this way that the progress of historical studies is often a danger for the nationality…Thus, the essence of a nation is that all the individuals have many things in common, and also that they have all forgotten many things."

2. Of the twenty-two anglophone universities studied in 2007–08, only six required students majoring in English to take at least one course on Canadian literature: Memorial, McGill, Ottawa, Calgary, Simon Fraser, and UBC.

3. I avoided including in my count courses such as "English for Engineers" that might skew these percentages. Only first-year English courses available to the English majors were counted.

4. As we know, it is rare that any English "Canadian Literature" course claims to represent the literature or people of Québec, but that's really my point here. This is not an insignificant part of the population or literary history that we are continually ignoring.

Afterword

1. Founded in 1981 at the Université Laval, CRELIQ joined forces in 2002 with the Université de Montréal's Centre d'études québécoises (CÉTUQ) and a team of researchers at the Université du Québec à Montréal to form CRILCQ.

2. Armed with what I had learned in Québec about CRELIQ, in 2003 I approached a senior administrator at the University of Alberta with a proposal to help create a similar centre focused on the literatures of Canada. I was confident we could find donors and government support for such a centre and that the centre could make a major contribution to research and teaching at the university and to the broader field of Canadian literary studies. The administrator, after jokingly reminding me that he remembered when "Canadian literature was an oxymoron," assured me that no faculty member would have time to contribute to such a centre, that no donor would ever be interested in funding it, and that I would be better off leaving Canada for the position awaiting me in the United States. This lack of institutional support or vision for Canadian literature and Canadian studies in general is something many Canadianists have felt and experienced at English-Canadian universities across the country.

Works Cited

Amis, Kingsley. *Lucky Jim*. London: Penguin, 1961. Print.

Anderson, Benedict. *Imagined Communities*. London: Verso, 1991. Print.

Anderson, Robert. "Education." *The New Oxford Companion to Literature in France*. Ed. Peter France. Oxford: Oxford University Press, 1995. 271–73. Print.

Arnason, David. "Critical Theory and the Canadian University." *Open Letter* 8.5–6 (1993): 57–63. Print.

Arnold, Matthew. "The Function of Criticism at the Present Time." *Essays in Criticism (First Series)*. London: Macmillan, 1865. 1–41. Print.

Baker, Ray Palmer. *A History of English-Canadian Literature to the Confederation, Its Relation to the Literature of Great Britain and the United States*. Cambridge, MA: Harvard University Press, 1920. Print.

Balibar, Étienne. "The Nation Form: History and Ideology." *Race, Nation, Class*. Eds. Étienne Balibar and Immanuel Wallerstein. London: Verso, 1991. 86–106. Print.

Barthes, Roland. *Le degré zéro de l'écriture*. Paris: Seuil, 1953. Print.

———. "Réflexions." *L'enseignement de la littérature*. Eds. Serge Doubrovskyand Tzvetan Todorov. Paris: Plon, 1971. 170–77. Print.

Bennett, Donna, and Russell Brown, eds. *A New Anthology of Canadian Literature in English*. Don Mills, ON: Oxford University Press Canada, 2002. Print.

Bertelsmann. "Random House—Bertelsmann SE & Co. KGaA." Web. 19 June 2013.

Biron, Michel, François Dumont, and Élisabeth Nardout-Lafarge. *Histoire de la littérature québécoise*. Montréal: Les Éditions du boréal, 2007. Print.

Bourdieu, Pierre. *Esquisse d'une théorie de la pratique*. Genève: Droz, 1972. Print.

———. "The Field of Cultural Production, Or: The Economic World Reversed." Trans. Randal Johnson. *The Field of Cultural Production.* New York: Columbia University Press, 1993. 29–73. Print.

———. *Homo Academicus.* Paris: Les Éditions de Minuit, 1984. Print.

———. *Leçon sur la leçon.* Paris: Les Éditions de Minuit, 1982. Print.

———. "Manet and the Insitutionalization of Anomie." *The Field of Cultural Production.* Trans. Randal Johnson. New York: Columbia University Press, 1993. 238–53. Print.

———. "Le Marché des biens symboliques." *L'Année sociologiques* 22 (1971): 49–126. Print.

———. "The Market of Symbolic Goods." Trans. Randal Johnson. *The Field of Cultural Production.* New York: Columbia University Press, 1993. 112–41. Print.

———. "The Production of Belief: Contribution to an Economy of Symbolic Goods." Trans. Randal Johnson. *The Field of Cultural Production.* New York: Columbia University Press, 1993. 74–111. Print.

———. *La reproduction.* Paris: Les Éditions de Minuit, 1970. Print.

Brown, Russell. Personal interview. Toronto, ON. 7 November 1997.

Brydon, Diana. "Cross-Talk, Postcolonial Pedagogy, and Transnational Literacy." *Home-Work: Postcolonialism, Pedagogy, and Canadian Literature.* Ed. Cynthia Sugars. Ottawa, ON: University of Ottawa Press, 2004. 57–74. Print.

Calvet, Louis-Jean. *Linguistique et colonialisme.* Paris: Payot, 1974. Print.

Cameron, David. *Taking Stock: Canadian Studies in the Nineties.* Montréal: Association for Canadian Studies, 1996. Print.

"Canadian Literature in English: Texts and Contexts, Vol. 1." *Pearson Education Canada Catalogue.* Pearson Education, 2009. Web. 7 June 2009.

Casgrain, Abbé Henri-Raymond. *Le mouvement littéraire au Canada.* Oeuvres Complètes. Vol. 1. Québec: C. Darveau, 1875. Print.

Corse, Sarah. *Nationalism and Literature: The Politics of Culture in Canada and the United States.* Cambridge: Cambridge University Press, 1997. Print.

Cullen, Burke. Personal interview. Toronto, ON. 4 November 1997.

Davey, Frank. "'and Quebec': Canadian Literature and Its Quebec Questions." *Canadian Poetry: Studies, Documents, Reviews* 40 (1997): 6–26. Print.

———. *Canadian Literary Power.* Edmonton: NeWest Press, 1994. Print.

———. "(Con)Figuring a 'Canada': Some Trends in Anglophone-Canadian Literature, Criticism, and the Arts." *Beyond Québec: Taking Stock of Canada.* Ed. K. McRoberts. Montréal and Kingston: McGill-Queen's University Press, 1995. 117–37. Print.

———. Personal interview. London, ON. 10 October 1997.

Davies, Gwendolyn. "J.D. Logan and the Great Feud for Canadian Literature: 1915–1923." *Canadian Issues/Thèmes canadiens* 17 (1995): 113–28. Print.

Davies, Robertson. *Leaven of Malice.* Toronto: Penguin, 1980. Print.

Department of English and Film Studies, University of Alberta. "Guide to Senior Courses." 2009. Web. 3 June 2009.

Dewart, Edward Hartley. *Selections from Canadian Poets, with Occasional Critical and Biographical Notes, and an Introductory Essay on Canadian Poetry*. Montréal: J. Lovell, 1864. Print.

Doyle, Brian. *English and Englishness*. London: Routledge, 1989. Print.

———. "The Hidden History of English Studies." *Re-Reading English*. Ed. Peter Widdowson. London: Methuen, 1982. 17–31. Print.

Dubois, Jacques. *L'institution de la littérature*. Brussels: Éditions Labor, 1978. Print.

Duffy, Dennis. Personal interview. Toronto, ON. 7 October 1997.

Dumont, François. "Le point de vue des professeurs: Quelques constats." *La littérature au Cégep, 1968–1978 : Le statut de la littérature dans l'enseignement collégial*. Eds. Joseph Melançon et al. Québec: Nuit Blanche Éditeur, 1993. 375–87. Print.

Edgar, Pelham. "Canadian Literature." *Acta Victoriana* 35.3 (Dec. 1911): 99–103. Print.

———. "A Fresh View of Canadian Literature." *The Search for English-Canadian Literature*. Ed. Carl Ballstadt. Toronto: University of Toronto Press, 1975. 110–14. Print.

Fee, Margery. "Canadian Literature and English Studies in the Canadian University." *Essays on Canadian Writing* 48 (1992–93): 20–40. Print.

———. "English-Canadian Literary Criticism, 1890–1950: Defining and Establishing a National Literature." Diss. University of Toronto, 1981. Print.

Findlay, L.M. "Prairie Jacobin: Carlyle King and Saskatchewan English." *University of Toronto Quarterly* 64.3 (1995): 417–30. Print.

Fortin, Nicole. "L'entrée en scène de la littérature québécoise." *Le discours de l'université sur la littérature québécoise*. Ed. Joseph Mélançon. Québec: Nuit Blanche Éditeur, 1996. 183–225. Print.

Friskney, Janet. "Re: NCL Dates." Message to Paul Martin. 28 May 1999. E-mail.

Gerson, Carole. "Cultural Darwinism: Publishing and the Canon of Early Canadian Literature in English." *Épilogue* 10.1–2 (1995): 25–33. Print.

Godard, Barbara. "The Critic, Institutional Culture, and Canadian Literature: Barbara Godard in Conversation with Smaro Kamboureli." *Canadian Literature at the Crossroads of Language and Culture*. Ed. Smaro Kamboureli. Edmonton: NeWest Press, 2008. 17–52. Print.

Graff, Gerald. *Professing Literature: An Institutional History*. Chicago: University of Chicago Press, 1987. Print.

Great Britain Board of Education, Committee on English in the Educational System of England. *The Teaching of English in England, Being the Report of the Departmental Committee Appointed by the President of the Board of Education to Inquire into the Position of English in the Educational System of England*. London: H. M. Stationery Office, 1921. Print.

Guillory, John. *Cultural Capital: The Problem of Literary Canon Formation*. Chicago: University of Chicago Press, 1993. Print.

Gunnars, Kristjana. *The Substance of Forgetting*. Red Deer, AB: Red Deer College Press, 1992. Print.

Harris, Charles B. "Canonical Variations and the English Curriculum." *ADE Bulletin* 90 (1988): 7–12. Print.

Harris, Robin S. *English Studies at Toronto: A History*. Toronto: University of Toronto Press, 1988. Print.

———. *A History of Higher Education in Canada, 1663–1960*. Toronto: University of Toronto Press, 1976. Print.

———. "The Place of English Studies in a University Program of General Education: A Study Based on the Practices of English-Speaking Universities and Colleges of Canada in 1951–52." Diss. University of Michigan, 1953. Print.

Hubert, Henry, and W.F. Garrett-Petts. "Foreword: An Historical Narrative of Textual Studies in Canada." *Textual Studies in Canada* 1 (1991): 1–30. Print.

Joyce, James. *Ulysses*. Trans. Hans Walter Gabler. London: Penguin, 1986. Print.

Kamboureli, Smaro. "Preface." *Trans.Can.Lit: Resituating the Study of Canadian Literature*. Eds. Smaro Kamboureli and Roy Miki. Waterloo, ON: Wilfrid Laurier University Press, 2007. vii–xv. Print.

King, Sarah. "The Failure of Canadian Literature: A Call for Revisioning the University English Curriculum." *Open Letter* 9.1 (1994): 5–24. Print.

King, Thomas. *The Truth About Stories: A Native Narrative*. Toronto: House of Anansi Press, 2003. Print.

Kreisel, Henry. "Has Anyone Here Heard of Marjorie Pickthall?: Discovering the Canadian Literary Landscape." *Canadian Literature* 100 (1984): 173–80. Print.

Lecker, Robert. *Making It Real: The Canonization of English-Canadian Literature*. Toronto: House of Anansi Press, 1995. Print.

Lecker, Robert, ed. *Open Country: Canadian Literature in English*. Toronto: Thomson Nelson, 2008. Print.

Lennox, John. Personal interview. Toronto, ON. 6 October 1997.

Logan, J.D. *Dalhousie University and Canadian Literature. Being the History of an Attempt to Have Canadian Literature Included in the Curriculum of Dalhousie. With a Criticism and Justification*. Halifax: The author, 1922. Print.

———. "Teaching Canadian Literature in the Universities." *Canadian Bookman* 2.4 (1920): 61–62. Print.

Logan, J.D., and Donald G. French. *Highways of Canadian Literature*. Toronto: McClelland & Stewart, 1924. Print.

Lucas, Alec. "Curriculum Crisis." *Canadian Dimension* 8.4–5 (1971): 58–60. Print.

Maclean, K. Seymour. "Education and the National Sentiment." *The Search for English-Canadian Literature*. Ed. Carl Ballstadt. Toronto: University of Toronto Press, 1975. 98–107. Print.

MacMechan, Archibald. *Headwaters of Canadian Literature*. Toronto: McClelland & Stewart, 1924. Print.

MacSkimming, Roy. *The Perilous Trade: Book Publishing in Canada, 1946–2006*. Toronto: McClelland & Stewart, 2007. Print.

Marquis, Thomas Guthrie. "English-Canadian Literature." *Our Intellectual Strength and Weakness, 'English-Canadian Literature,' 'French-Canadian Literature'*. Eds. J.G. Bourinot, T.G. Marquis, and C. Roy. Toronto: University of Toronto Press, 1973. 493–589. Print.

Martin, Paul. "Re: Producing Culture(S): The Politics of Knowledge Production and the Teaching of the Literatures of Canada." Diss. University of Alberta, 2001. Print.

Mathews, Robin. "Research, Curriculum, Scholarship, and Endowment in the Study of Canadian Literature " *English Quarterly* 5.3 (1972): 39–46. Print.

Mathews, Robin, and James Arthur Steele. *The Struggle for Canadian Universities: A Dossier*. Toronto: New Press, 1969. Print.

"McClelland & Stewart." *Random House of Canada*. N.d. Web. 19 May 2013.

McDonald, Larry. Personal interview. Ottawa, ON. 16 October 1997.

McDougall, R.L. "A Place in the Sun." *Totems: Essays on the Cultural History of Canada*. Ed. R.L. McDougall. Ottawa: Tecumseh Press, 1990. Print.

McKillop, A.B. *Matters of Mind: The University in Ontario, 1791–1951*. Toronto: University of Toronto Press, 1994. Print.

Melançon, Joseph. "La conjoncture universitaire." *Le discours de l'université sur la littérature québécoise*. Ed. Joseph Melançon. Québec: Nuit Blanche Éditeur, 1996. 63–93. Print.

Melançon, Joseph, Clément Moisan, and Max Roy. *Le discours d'une didactique: La formation littéraire dans l'enseignement classique au Québec*. Québec: Centre de recherche en littérature québécoise, Université Laval, 1988. Print.

Melançon, Joseph, et al. *La littérature au Cégep, 1968–1978 : Le statut de la littérature dans l'enseignement collégial*. Québec: Nuit Blanche Éditeur, 1993. Print.

Moisan, Clément. "Histoire des structures institutionnelles." *Le discours de l'université sur la littérature québécoise*. Ed. Joseph Mélançon. Québec: Nuit Blanche Éditeur, 1996. Print.

Monkman, Leslie. "Canadian Literature in English 'among Worlds.'" *Home-Work: Postcolonialism, Pedagogy, and Canadian Literature*. Ed. Cynthia Sugars. Ottawa: University of Ottawa Press, 2004. 117–33. Print.

Morgan, Robert. "English Studies as Cultural Production in Ontario 1860–1920." Diss. University of Toronto, 1987. Print.

Moss, Laura, and Cynthia Sugars. *Canadian Literature in English: Texts and Contexts*. Vol. 1. 2 vols. Toronto: Pearson, 2009. Print.

Murray, Heather. *Working in English: History, Institution, Resources*. Toronto: University of Toronto Press, 1996. Print.

O'Connor, John. Personal interview. Toronto, ON. 7 October 1997.

"Open Country," Instructor product details page. *Nelson Education*. Nelson Education, 2007. Web. 7 June 2009.

Pacey, Desmond. "Literary Criticism in Canada." *Essays in Canadian Criticism 1938–1968*. Ed. Desmond Pacey. Toronto: Ryerson Press, 1969. 45–52. Print.

———. "The Study of Canadian Literature." *Journal of Canadian Fiction* 2.2 (1973): 67–72. Print.

Palmer, D.J. *The Rise of English Studies*. Oxford: Oxford University Press, 1965. Print.

Pierce, Lorne. *An Outline of Canadian Literature (French and English)*. Toronto: Ryerson Press, 1927. Print.

Québec, Commission royale d'enquête sur l'enseignement dans la Province de. *Rapport de la commission royale d'enquête sur l'enseignement dans la Province de Québec (Rapport Parent)*. Québec: Commission royale d'enquête sur l'enseignement dans la Province de Québec, 1963–1966. Print.

Renan, Ernest. "Qu'est-ce qu'une nation?" *Qu'est-ce qu'une nation?; Suivi de préface aux discours et conférences; et préface à souvenirs d'enfance et de jeunesse*. 1882. Marseille: Le Mot et le reste, 2007. Print.

Robert, Lucie. "Institution, forme institutionelle et droit." *L'institution littéraire*. Ed. Maurice Lemire. Québec: Institut québécois de recherche sur la culture/Centre de recherche en littérature québécoise, 1986. 17–26. Print.

———. *L'institution du littéraire au Québec*. Québec: Presses de l'Université Laval, 1989. Print.

Roy, Camille. *Manuel d'histoire de la littérature canadienne-française*. Québec: Imprimerie de l'Action Sociale, 1918. Print.

———. "La nationalisation de la littérature canadienne." *Essais sur la littérature canadienne*. Ed. Camille Roy. Québec: Librairie Garneau, 1907. 187–201. Print.

Roy, Max. *La littérature québécoise au collège (1990–1996)*. Montréal: XYZ éditeur, 1998. Print.

———. "Les oeuvres littéraires étudiées dans les cours communs de français." *La littérature au Cégep, 1968–1978 : Le statut de la littérature dans l'enseignement collégial*. Eds. Joseph Melançon et al. Québec: Nuit Blanche Éditeur, 1993. 155–227. Print.

———. Personal interview. Montréal, QC. 22 October 1997.

Said, Edward. "Opponents, Audiences, Constituents, and Community." *Postmodern Culture*. Ed. Hal Foster. London: Pluto Press, 1985. 143–62. Print.

Saint-Jacques, Denis. Personal interview. Québec, QC. 23 October 1997.

Sartre, Jean-Paul. *Existentialism and Human Emotions*. New York: Philosophical Library, 1957. Print.

———. *Situations, II: qu'est-ce que la littérature?* Paris: Gallimard, 1948. Print.

Saul, John Ralston. Interview. CBC *Newsworld*. 4 Feb. 1998. Television.

———. *Reflections of a Siamese Twin: Canada at the End of the Twentieth Century*. Toronto: Viking, 1997. Print.

Shumway, David R. *Creating American Civilization: A Genealogy of American Literature as an Academic Discipline*. Minneapolis: University of Minnesota Press, 1994. Print.

Smyth, Donna E. Personal interview. Wolfville, NS. 29 October 1997.

Spivak, Gayatri Chakravorty. *A Critique of Postcolonial Reason: Toward a History of the Vanishing Present*. Cambridge, MA: Harvard University Press, 1999. Print.

Stevenson, Lionel. *Appraisals of Canadian Literature*. Toronto: Macmillan, 1926. Print.

Stratford, Philip. "Canada's Two Literatures: A Search for Emblems." *Canadian Review of Comparative Literature/Revue Canadienne de Littérature Comparée* 4 (1979): 131–38. Print.

Sugars, Cynthia. "Postcolonial Pedagogy and the Impossibility of Teaching Outside in the (Canadian Literature) Classroom." *Home-Work: Postcolonialism, Pedagogy, and Canadia Literature*. Ed. Cynthia Sugars. Ottawa: University of Ottawa Press, 2004. 1–33. Print.

Symons, T.H.B. *To Know Ourselves: The Report of the Commission on Canadian Studies*. Ottawa: Association of Universities and Colleges of Canada, 1975. Print.

Tausky, Thomas E. Personal interview. London, ON. 9 October 1997.

TransCanada Institute. "TransCanada Institute," 2008. Web. 27 Aug. 2009.

Trout, Paul. "Contingencies of Canonicity." *Weber Studies* 13.2 (1996): 86–99. Print.

Viswanathan, Gauri. *Masks of Conquest: Literary Study and British Rule in India*. New York: Columbia University Press, 1989. Print.

Weiss, Allan Barry. "The University and the English-Canadian Short Story, 1950–1980." Diss. University of Toronto, 1984. Print.

Willinsky, John. *Learning to Divide the World: Education at Empire's End*. Minneapolis: University of Minnesota Press, 1998. Print.

York, Lorraine. Personal interview. Hamilton, ON. 9 October 1997.

Index

Aboriginal writing. *See* First Nations writing

Acadia University, 20–21

aesthetic quality, 47–48, 51–52, 55, 87

Alexander, W.J., 9

American-Canadian courses (AmCan), 20, 25–27

American literature, 20, 21–22, 25–27, 73

anglophone universities

American literature taught at, 20, 21–22, 25–27, 73

arbitrariness of literature choices at, 105, 174, 183

bias toward British literature, 18–25, 30–31, 71, 73, 144

courses offered in 1997–98, 117–23, 193–220

courses offered in 2007–08, 174–78

devaluing of English Canadian literature, 25–31

earliest courses of English Canadian literature, 18–25

effect of curricula on book sales, 83–85

effect of curricula on canon, 88–89, 135–36, 150, 178, 182–83

effect of department structures on literatures of Canada, 115–17, 119, 122–23, 130, 134, 136–37, 150–52, 185

and field coverage, 136–37, 149–52

focus on contemporary literature, 41–42, 129, 140, 175, 182

isolation of, xxi–xxii, xxvii–xxviii

and monolingual approach to literature, xviii, xx, 91–93, 185

place of literatures of Canada in 1997–98 curricula, 106–14

place of literatures of Canada in 2007–08 curricula, 167–74

Québécois literature taught at, 23, 38, 81, 114, 156, 176–77

recent decline in Canadian literature courses, 105–06

resistance to literatures of Canada, 47–48, 90–91, 122, 144–46

summary of texts used in 1997–98, 123–31, 221–33

summary of texts used in 2007–08, 174–82, 184, 249–65

survey of Canadian literature courses
in 1960s–70s, 37–39

survey of Canadian literature courses
in 1980s–90s, 42–43

tie to publishing, 75–77, 79–83, 85–86,
87–88

using graduates to support canon,
89, 116

using Québec universities as model,
188–90

See also faculty; professors; survey
courses

anthologies, 79–83, 127–28, 129, 153–54,
180, 183–85, 289n8

*An Anthology of Canadian Literature in
English*, 153

The Apprenticeship of Duddy Kravitz
(Richler), 84

Arnason, David, 83, 84

Arnold, Matthew, 9, 13, 22, 24, 28, 51, 52,
55, 58, 87, 91

As For Me and My House (Ross), 125,
180–81

Association of Canadian and Québec
Literatures, xix

Atwood, Margaret, xiv, 41, 77, 88, 123,
125–27, 129, 152, 157, 181–83

authors
courses based on, 120, 123
effect of curricula on book sales, 83–85
factor in professors' choice of texts,
156–57
primacy of, in literary institution, 54
and publishing choices, 67–69
as subjects of scholarly research,
87–88
tie to universities, 77–79
works included in 1997–98 university
curricula, 124, 125–30, 235–47

works included in 2007–08 university
curricula, 179–82, 183, 267–82

Barbour, Douglas, 76, 78

Barthes, Roland, 52, 54, 55

Bear Bones and Feathers (Halfe), 127

Les Belles Soeurs (Tremblay), 128

Bennett, Donna, 80–81

Bentinck, W., 7

Bessai, Diane, 76

Bibliothèque Québécoise, xxix, 154, 290n3

Blodgett, E.D., x, xxx, 77, 98, 115, 285n3

The Book of Jessica (Griffiths and
Campbell), 128

Bouchard, Lucien, 70–71

Bourdieu, Pierre
and conditions of cultural production
and reproduction, xxiii, xxvii,
52–57, 58–59, 62, 87–89
on educational process, 91, 92
on role of professors, 52, 88
on symbolic profit v. economic profit,
67–68
on university role in maintaining
status quo, 60–61, 93, 116

Brand, Dionne, 182

British literature
bias toward at anglophone
universities, 18–25, 30–31, 71, 73,
144
taught in colonies, 4–5, 6–11
taught in England, 7, 9

Brown, Russell, 80–81, 140, 142

Callaghan, Morley, 129

Cameron, David, 42

Cameron, Susan, 20

Canada, 62–63. *See also* nationalism

Canada Council for the Arts, 63, 67, 68, 69

Davies, Robertson, 26–27, 120, 123, 125, 157, 182
Davies, Tony, 55
Dewart, E.H., 17
The Diviners (Laurence), 125
The Double Hook (Watson), 84
Doyle, Brian, 5, 58
Dragland, Stan, x, 98, 139
drama, 128–29, 177
Dubois, Jacques, xxiii, 52, 53, 54, 57–58, 60–62, 79, 89, 93, 135, 185
Duffy, Dennis, 163–64
Dumont, François, 162, 191

ECW Press, 76
Edgar, Pelham, 17, 18
England, 3–4
English Canadian literature
    and building nationalism, 17–18
    devalued at anglophone universities, 25–31
    effect of being on university curricula, 81, 83–86, 88–89
    ignorance of Québec model, 190
    and nationalism, 17–18, 39
    and regionalism, 64
    as subject of scholarly research, 87–88
    survey of courses in 1960s–70s, 37–39
    survey of courses in 1980s–90s, 40–42
    on university curricula in early years, 1–2, 18–25, 28–29
    university departments monolingual approach to, xviii, xx, 91–93, 185
    See also literatures of Canada
ethnic literature, 66, 158, 191
experimental literature, 161

faculty
    availability of, to teach literatures of Canada, 39–40, 113, 114–15, 168, 177

distrust of focus on Canadian literature, 24–25, 28
    hiring of US professors, 285n12
    and Pacey's vision, 30–31
    role in consecration of texts, 86
    and scholarly publishing, 87–88
    See also professors
Fee, Margery, x, xv, xxvi, 6, 19, 20, 42, 196, 285n3
feminist writing, 161
field coverage, 136–37, 149–52
15 Canadian Poets x 2 (Geddes), 153
Findlay, Len, 27
Findley, Timothy, xxix, 77, 125, 157, 182
First Nations writing
    in anthologies, 80–81, 82, 127
    chosen as university texts in 1997–98, 158–60
    chosen as university texts in 2007–08, 182
    courses on university curricula in 1997–98, 120, 121
    courses on university curricula in 2007–08, 168, 175
    first university courses offered on, 44
    professors' attitudes toward in 1997–98, 145
    on University of Alberta curricula, 45, 46, 47
Fortin, Nicole, 35–36, 43–44, 46–47
France, 3
francophone writers outside Québec, 65, 70, 105
French (France) literature, 5–6, 7, 11–13, 31, 32, 72. *See also* Québécois literature

Gerson, Carole, ix, 86, 87, 88, 127, 285n3
Godard, Barbara, x, xix, xxvi

Goodnight Desdemona (Good Morning
Juliet) (MacDonald), 129
Goto, Hiromi, 78
government funding, 90. *See also* Canada
Council for the Arts
graduate courses, 24, 38, 39, 40, 116
Graff, Gerald, 136
Green Grass, Running Water (King), 154,
159, 160, 180
Guillory, John, 62, 135, 160, 163

The Handmaid's Tale (Atwood), 126, 154,
181
HarperCollins, 68
Harris, Charles B., 188
Harris, Robin S., 8, 19, 24, 25–26, 28–29,
30, 40
Highway, Tomson, xiv, 128, 159, 175, 177,
182, 186
A History of Canadian Literature (New), 80

Icefields (Wharton), 78–79
immigrant literature, 66, 158, 191
imperialism, 8, 10–11
India, 6–7
In the Skin of a Lion (Ondaatje), 125, 154,
158, 180
The Journals of Susanna Moodie (Atwood),
126, 127

Kamboureli, Smaro, xvi, xvii, xx
King, Carlyle, 27–28, 30, 141, 186
King, Sarah, 25, 136
King, Thomas, xiv, 77, 157, 159–60, 180,
182, 186, 187
Kingsley, Charles, 4
Kiss of the Fur Queen (Highway), 175
Kogawa, Joy, 118, 158
Kreisel, Henry, 47
Kroker, Arthur, 130

Langevin, André, 31
Laurence, Margaret, 41, 77, 83–84, 120,
123, 125, 141, 157, 181, 182
Leacock, Stephen, 125, 129, 180
LeBlanc, Léopold, 31
Lecker, Robert, x, xv, 76, 82–83, 127, 165,
166, 178, 182, 184, 285n3
Lennox, John, 157
literary awards, 70
literary consecration, 52–59, 63–64,
68–69, 74–79, 86–90
literary institution, 53–62
literatures of Canada
and advocating nationalism, 143, 149,
161–62, 165–66
and anthologies, 79–83
availability of faculty to teach, 39–40,
113, 114–15, 168, 177
complex overlapping production of,
63–69
consecration of, through publisher,
68, 69
courses offered in 2007–08, 167–78
course types in 1997–98, 117–23,
193–220
effect of limited university coverage
on, 85–86
effect of excluding translated works
on, 184–86
effect of university department
structures on, 115–17, 119, 122–23,
130, 134, 136–37, 150–52, 160, 185
elitism in, 69–71
explanation of preference for
terminology, xxviii–xxx
factors in professors' choice of texts,
152–61
and field coverage, 136–37, 149–52
first acceptance of, in university
curricula, 2–3

tie with literature in English Canada, 17–18, 39, 165–66

Native writing. *See* First Nations writing

Nepveu, Pierre, ix, xxvi, 77, 162

New, W.H., 76

A New Anthology of Canadian Literature in English, 80–81, 184

Newbolt Report, 10

New Canadian Library, 75, 76, 79, 83–84, 154, 283n4

NeWest Press, 76, 78

non-fiction, 129–30, 161

Obasan (Kogawa), 154, 158

O'Connor, John, ix, 148, 153, 163

Ondaatje, Michael, xiv, 77, 125, 127, 157, 158, 180

Ontario Agricultural College, 19–20, 29, 30

Open Country: Canadian Literature in English (Lecker), 82–83, 184

Pacey, Desmond, 30–31, 38, 40–41, 48, 284n8

Parent Report (Commission royale d'enquête sur l'enseignement au Québec), 32, 33

Phelps, Arthur, 20

poetry, 119, 127–28, 177–78, 290n10

postcolonial studies, xix–xx

price of texts, 152, 153, 154

professors

    attitudes toward translated works, 145, 162–64

    Bourdieu on, 52, 88

    choice of texts in 1997–98, 152–61

    and choice of texts' influence on cultural reproduction, 122, 145–46, 153

    course objectives in 1997–98, 147–52

    hiring of, from US, 285n12

    influence of background on teaching in 1997–98, 138–47

    influence of text choices on canon, 74, 86, 87, 154–55, 178, 182–83

    role in maintaining status quo, 61

    tie to publishing, 75–77

    tie to writing, 77–79

    views of advocating nationalism, 143, 149, 161–62

    views on gaps in curricula, 162–64

    views on working around the canon, 134–35

    who have graduate degrees in Canadian literature, 140, 141

    See also faculty

publishing

    government support of, 63, 67, 68, 69, 90, 287n23

    scholarly, 87–88

    small presses v. large presses, 68–69, 287n15

    tie to university curricula, 79–83, 85–86

    tie to university teaching, 75–77, 78–79

Québec government, 90

Québécois literature

    aesthetic view of, 51

    anglophone writers of, 64–65

    belief in its own worth, 35–37, 63

    disavowing nationalism, 36–37

    early development of in colleges, 14–17, 31–33

    early examples in university curricula, 1, 2–3

    effect of being on university curricula, 85, 88–89

    as focus of Québec university courses, 73–74, 81, 144, 156

and francophone writers outside
Québec, 65, 70, 105

importance of CÉGEPs to, 34–35

more rounded view of, xx

as subject of scholarly research, 87–88,
146–47, 190

taught at anglophone universities, 23,
38, 81, 114, 156, 176–77

on university curricula in 1997–98,
146–47

university departments monolingual
approach to, 91–93.

See also literatures of Canada

Québec universities

anglophone literature taught in, 158,
162

availability of faculty to teach
literatures of Canada, 113, 114–15

and canonizing texts, 88–89, 135–36

changes in 1990s to CÉGEP, 71–72

changes to in 1970s–80s, 43–44

course types in 1997–98, 117–23,
193–220

creation of CÉGEP, xxiv, 34–35

in early years, 11–13

effect of curricula on book sales, 85

effect of department structures on
literatures of Canada, 115–17, 119,
130, 134, 150–52

focus on Québécois literature in,
73–74, 81, 144, 156

introduction of new literature classes,
35–36, 37

isolation of, xxi–xxii

literature from France taught in, 5–6,
11–13, 31, 32, 72

and literature research, 87–88, 146–47,
190

as model for anglophone universities,
188–90

and monolingual approach to
literature, 91–93

and nationalism, 32, 35, 36–37, 105

and Native language texts, 158

and Parent Report, 32, 33–34

place of literatures of Canada in
1997–98 curricula, 106–14

reproducing old view of literatures of
Canada, 122, 144–46

role in early development of
Québécois literature, 14–17, 31–33

and scholarly publishing, 87–88

and survey courses, 150–51

texts used in 1997–98, 123–31, 221–33

See also faculty; professors

Queen's University, 23, 25, 29

Random House, 68

regionalism, 64, 120–21, 156

research, 87–88, 116, 120, 142, 146–47,
190, 290n2

Rhodenizer, Vernon B., 21

Rimstead, Roxanne, 113

Robert, Lucie, x, 65

Robinson, Eden, 175, 182

Robinson, H.G., 5

Ross, George, 8

Ross, Malcolm, ix, xxvi, 75, 79, 98

Ross, Sinclair, 125, 180–81

Roughing it in the Bush (Moodie), 158

Routh, H.V., 10–11

Roy, Camille, 3, 15–16, 32, 75, 141

Roy, Max, x, xxiv, 48, 72, 85, 115, 287n16

Said, Edward, xxvii–xxviii, 133

Saint-Jacques, Denis, x, xxvi, 98, 146, 158

Sartre, Jean Paul, 54

Saul, John Ralston, 62, 64, 70, 71, 73, 93

scholarly publishing, 87–88

Shields, Carol, 70

short stories, 129, 177

Smyth, Donna, ix, 139, 141

social class, 62–63

Staines, David, 76

The Stone Angel (Laurence), 83–84, 141, 181

structuralist theory, 36

Sugars, Cynthia, xv, 82–83, 184–85

Sunshine Sketches of a Little Town (Leacock), 125, 129, 180

Surfacing (Atwood), 126

survey courses

  and anthologies, 79, 183

  and difficulty of coverage, 150–52, 157–58

  effect on texts chosen, 117–18, 152–53

  offered at anglophone universities in 2007–08, 174

  offered at universities in 1997–98, 117–18

  and professors' difficulty of coverage, 155–56

  as solution to increased demand for literature courses, 40–41, 43, 106

Symons Report, 42, 131, 285n13

Tausky, Tom, 141

TransCanada Institute, xvi

TransCanada project, xvi

translated works

  courses using in 2007–08, 176–77

  departments' refusal to use, 93, 156

  effect of omission on production of knowledge, 185–86

  exclusion from anthologies, 184–85

  funding for, 65

  professors' attitudes toward in 1997–98, 145, 162–64

  of Québécois literature into English, 82, 83

Trout, Paul, 135

Université de Montréal, 12, 13, 16, 17, 44–45, 46–47, 146

Université du Québec à Montréal (UQÀM), 36, 46–47, 113–14, 146

Université Laval

  curriculum in 1997–98, 146

  early courses on Québécois literature, 16, 31, 32–33

  establishment of, 12–13

  and literatures of Canada, 116

  poetry courses at, 119

universities and literary institution, 57–62

University of Alberta

  courses in 1997–98, 121–22

  Creative Writing Program, 78–79

  earliest Canadian literature courses, 29

  and literatures of Canada, 114, 115

  problem-based curricula of, 45–46, 47

  and research, 190, 290n2

University of British Columbia, 29

University of Manitoba, 23

University of New Brunswick, 113

University of Ottawa, 16, 17, 31–32

University of Toronto

  and AmCan course, 25–26

  courses in 1997–98, 119, 122–23

  reluctance to teach Canadian literature, 23–24, 25, 38

  use of anthologies, 80, 81

  use of translated woks, 145

University of Victoria, 110, 114, 115, 117, 130, 144, 171, 176, 178, 288n26

University of Western Ontario, 23, 25, 122

Vanderhaeghe, Guy, 76

Vautier, Marie, ix, 114–15

Viswanathan, Gauri, 6

Volkswagen Blues (Poulin), 176